THE PEACE CORRESPONDENT

Asian travel stories from a restless writer

Garry Marchant

EARNSHAW
BOOKS

The Peace Correspondent

By Garry Marchant

ISBN-13: 978-988-18154-6-0

This book has been reset in 10pt Book Antiqua. Spellings and punctuations are left as in the original edition.

TRV003000 TRAVEL / Asia / General

EB022

Published by Earnshaw Books Ltd. (Hong Kong)

PREFACE

WAR correspondents are the glamorous stars of journalism, dashing around to the world's hot spots, filing stirring accounts of historic events. I call myself a peace correspondent. I prefer to go to mainly untroubled, but exotic areas to write about the places and the people I meet there.

As a youth growing up in the dead center of Canada, I became obsessed with travel. As soon as I was able, I left home and wandered the Earth for many years. To support my "habit," I worked at odd jobs such as a burglar alarm installer in Sydney, Australia, a movie extra in Tokyo and a malaria control officer in Papua New Guinea. I also made a living in journalism, first in small-town newspapers in Canada, then in Rio de Janeiro, where I edited the Brazil Herald, the country's only English-language daily newspaper. Finally, I went to Hong Kong, where I was a reporter for the South China Morning Post and an editor for the Far Eastern Economic Review.

Only later did I discover that I could combine my trade and my passion, and make a living from travel writing. This book is a result of Asian travel in those later years, reporting on my journeys for newspapers and magazines. As an independent traveler, and later as a travel writer, I visited every continent on Earth, including the Antarctic. Although I was able to travel anywhere in the world, Asia generally provided the most powerful experiences, and the best stories. I returned to the area frequently, drawn by its magic and mystery, and quickly developed a deep love for this part of the world.

On assignment, I visited, and wrote about, most of the great cities of Asia, including Hong Kong, Tokyo, Singapore, Peking and Bangkok. I also wandered from the remote islands of Korea and Indonesia to the swarming streets of Southeast Asian cities, and from the Indian plains to the Mongolian steppes and beyond to the Himalayas of Nepal, Tibet and Bhutan.

I met and talked to fascinating local people (though no world leaders) and witnessed extraordinary events and festivals. I also traveled to harder-to-reach or less desirable places in search of a good story, or mainly to satisfy my curiosity.

I was fortunate that I started travel writing when it was still a thriving occupation - before newspapers and magazines started closing down, and the Internet started providing "content" instead of stories. Also, that I had several editors who appreciated travel writing beyond the usual bland tourist brochure stuff that so many publications ran, and that they let me develop my own style.

The idea for this book, as so many ideas good and bad, was hatched in a bar, in this case the venerable Hong Kong Foreign Correspondents Club. It was there, in 2008, where I re-acquainted with Graham Earnshaw, an old friend and fellow reporter from the 1970s South China Morning Post. While I still make my living as a merchant of words, he has gone on to other things, including, among many others, a marketer of words as a publisher of magazines and books. This anthology, his idea, is a direct result of that meeting at the FCC bar. I am grateful for his suggestion, and for making this book possible.

I am also fortunate to have my own in-house editor - my wife, Marnie, who helped select and check all of my stories, saving me from some mistakes and embarrassments. She also accompanied me on many of these journeys, experiencing luxury and hardships with equal good cheer and resourcefulness.

The many friends, editors, fellow writers and people in the airline and hotel industries who helped along the way are too numerous to thank individually here. Their advice, assistance and especially friendship are much appreciated.

This is a collection of those dispatches from the peace trenches I filed for various publications over the course of several de-

cades. Most are about lesser-known places, away from what social anthropologists term a "tourist bubble." A well-known war
correspondent turned travel writer once told me that although it
was not as glamorous, he preferred travel writing, as it brought
people pleasure. I hope these 40-odd stories from some 16 countries bring enjoyment to readers who share my deep love for
Asia.

TABLE OF CONTENTS

CONTENTS

THE PEACE CORRESPONDENT

JAPAN

HOKKAIDO

Bathing with the Ladies

SEPTEMBER 1979

IT was old Nemoto-san's lyrical reminiscences that induced me to go north. We were sitting at one of the cramped yakitori stands that line an alley under the railway track in Ginza, Tokyo's night-life district, eating skewers of barbecued chicken, when the subject of onsens, the hot mineral springs, came up.

"Ah," my friend sighed, recalling a scene from long ago, "It was so beautiful in that ofuro, men and women bathing together." We poured more sake into our tiny cups and, following proper etiquette, downed it in one gulp.

Nemoto-san continued, his eyes clouding at the memory, "It was like a dream. Everything looked soft through the steam rising from the bath water.

"And then," the old man became agitated, the light from the paper lanterns overhead glinting from his gold fillings, casting a reddish sheen on his pearl grey hair, "and then a class of young schoolgirls came through the rock garden, into the ofuro. They were so young and soft, so round through the mist." Lost in the revery of that treasured moment, Nemoto-san fell silent, oblivious to the bullet train overhead, rumbling south to Osaka.

Early next morning, I squeeze onto the crowded monorail at Hamamatsucho station with thousands of sarari (salary) workers, and arrive at Haneda airport in time for the first Japan Airlines flight to Hokkaido, Japan's northern island. Before noon, we land at Chitose, where broad farmlands and distant, snow-capped mountains give a spacious feel atypical of this country. The Japanese consider the lightly populated northern island, with its rugged mountains, volcanoes, forests and lakes, its "Wild West." Short on temples, shrines and castles (which weary tourists may find a blessing), Hokkaido offers instead spectacular scenery and outdoor sports. And hot springs.

Sapporo, the island capital 41 kilometers south of the airport, is an oddity among Japanese cities. Wide streets set at right angles on the "American plan" make it easy to find an address - a rare luxury in the chaotic maze of streets elsewhere in Japan. So I strike out without a guide to see the city of Asia's first Winter Olympics (1972), famed for its snow festival with fantastic ice sculpture and its beer.

A hilltop observation platform 40 minutes by bus overlooks the neat city and the vast farmlands of the Ishikari Plain. Here stands a statue of my favorite Hokkaido character, Dr. William S. Clark, his right arm flung boldly outward. Dr. Clark came to Hokkaido from the U.S. in 1876 as colonization minister, established the Sapporo Agricultural College and left a deep Christian influence upon his students. His parting words, inscribed on the statue, were: "Boys, be ambitious."

The Botanical Gardens near the center of town reminds us that Hokkaido is, both physically and culturally, more a northern than an eastern area, with familiar elm, fir and spruce trees. Two museums, in decidedly Western-style buildings, house exhibits that could almost come from Canada's north country, or Alaska: stuffed bears, seals, wolves and other animals; Ainu artifacts similar to those of Eskimos, such as dogsleds, dugout canoes, harpoons, skis, mukluks; and native costumes.

Back in the streets, I find yet another similarity to North America's Wild West. Tanuki Koji (Badger Alley) is a long, enclosed shopping arcade with restaurants, bars and souvenir shops. In one, a pseudo-Ainu in long hair and native jacket carves a bear. And all along the street, shops peddle Hokkaido-nalia: stained wooden carvings of bears with oversized fish in their mouths, or clutching a Suntory whiskey bottle; endless shelves of Ainu artifacts; wall plaques, native costume dolls, doorway curtains, key chains, purses, Hokkaido maps on tea towels; and pictures of the famous Sapporo Tower, cheap jewelry and handicrafts. There is hemp junk, wood junk and stoneware junk, all reminiscent of the worst kind of fake Indian souvenirs sold in American West resort areas, proof of the universal poor taste of tourists.

There is nothing fake, though, about the Sapporo Brewery, the oldest in Japan, where young guides in long plaid skirts, cowboy hats and black Sapporo beer T-shirts conducted tours daily. Our guide points out the significant fact that Sapporo is on the same latitude as Munich and Milwaukee, but refuses to sell me a T-shirt which, she insists, is a uniform and not a souvenir.

The brewery's wood-beamed, red-brick beer hall, which has been designed for serious eating and drinking, offers one of the best bargains in Japan. It is an almost irresistible invitation to gluttony: all the beer you can drink and all the Jingsukan you can eat for two hours for about $12. (Jingsukan is a Hokkaido specialty of mutton and a little cabbage, cooked on a grill at the table, Korean style).

My own modest appetite can not do justice to this offering, so I take instead a small draft beer for about $2, which seems a little steep for wellhead prices. Normally, Japanese and Chinese do not like mutton (they say it stinks), but three Japanese businessmen at the next table have risen to the challenge with gusto. They are into their second hour, still going strong, with mutton-splattered paper bibs, ties loosened, faces lobster red. They wipe the sweat from their faces, call for more massive mugs of beer, and gorge on plate after plate of meat. The whole busy, cavernous room reeks of mutton grease, and I leave smelling like a New Zealand barbecue chef.

Later, I rest in Odori Park, the wide boulevard intersecting the city, noting more "Western" influence in the form of a horse with a Calgary-style chuck wagon waiting for tourists. I am distracted by a rushing sound that brings to mind a verse by the great 17th-century Japanese traveling poet, Basho:

Bitten by fleas and lice,
I slept in a bed,
A horse urinating all the time
Close to my pillow.

Basho Matsuo traveled on foot or horse throughout medieval Japan, writing of his experiences and of his love of nature using the strict, 17-syllable haiku form. His journeys are recorded in prose and verse accounts such as The Narrow Road to the Deep North, The Records of a Travel-Worn Satchel and The Records of a Weather-Exposed Skeleton.

It is an evening for poetry. Another sound reminds me of another poem an American Zen friend (appropriately named Abbot) wrote back in Tokyo:

Summer night,
Sitting,
Zzzzzzzzz,
Giving blood.

It is time to move on.

Sapporo's busy, neon-lit wonderland of 3,000 bars, cabarets, restaurants, snack shops and gaming houses, while perhaps pale compared with Ginza and Shinjuku, out-dazzles anything this side of the Pacific. My finances dictate that my appreciation of the nightlife leans toward the voyeuristic, but after a few hours of just looking, my journalistic code of ethics and curiosity demand that I experience as well.

Amidst the jumble of signs, I spot the one bit of Japanese script I know, the kata-kana for beer. It is 300 yen, almost $2. (I also know the sign for "big", but this does not precede the beer symbol here.) At the bottom of the steps, a wood and paper door leads to a traditional restaurant, while a Naugahyde door opens into a dark bar. Inside, where student types sit and listen to music, a dimply schoolgirlish barmaid serves me a small beer and a saucer of what appear to be jellied fish intestines.

The saucer is untouched when I call for the bill and produce 300 yen. The smiling lady behind the bar rings up 850 yen on the cash register -- for a mini-beer and a plate of fish guts I didn't touch. There is some mistake here, and I made it: The price list in the street refers to the restaurant.

I sulk back to my hotel room to watch television. On one channel, I catch the Japanese women's wrestling championship bout, and cheer up while a lady as big and ugly as a Hokkaido bear slams into submission a pretty, delicate girl who resembles my barmaid. On another channel, two disco ladies dance and sing in perfect unison to the tune In the Navy (all in Japanese, except for a chorus of One, Two, Three, sung in English).

But I am not here for the beer or even the striking mountain scenery we pass next morning as the bus winds up through the forests. We stop to view the perfect cone of a far off volcano, as perfect, to my eyes, as Fujisan, though not as sacred to the Japanese.

Toyako Onsen, on the shores of Lake Toya, is considered one of the finest hot spring resorts in Japan, partly because of its striking setting. But also, the official guidebook says, because "The spa has colorless, weak common-salt springs and sulfated common-salt springs, with temperatures ranging from 55 to 60 C. The springs are said to be efficacious against rheumatism, nervous diseases and abrasions, while the spring water taken internally is good for chronic stomach catarrh, hyperacidity of the gastric juices and constipation from atonic dyspepsia." Have I stumbled into a hypochondriacs' haven?

My particular problem is not chronicled here, but I retire to my lakefront room in the Hotel Manseikaku to wait for the baths to open. Distracted by the sound of music outside my window, I put aside my Japanese novel and walk out to the balcony.

My heart leaps. There, below me, an entire high school girls' band is pumping out the best of Souza. They are demurely dressed in traditional uniform of white blouses, black, calf-length skirts, black shoes, black bangs and baby fat. It is two hours before the hotel bath reopens.

Cognizant of the punctilio of the ofuro, I don the hotel's white-and-indigo striped yukata (light, indoor kimono) and, miniature towel in hand, stride eagerly through the lobby. My swagger is carefully patterned from the samurai movies: shuffling along, slightly sway-backed, belt pulled down almost to crotch level, kimono pushing out slightly to accentuate the manly paunch, feet slopping carelessly along the floor in green hotel slippers. I am a samurai, returning from battle for a hot, restive soak in the curative waters.

The lobby this evening is full of young Japanese men, all attired in the same way, swaggering along in twos and threes. Meek, clerk-like creatures in Western business suits, they suddenly change their entire demeanor in native costume. We are the 47 Ronin, the leaderless samurai from the classic tale Chushingura, gathered to plot revenge for our disgraced feudal lord, then to commit suicide.

The first hint that all may not be as hoped for comes as I strut down the stairs: there are separate entrances to the bath. But years of dealing with the idiocy of Canadian liquor laws tell me that this is the same as the separate Men's and Ladies and Escorts' entrances to beer parlors, leading to one big communal pleasure room.

It is not. The Hotel Manseikaku ofuro is a substantial tiled room with three separate kiddie-pool-sized baths and a glass wall overlooking a garden of miniature pines and jagged rocks. It is also decidedly segregated. Along the wall opposite the window facing the lake, naked men squat on low, plastic stools before hot and cold water taps, shaving, washing, shampooing and rinsing. Then, with great sighs and groans of satisfaction, they immerse themselves to the neck in the hot water.

An hour later, a crowd of exuberant hoydens, their firm bodies tightly wrapped in yukata, wet black hair hanging in strings above lively brown eyes, gambol about the games room outside the ofuro. Chattering, laughing and playing electronic Star Wars games, they do not even notice the streaming pink body of a thwarted Humbert Humbert (of Lolita fame) stalking through their midst, grumbling about the loss of Japanese customs in the hotel.

Back again in mufti, I wander the few streets of the town, peering into soba (noodle) stalls, poking among the mementos. A life-size wooden carving of a urinating bear forms an ursine fountain at the entrance of a souvenir shop. On a side street, crude paintings touting a strip show portray naked women with enormous mammaries, putting to rest that misguided notion about breast worship being singularly American.

Middle-aged Japanese couples (I am the only gaijin, or foreigner, in town), now in heavy brown outdoor kimono, clatter along on wooden geta (clogs). It is the sound I once heard from my paper-walled apartment in Meidaemai, in Tokyo, lying awake on the tatami floors. The little house was across the street from the neighborhood public bath, and every evening the noodle cooks, just finishing their shifts, would clop-clop down the road (dragging their feet for maximum effect) for their baths. On cold winter nights, I would see them leaving the bath, steam rising from their reddened bodies as they tottered home in high spirits.

Reluctant to repeat my performance of the previous night with the $5 beer, I buy a cup of sake from a dispensing machine in the street and heat it under the hot water tap in my sink. Then I return to the novel that Nemoto-san has given me for this journey: Junichiro Tanizaki's classic Diary of a Mad Old Man. It is the story of an elderly gentleman's obsession with his young daughter-in-law, a sort of Japanese Lolita. I read:

7

"Today, you can kiss me." The shower stopped. A leg appeared between the curtains.

"Nothing above the knee..." Then she added: "Today, I'll let you use your tongue, too."

Noborogetsu Spa, the most famous in the country, sits 200 meters up in the mountains. Nestled in a large ravine of the Kasurisambetsu River, walled in by timbered mountains, the spa is said to contain 11 springs of various kinds, with temperatures ranging from 45 to 93 C. My guidebook assures me it is one of the few remaining mixed bathing places in Japan.

A half-kilometer from my hotel, the Takimoto, the Jigakundani (Valley of Hell) festers and bubbles in the miasma of a backed-up toilet. Fierce red devil statues guarding the road add to the impression of entering a hell, which on this breezy day attracts a number of visitors. In the floor of the valley, honeymooning couples pose amid the bubbling, steamy, dirty, stinking sulfur pools. Wind whips sand from the cliffs, and between the sulfur steam and dust gritting in my eyes, I feel like I need a bath.

The Takimoto ofuro is a small, unimpressive affair, so after a perfunctory soak, I cross the street to its sister establishment, the Daichi (or big number one) Takimoto. True to its name, this has the largest bath in the country, some 40 tubs and pools and 10 different kinds of water so bathers can select that which is best for what ails them.

Faded photographs outside the bath show water nymphs disporting themselves in the mineral waters, ignored by men performing their ablutions along the wall. This, finally, is the place. I undress in the locker room, tended by an old woman inured to even the strange sight of foreign flesh, and enter Japan's largest bathroom.

It is a massive, steamy tiled cavern, noxious fumes rising from the many tubs, rows of washing places along the wall, a swimming pool with a slide running into cold water. Each pool is identified by a small sign in Japanese, listing its curative properties. Wrinkled elderly men go from one to another, sampling the waters like wine connoisseurs.

At the far end, a tiled wall some three or four feet high blocks the view. A scrawny septuagenarian in flimsy shorts and head band walks along the wall, the only man in an all-female world. I move over to the pools near the wall to test the waters with my toes, trying not to be too obvious. Across the effluvia of the bath, I catch a quick glimpse of female flesh, cursing my lack of peripheral vision as I slide into the stinking water.

How old are those photographs outside the bath? Nemoto-san, you old rogue, how long is it since you were here? Customs change, even in the Land of the Rising Sun. I have taken a dozen baths in three days; my skin is wrinkled and I feel like a water-logged rat. But I am protected from atonic dyspepsia and even chronic stomach catarrh. It is time to go home.

I meet Nemoto-san again in our favorite sushi and sake shop where I relate my failures in the onsens. Nemoto-san selects a piece of raw tuna, shakes his head at my Western timidity as I tell him of the big bath and the low wall. "Ah, Marchant-san," he remonstrates, "but why didn't you climb over the fence?"

NAGANO

The Mysterious Disappearing Matsumoto Ball

June, 1994

BY day three of the official North American Press Tour to the Japan Alps, we are laden with gifts and our wallets are thick as Japanese toast with business cards, but we have seen precious little of the region's attractions and nothing of the ski slopes we came for.

As official guests of the Japan National Tourist Organization, we four visiting scribes quickly learn the truth of the old Japanese adage, "There is no such thing as a free bento (box lunch)."

Nagano Prefecture in central Japan has invited us to publicize its bid for the 1998 Winter Olympic Games (the largest international event marking the end of the century) and to show off its winter sports facilities.

But this is no casual jaunt around picturesque, pastoral Japan. The tourism officials meeting us at the Matsumoto city train station set the tone of the tour: "At 12:40 we will have lunch. At 1:45 we will meet the mayor, then sightseeing. At 5:40 we will arrive at the hotel and at 6:30 we will have dinner."

The hospitality is grandly bounteous, if structured. The "noodle shop" on the itinerary is a stylish Japanese specialty restaurant with low tables made from foot-thick slices of an oak tree. Lunch in the private tatami room upstairs is somewhat demanding for first time foreign visitors; roasted, sugared bees (the town specialty), horse meat sausage and rainbow trout soaked in soya and smoked.

National tourist organizations habitually ply visiting travel press with the finest of food and drink. In Japan, it is local delicacies such as potatoes smeared with a kind of custard that makes our lips itch, alien tubers and strange sealife and grasshoppers in a tiny sake cup. After a few days, we long for a simple bowl of soba noodles.

At Matsumoto city hall, where Japanese, American and Canadian flags poke from a tabletop stand, there is much exchanging of cards and bowing with local officials. When the mayor and his entourage enter, the ceremony is repeated.

We are celebrities, or at least curiosities, here in the hinterland. TV crews, news photographers and reporters crowd into the board room, strobe lights flashing as they photograph us like eager paparazzi. The reporters have become the news, the watchers the watched.

The mayor extols the virtues of the region's mountains and facilities, and joshes gently with a Salt Lake City, Utah, reporter because his city is also bidding for the Games. The brief press conference introduction over, we pose questions over ritual green tea.

Calgary applied for 17 years before it got the 1988 Games. Will Nagano bid again if they do not get the 1998 Games? The mayor does not anticipate failing (and Nagano does win the right to host the Games).

What budget have they set aside for hosting the Games? Financial details are not yet decided.

The traditional Japanese gift-giving rite follows, with our generous hosts bestowing on us an embroidered bag, 500 yen telephone calling card, carved hand mirror and a glossy souvenir book of the region. We have shamefully neglected to bring even national lapel pins of our homelands.

Finally, we traipse off to visit the six-story stone castle, oldest of four designated as National Treasures, trailing the local media who photograph us photographing the sights.

With all the formalities, there is little time for the sightseeing that is so crucial to travel writers. Our visits to the important sites are not serious research but Japanese-style, token gestures, the way they visit a temple, clap, bow, buy a small memento and depart, chalking it up on a list. At the Ukiyoe museum, with the world's greatest collection of 100,000 wood block prints, we admire Hokkusai and Kuniyoshi masterpieces before the curator rushes us to a slide show of these very prints, with taped Japanese and English explanation. He then distributes books on wood block prints, in Japanese.

Following a perfunctory tour of the Sasai Sake Brewing Company, an industrial plant of vats and pipes and drying rice, we retire to a small tatami room to discuss and sample the wares. It is like a European wine tasting, without the vulgar spitting. The beaming brewmaster bestows on each of us a bottle of the expensive house brand to add to our booty. The Utah Mormon offers to exchange his for one of the silk ties we picked up on the way.

Dinners, where all of the Japanese and none of the foreigners wear ties, are long, liquid and loquacious, with copious sake and beer and endless polite introductory speeches. Mr. Sato from the San Francisco JNTO office, our overseer, introduces each of us in a ceremonial litany. "Rynn Ferrin-san, Motorland Magashine -- Petah Callahan-san, Travelage Westo ... Jerry John-stone-san, Salt Lake City shimbun ... Marchant-o san, Bancouber Magazine..." We now appreciate that much of Japanese food is not heated because it would turn cold anyway during the endless obligatory discourses.

Between speeches and liberal mutual pouring of drinks, our hosts present their cards: the chairman of the village council, treasurer, vice mayor, director of the Nagano prefecture, director of tourism for the prefecture, principal of the ski school, chairman of the tourism committee, president of the tourism association, manager of the tourism division ...

Later, the party gets somewhat ribald, with the flushed senior bureaucrat filling my tiny sake cup suggesting with a wink and a nudge that I should see the Ukiyoe museum special prints, "For adult people."

Donning lime-green happi coats, we perform a fan-waving, hand-clapping festival dance around the tables, chanting choruses of the "Matsumoto Bonbon" song. Tonight's gifts include the happi coat, a cassette of the festival song and the town trademark souvenir, the Matsumoto Temari (hand ball) a basketball-sized, silk-embroidered ball on a wooden stand. My concupiscent male dinner companion slips it under an American writer's happi coat, like a giant breast, shocking her speechless in a lively cross-cultural encounter.

After much drinking and camaraderie, our hosts dismiss the women, saying they should rest, and take us to a karaoke bar for whiskey, beer, and singing of national songs. They have nothing Canadian, so I escape performing, (although I do hear Paul Anka's Diana played later). Late in the night, the Mormon reporter sings a touching Tennessee Waltz.

Over a Western breakfast of bacon, eggs and salad, Sato-san distributes two local newspaper clippings with photographs of the visiting foreign press.

At checkout, an earnest housemaid shuffles to the lobby with the bulky Matsumoto ball, which I have thoughtlessly left behind. On the crowded train higher into the mountains, I shove the hatbox-sized container safely behind the seat and settle back to savor the view. Twisted, stark apple trees flit by, and rustic homes with shiny blue and grey tile roofs, fed with messy tangles of power and telephone wires. Straw, kindling, and round, vermilion-red daruma wish dolls, both eyes blackened in, are piled up in frosty fields ready for Bonfire Festival burning.

In Nagano, I am first off the train and down the platform, but a skier chases me with the large box I had somehow forgotten.

Our new retinue includes three driver/escorts and Sarah, an American who works for the prefecture. Sarah, who appreciates all things Japanese, expresses admiration for the ungainly Matsumoto ball I still clutch, but declines the offer of it as a gift.

First stop is the city hall board room, crowded with more

officials and local press, for introductions and card exchanges (Wago-san, Yamazaki-san, Usui-san...). Available light fades over the temples and castles we wish to photograph as the speeches and a few polite questions (nothing pointed now) drone on. Finally, they bestow their largesse: an international digital time zone clock, cassette tape, Japanese noren door curtain and press kits with musical guidebooks which play a Nagano song when opened. By now, the tiny closets in our hotel rooms are piled high with souvenirs.

In three cars, we take to the countryside, our Japanese companions desperately chewing gum to avoid upsetting the gaijins (foreigners), who, they understand, do not like cigarette smoke.

In Obuse, the town that artist Hokkusai visited for inspiration, we admire what has been designated as one of the country's 10 best toilets. It is closed for the winter, so we do not experience it.

Near the town temple, we happen on a winter festival, with food kiosks and souvenir tents displaying blank-eyed, legless daruma dolls from the size of a fist to bigger than a beach ball. When we separate to wander on our own briefly, our guides, armed with walkie talkies, follow each of us, concerned we might get lost, while also exhibiting the Japanese love of high-tech gadgetry. There will be a traditional parade and fire-walking ceremony within the hour, but we have to move on. It is not on the itinerary.

At Nozawa Onsen village, a scenic ski resort town, the skiers look longingly at the slopes as we are ushered into city hall for tea and talk. A resort official explains that of Japan's 650 ski resorts, including 107 in Nagano prefecture, Nozawa Onsen has the finest facilities, with 23 hot springs, two gondolas and 30 lift systems. With 26 ryokans and 360 minshukus (family run inns), the town accommodates 20,000 skiers, or about 800,000 a season.

The mayor (his card identifies him as the burgermeister) then hands out peach-colored silk scarves for the ladies and moss-green ties for the men, as well as life-sized woven pigeons on wheels. A printed explanation of their legend points out that the straw birds are designated as a number one craft in Japan.

On this, our last day, it appears the outdoor writers will finally get on the slopes when the chief ski instructor and village officials lead us past long lineups to jump queue onto the gondolas for the 18-minute climb up Mount Kenashi.

At the summit, they lead us past the lifts, straight to the lodge. Looking longingly at the cafeteria yakisoba, curry rice and other basic dishes, we are ushered into a private room for the official lunch, an exotic Western hybrid of oyster soup and tender steak accompanied by a local mashed radish and onion dip. During the gift-giving (head bands and gloves for tonight's festival), Sato-san mentions that he has received a telephone call that a Matsumoto ball was found in our Nagano hotel, and will be returned. Welcoming speeches, lunch and card-passing leaves just a few hours for the visiting skiers to get on the slopes, finally.

Tonight is the Himatsuri Bonfire Festival, held every January 15 since 1839 to eliminate evil spirits and honor the male offspring born that year.

In the evening, a restive air of excitement hangs over the town, with roving revelers getting into the festival spirits. A group of wandering minstrels sings "Sake is my Friend," a long paean to the rice wine with much hand-clapping and jolly, red-faced drunkenness. Men in head-bands appear bearing straw torches the size of apprentice sumo wrestlers, like blazing, smoking battering rams. Reeling down the narrow streets, they pass liter boxes of iced sake to shopkeepers and bystanders to sip from.

Despite the sub-zero temperatures, 8,000 excited skiers and townsfolk jam the town square. From the press stands, where they have set aside a section for us, we look down to a floodlit, three-story tower of sticks and branches standing on a small, icy rise. Where it spreads out slightly at the top, dozens of the town's 42-year-old men are jammed together as though on a front row balcony. Clad in hard hats and blue coveralls, they wave white Japanese-style paper lanterns, clap white-gloved hands and sing.

Several dozen 25-year-olds, the defenders, circle the base of the tower, while the attackers gather round a giant bonfire several hundred feet away.

When I try to slip away by myself, one of our guides, armed with his walkie-talkie, escorts me through the dense crowd to the public toilet where municipal workers squat on the ground swigging sake. Standing in the cubicle, I hear him hollering into his radio, "Ahhh, Marchant-o san ..." The media gathered on the platform get a full report of my progress.

The festival is a fierce mock battle with bands of young men charging the tower with flaming torches. The defenders beat them off with kicks, punches and shoves, throwing the attackers down the hill, and thrashing at the flames with pine branches. The men atop sing, and chant, wave the lanterns and taunt the attackers, throwing down long bundles of sticks to give them more firewood. From back here, it appears vicious, with the attackers shoving flaming torches in the defenders' faces.

The crowd roars whenever the tower catches fire. Huge billows of smoke, cinders and sparks rise into the black night, and flames lick up around the men on the tower who appear to chant even more vigorously. The battle wages for hours until, when it appears that the men on the tower will be grilled like human yakitori, they exit down a ladder out back.

With the tower blazing like a steam locomotive's boiler, flames and cinders rising hundreds of feet in the air, our guides abruptly announce, "Let's go," and we head back to the cars.

Forty minutes later, we arrive back at our hotel in nearby Iiyama. The itinerary I got weeks ago in Vancouver said "22:40 Transfer to your accommodation. Arrive at 11:20." Tumbling out of the car, I spot the clock on the front of the hotel. It says 11:22.

Next morning, the foreign press all have lighter luggage, while Sarah's duffel bag looks suspiciously like a ripe pod bearing three peas. We bow our last good-byes to her and the relieved prefecture officials, who frantically light up Hope cigarettes as soon as we turn to board the Tokyo train. It has been an educational and useful trip, we all agree.

At the brief Nagano stop, city emissaries meet us at the platform with more smiles, handshakes and bowing. And they graciously return my wayward Matsumoto ball.

SENDAI

The Poet's North

June, 1994

MATSUO Basho, Japan's famous bard of the back roads, was delighted by Matsushima, a bay of hundreds of odd islets near the city of Sendai.

"Much praise had already been lavished upon the wonders of the islands of Matsushima," the 16th-century itinerant poet wrote. "Yet if further praise is possible, I would like to say that here is the most beautiful spot in the whole country of Japan."

The early travel writer and master of the haiku form of poetry traveled to northern Honshu Island when it was considered a wild, unexplored territory, a "far province beyond the roads." His famous book The Narrow Road to the Deep North describes his two-and-a-half year trip in prose and poetry.

Sendai, 350 kilometers north of Tokyo, is now the hub of northern Japan. The Shinkansen bullet train reached it in 1981, and international flights began in 1990, with direct connections now to Seoul, Chengdu, Guam/Saipan, Singapore and Hong Kong.

Basho strapped on his straw sandals and walked to the north from Edo (now Tokyo). Taking an easier route, I hailed a cab to Hong Kong's Kai Tak Airport and flew on Dragonair's new direct flight.

On the plane, over pre-dinner drinks, I learn something about the city from my seat mate who is returning home from a holiday in Hong Kong. "Sendai is the center of everything," she says, not meaning to be as immodest as she sounds.

This former "unexplored territory" has become a modern industrial, commercial and cultural center for Tohoku, Japan's northeastern district. It is a city of learning, with 10 universities and 10 junior colleges, high-tech industries, 30 labs and research institutions such as the 21st-Century Plaza Research Center. The Tohoku Intelligent Cosmos Plan aims to turn the region into an international high-tech center.

After dinner, she shows me photos of her home in the Izumi Park Town, an industrial and residential area on the outskirts of Sendai. It is Japan's version of a pleasant American suburbia, with spacious houses (rare in Japan), real yards, and a futuristic research center where outside companies rent time on computers and advanced lab equipment.

"With so many branch offices of major companies there, men are often transferred without their families. We call them 'Sendai bachelors,'" the young lady says with a slight glint in her eye.

Feudal lord Masamune Date, the warrior who established Sendai as his castle town in 1600, was known as the One-Eyed Dragon, because he lost his right eye as a child. We agree that Dragonair and Dragoneye make a fortuitous sounding parallel, and toast the new flight.

However, this is not just a Japanese Silicon Valley, but a scenic area with historical sites, ancient temples, shrines and castles and famous local delicacies. Numerous hot springs and ski slopes are within easy reach of Sendai, a major outdoor recreation center.

The first impression when the plane doors swing open is that this is a northern country, the air as sharp and clear as the famous local sake -- the best in Japan, Sendai aficionados insist.

After the crowds of Hong Kong or Tokyo, Sendai is a spacious, uncrowded city with parks, broad streets and the scenic Hirose River winding through the center. "We call this Mori no Miyako, City of trees," explains my friend. "Families of trees line the streets."

Although Sendai means one thousand years, or longevity, the

city was destroyed in an air raid in 1945, so most buildings are new. And it is growing rapidly. The suburbs we drive through from the airport were rice paddies just 10 years ago. Despite its newness, there are beguiling traces of old Japan -- cherry trees growing along the riverbank, satellite dishes sprouting on tile roofs, traditional low houses among the modern office buildings.

The Sun Mall Ichiban-cho typifies modern, prosperous Japan, where East and West meet and mix. A life-size plastic Santa Claus -- with a slightly Asian face -- stands outside one store, American fast-food places such as Mister Donut, Baskin Robbins, Kentucky Fried Chicken and McDonald's feed the strollers, while American brand names such as Levi's and Lee clothe them. But a few place names in Western script and signs such as "I feel Coke" and "Let's sport" are the only concessions to a foreign language.

My stay coincides with the winter Pageant of Starlight, when half a million tiny bulbs glow like fireflies in the branches of the zelkovas (a kind of elm) on Aoba and Jozenji Avenues. The happy young people walking along the fantastic streets of lights give the evening a festive, college-town atmosphere.

Next day, I visit the forested park on Aobajo Hill in the center of the town, where Date built his castle in 1602. With the evergreen forests of giant pine and cedar, the morning chill in the air and ducks swimming in the pond, Sendai feels like a town on the Canadian Pacific Coast. But among trees growing tall and straight are some that are twisted and gnarled and topped, as in Japanese prints.

And at the local temple, devotees' wishes scribbled on pieces of paper and tied to tree branches resemble winter blossoms. A stone tower, like a chess castle hidden in the woods, and the famous mounted statue of Date, the one-eyed dragon, are reminders of the hilltop's military origins, but below, the river now twists through a contemporary city of a million people, instead of forest or rice paddies.

Down there among the 20th-century buildings, the Shokeikaku restaurant is a remnant of an earlier Japan that Basho might have recognized. The Date clan's former summer home is a classic low Japanese structure with tile roofs, cedar beams, woven tatami mats, sliding paper partitions and doors and windows overlooking an outdoor stone garden. The menu is as traditional as the building, presenting local delicacies, excellent Sendai sake, and the area's fine rice, especially a sticky version called Hitomei Bore, "Love at first sight" rice.

"Sendai people like to eat and drink, and once we start, the party never ends," a man sitting across the tatami mat assures me, over tiny cups of the local brew.

The distinctive Japanese feast starts with familiar sushi dipped in soy sauce mixed with wasabi (horse radish), but from there everything is new, and mostly unrecognizable. A dozen dishes of all shapes are spread before us on the low table, with pickles, vegetables, including a bright green leaf in batter, some fish products and rice with a fine powder sprinkled over it. It is dried, crushed plum leaf, my lunch companion explains.

Now into our sake cups, we talk about the city's quirks. "Lord Date was a stylish man, a dandy, so there are many dandies in Sendai," he boasts. In winter they have a naked festival. "Naked men and half-naked women pay homage to a shrine."

Japan's tallest Buddha statue, 30 meters high, a female incarnation (like the Chinese Kwan Yin? I wonder), stands on a hill near the city center. "Inside are 108 small Buddha statues," my companion says. "She holds a rice wine bottle in her hand, blessing the harvest and the pleasures of alcohol. Kampei (cheers)."

Skiing is a popular winter sport in Northern Japan, and special buses take skiers directly from the city to places such as Zao Mountain, where visitors can rent equipment. But with limited time, I can only see the nearest slopes, the Spring Valley (spring, as in stream) on the outskirts of Sendai. Because it is warmer than other mountains, they use snow-making machines on these runs, but the dryness creates the famous powder snow so beloved by skiers.

However, part way up the hill, icy patches stop the bus from going further without tire chains. So the passengers get out, have a snowball fight, then hurry into a well-equipped, spacious ski lodge for tins of hot coffee from a vending machine and look out at the city spread out just below in the fading afternoon sunlight.

From the mountain, I turn to the sea, to see Matsushima, just 20 kilometers from Sendai and accessible by bus or fast train. The methodical Japanese rate this area that so enthralled Basho as one of the country's three most beautiful places. On an afternoon trip, I find it both changed, and the same, as the poet saw it. Souvenir shops along the waterfront sell local food delicacies, attractive wooden Kokeshi dolls, lacquerware and postcards and books advertising the "Three noted views of Matsushima."

It is raining when I arrive, so I slip into a traditional shop with great iron kettles hanging over beds of charcoal for a cup of tea and some fish cake. This is old, unchanged Japan. Back in the street, I happen on a cartoon character statue outside a store: Basho in his trademark straw sandals and turtle-shell shaped hat.

Further on, I encounter more ancient Japan, where a small vermilion bridge leads to Godaido, a traditional Buddhist shrine the size of a summer cottage. It is a classic scene, the natural weathered wood building surrounded by gnarled trees, standing exposed out on the tiny island. Then the sun breaks out of the clouds, illuminating one of Matsushima's most photographed sites in a pale winter light.

Later, at the entrance to the famous 9th-century Zuiganji Temple that Date rebuilt in 1609, a marker mentions Basho's visit more than 300 years ago. Now a national treasure, the temple is set in a large park with giant, rough-barked cedars, the tall trees in front of the temples acting as lightening rods.

The temple, made from the same kind of white cedar, shows Chinese influences such as an elegant golden screen with exotic peacocks. Delicate, ornately carved peonies, chrysanthemums and melons grace the enormous door. "These magnificent and glorious images seem to take us to JODO (The Pure Land of Paradise)," a sign says.

Outside, I contemplate the stone garden with its gracefully raked patterns, like the one in Kyoto, until a foreign tourist spoils my revery: "Why do they have the rock like that? It makes it hard to stand there."

Again, I sample the distinctive local fare. Many famous Japanese temples have restaurants serving the priests' type of food. In the Zuiganji Temple's Ungai (Out of the Crowd) Restaurant, the Buddhist meal is all vegetarian except for the squid sushi (the best part) and some oysters baked in their shell. Taro, coconut, seaweed, shredded mushroom, sago (which, they explain, approvingly "is like rubber") complete the pious repast, along with several small cups of hot sake, the Zen priests' favorite beverage.

It is an authentic experience, unlike the short, instant tea ceremony that follows, which seems about as real as the Kodak hula show in Honolulu. Outside in the garden, it starts to snow, beautiful fluffy snowflakes swirling around the temple rooftops.

Back at the pier, gaudy, over-embellished boats shaped like dragons, or like peacocks with prows of giant heads and fantails of feathers, wait for tour groups. The contrast with the simple, minimalist Zen temples on the island behind is striking.

Avoiding these kitsch craft, I take a large, modern tour boat, with comfortable swivel seats set before huge windows in the upper deck lounge. Right on time, we pull out of Matsushima harbor trailing a slipstream of gulls for a one hour tour of the unusual archipelago, like a Japan Sea miniature. The sight of these phenomenal, rugged islets eroded into bizarre shapes like some modern sculptures, is marred only by the power station with its gigantic smoke stacks on the far shore.

"Tall islands point to the sky and level ones prostrate themselves before the surges of water," Basho wrote. "Islands are piled above islands, and islands are joined to islands, so that they look exactly like parents caressing their children or walking with them arm in arm," he added with imagination run wild. "The pines are of the freshest green, and their branches are curved in exquisite lines, bent by the wind constantly blowing through them."

Basho was so awed by Matsushima, he did not compose a single haiku to its beauty. He did, however, quote an appropriate work by his companion, Sora:

> Clear voiced cuckoo,
> Even you will need
> The silver wings of a crane
> To span the islands of Matsushima.
> Or, in our case, the silver hull of a sleek tour boat.

SOUTH KOREA

HONGDO

Seeing in the Rain

September 1994

ALL that gloomy day on Korea's Hongdo Island in the damp mist and drizzly overcast, I felt sorry for myself. But a young woman on the hydrofoil back to the mainland set me right.

"I came here before, but it was sunny so I did not see it at its best," she said. "I had to come back to visit in this weather."

I am baffled.

"We Koreans believe the wet, grey scenery is better," she explains. "It is closer to Genesis, to true nature." So I am wrong to let the nasty weather spoil my visit. I am, in fact, lucky after all. It is better to see Hongdo in the rain and fog.

With a few spare days to spend in Korea after a visit to Seoul, I searched for a pastoral excursion. A man of extremes, I have stood on the southernmost tip of Africa (Capetown) and South America (Ushuaia), the western extremity of Europe (in Portugal), the westernmost part of the U.S. (Hawaii) and the easternmost (American Virgin Islands), the western edge of the North American continent (the coast of Vancouver Island, British Columbia) and the easternmost (Newfoundland). On a previous visit, I traveled to Korea's far east -- Ullungdo island.

So from the map, I pick out Hongdo, the farthest southwest piece of the country accessible by public transportation. From the postcard and coffee table book photographs, it looks like a bright, sparkling place.

Considering its remoteness, the island is remarkably easy to reach -- the only sacrifice being waking up at 5am after a night of sampling Seoul's vaunted hospitality. But the taxi driver taking me to the Seoul train station has never heard of Hongdo, an ominous sign.

"What's that, an island?" he asks, because of the "do" suffix.

The train, which leaves right on time at 7:05am, provides a leisurely transition from industrial Seoul to the tidy Korean countryside. Further south we pass ancient stone houses and agrarians in traditional costume, the women with baggy pants gathered in at the ankle, and a bright blouse or jacket, in different, mix-and-clash paisley or flowered patterns.

After the hothouse warmth of Seoul, Mokpo (the port for the Hongdo ferry) is cooler and decidedly grey, with the fresh, natural smells of strawberries and seaweed. Hundreds of outdoor tour group types in bright hiking jackets and rucksacks pack the spacious, modern catamaran with its comfortable airline-style seats. A TV set at the front shows a video of sunny Hongdo, which a crew member peddles to the passengers.

The little island, a rocky outcropping 115 kilometers southwest of Mokpo, was designated as a Nature Reserve in 1965 and became part of the Tadohae (Sea of Many Islands) Maritime National Park in 1981. Large groups of Koreans come on organized overnight tours, or even day excursions, but foreign visitors seldom make the trip.

Guidebooks even a few years old say that the only way to reach Hongdo is by a slow ferry, but these modern craft make the crossing several times a day in two-and-a-half hours. So, soon after the second showing of the video of Hongdo sparkling in the bright sunshine, the island looms in the haze ahead like a menacing, jagged piece of granite. Only mountain goats and a few rugged Korean fishermen could survive on this steep, rocky island. We drop anchor and a small, open motorboat shuttles us ashore. Stepping off on the old pier slippery with moss, I pay 1,200 won national park entry fee at a small booth, and here I am, the only non-Korean on the whole island, where no English is spoken.

There are no hotels on the island, but elderly ladies meet the ferry, offering rooms in their homes. I follow one up a steep, rocky path, through the little town, across to the far side of the island.

We pass some bright, inviting inns, with sparkling, modern toilet facilities, but I discover I have chosen unwisely. The woman's old house up on the hill is untidy (unusual in Korea), with a grubby bathroom, but it is too late to change, and it is only 10,000 won a night.

There is not much to Hongdo. In the otherwise somber village, huge, brightly colored plastic water-storage drums sit on most buildings, and garden hoses run down the steep streets like squid tentacles.

Aged women in traditional costumes squat in the doorways, sorting out fishing lines and cutting up sea creatures. Small stores sell the local delicacy, sheets of paper-thin, blackish seaweed, bundled up like small mattresses. Other souvenirs are dried fish and squid, gaudy seashell wall decorations and chandeliers, and videos of Hongdo in the sun.

On a steep path up from the beach, I encounter a bevy of rugged women in shiny black wetsuits, some quite young, others middle aged or as weathered as grizzled sea otters. They are haenyo, women who dive for abalone, crabs, fish and other sea delicacies, which they now carry home on baskets atop their heads. Suddenly, a long, slithery eel wriggles out of a basket, and the diver struggles like a Medusa, fussing with her hair, trying to put it back with one hand, while balancing the basket and giggling at the strange foreign apparition on the path ahead of her.

At the top of the hill, the only English sign on the island, un-

der the title "Natural Monument No. 170 Hongdo-Ri (village),"
explains that the island is 6.4 kilometers north to south and 1.6
kilometers east to west, with a total coastline of only 20 kilometers. The 545 kinds of plants in the reserve include big-leaf orchids and white camellia (Camellia japonica), and there are 170
species of animals. Since a Mr. Ko first settled here in 1679, the
population has increased to 250 people in 141 households.

All 250 are now at home, and the streets are already deserted,
with the only sign of life a small place decorated with bright,
Christmas-like lights. Inside, what looks like a bleak karaoke bar
is abandoned.

It is cold and blustery now, so I escape into a simple restaurant overlooking the dark sea. The woman proprietor produces
a large OB beer, then through sign language I order a basic meal
of rice, seaweed soup, kimchi and a plate of tasty little wriggly
things that I hope are dried noodles.

We struggle haplessly to communicate through sign language, then the woman's husband invites me to the adjacent
living room to see a video of the island in 1960. It is fascinating, like a National Geographic special from an earlier time, with
stone houses, women with large wooden tubs diving for fish and
seaweed, and no apparent sign of modern dress or implements.
Having exhausted the possibilities of Hongdo nightlife, I walk
back to the guest house through the narrow streets, buffeted by
the stiff wind howling from the sea.

Back in the traditional room, I watch Korean news on TV, then
drift to sleep, my head on the hard, wheat husk pillow, feeling
the comforting warmth coming up from the ondol floor (heated
underneath), while a storm rages outside.

Dawn comes, chilly, grey, drizzling and so foggy I can barely
see across the little harbor below. My proprietress fetches me to
join her other three guests. The breakfast we eat seated on the
floor is the same as dinner, along with black wafers of seaweed
taken from a bag like a bale of hay in the corner. Over a warming
instant coffee, another guest tells me with sign language about

the morning round-island boat tour.

Passing village storekeepers out on the street early, greeting tourists and offering their wares, I head back to the pier. On the beach, people bow as they pass several Buddhist monks in broad straw hats and baggy traditional garb, and a nun, her shaved-head topped with a straw pith helmet. They are tourists like us. Clumps of visitors in matching yellow, blue or clear disposable rain jackets stand around chattering happily in the drizzle. Koreans travel not so much for the "where" but for the "who with." For these Confucians, travel is a structured social occasion, so they are unfazed by the dismal weather.

We all board several wood-hulled boats with about 50 or 60 passengers each, and disappear into the mist for the round-island tour. For several hours, we circle the island, the long boats nosing forward into caves or running close along bizarre rocks shaped by the elements. Like so many other "end of the earth" places, it is a dramatic setting. A tour guide chatters on about the rocks and all their stories, and maintains an energetic sales patter, hawking the Hongdo video and Polaroid photos.

The only words I understand are "Ko-ka Ko-la." The over-hanging rock with a cleft in it does look like an old-style Coke bottle. It is frustrating, missing the commentary, until a young Korean, part of a Presbyterian Church group from Seoul, asks me in good English if I can understand what is being said. Then he translates for me, and I can appreciate the Korean imagination, applied to these geographic oddities. There is the Number 1 Rock, the most beautiful in Hongdo, and Sad Rock, which is separated from the island when the tide comes in. He points out the Pregnant Monk -- hastening to add it was a virgin pregnancy.

With a little imagination, I can now make out The Perfect Couple, Candle, ET Rock, Squirrel Rock, Tall Rock, Kettle Rock and Lucky Turtle Rock, lucky because turtles represent longevity. Birds' Apartment Rock is named for the many birds living there. My unofficial guide and rock guru points out a white mark high on a cliff. Long ago an old man fell asleep while fishing there. He woke suddenly when he caught something, pulled it up quickly, and it made that impression.

"We Koreans like stories," the young man explains.

Later we pass the Solitary Ladies, a row of nine small islands. When the women's father went to the mainland to buy festival costumes, he got caught in a violent storm and never returned. Bad-Minded Man Rock is a big, solid block balancing precariously high on a cliff. If a bad man passes under it, the rock will fall down on him, the tour guide explains, as we pass close underneath. It is an old local joke.

Independence Rock is shaped just like Independence Gate in Seoul, and another resembles a map of Korea, complete with the North-South demarcation line. We peer into the Cave of a Korean harp player, and another where 10-meter long snakes are supposed to dwell.

When Korean music comes on the tinny PA speakers, the middle-aged Korean women start dancing energetically on the deck. Below deck, where others huddle from the wind, jovial ladies stumble around pretending to be seasick, and clap their hands to the music, creating a party atmosphere. Some of the less spirited young ladies from the church group are genuinely drowsy and seasick.

Later, we stop alongside a fishing boat that appears to float in on the mist. On deck, fishermen fillet and slice live fish, putting the pieces on plates of shredded onions to sell to hungry passengers.

Back at the bay I rush to the dock to get my ticket to the mainland, but there is gloom of another type. The ferry is full, so I will miss my train to Seoul, and my flight home. But just when things looked bleak as a Hongdo day, help comes from the Christian group. The young man tells me that the local parson will talk to the ferry captain to try to get me a seat.

While we wait on the wet, slippery dock for the boat, friendly, lively group members tease the gray-haired, jovial parson.

"He only knows three English phrases," they tell me. "I'm

hungry, help me and I can't speak English."

When the hydrofoil arrives, they slip me aboard past the ticket taker, find me a seat on the upper deck, and I am able to buy a ticket from the captain.

Here I meet Miss Lee, an earnest young reporter from a weekly religious newspaper, who provides an enlightening insight into the Korean approach to appreciating the view.

Millions of Koreans collect natural stones, a national hobby called Su Sok (or susok), meaning Live Stone. Miss Lee carefully writes it out in Hangul (Korean script) for me, then writes, "Collecting stones strive to imitate and express the liveliness of the universe and earth."

The treasured rocks are not just beautiful, natural objects, but reflect Taoist and Confucian philosophy, stressing man's harmony with nature. "It is part of yin and yang," Miss Lee explains. And these stones, like Hongdo, look better when they are wet.

Although I don't entirely understand, I begin to appreciate the idea, the emotion. I recall the people on the boat dancing, singing and reveling in the misty atmosphere. And the rocks do take on a haunting, eerie, but compelling aspect on this grey day. Yes, I was lucky for the misty, murky weather.

Still, I would like to return to see Hongdo in the sunshine, just like in the postcards.

CHINA

CANTON

The Door Creaks Open

June 1978

THIS incident was highly amusing to the journalists and hangers-on at the Hong Kong Press Club in Wan Chai. Some six or so years ago, a number of Royal Australian Navy sailors bought tickets for a weekend trip to Canton from a man in a bar in Wan Chai, Hong Kong's Suzy Wong district. The trip was to include return train tickets, meals, hotels and guided tours. Of course the hapless seamen were stuck with worthless tickets - and the friendly man at the bar could not be found. A weekend in Canton? Preposterous. Everyone knew then that China was a closed country, that no one was let in except socialist politicians, left-leaning journalists and special interest groups, and then only by invitation.

Now, however, the preposterous is the possible.

There is a rent in the Bamboo Curtain. Since January of this year, travel to China has become simple for residents and visitors to Hong Kong. The faceless bureaucrats in Peking have decided that the Year of the Horse is to be the Year of the Tourist, and it is now as easy to organize a trip to China as to China Bar (a small town in British Columbia, Canada).

A trip to Canton is not a "holiday" in the normal sense. There are no beaches, few architectural or artistic gems to marvel at, only mediocre food (better Chinese food is served in Hong Kong) and the city, like the weather, is grey and grim. The weekend features the thrills of a ceramic factory, the excitement of a visit to a people's commune, the delights of Chinese nightlife, highlighted by a three hour acrobatic show, a sort of Sino Ed Sullivan Show.

The trip starts at Kowloon's ugly new Hong Hom Station, where Hong Kong secretaries and civil servants, backpacking Americans, Canadians, Europeans and Japanese, and Filipino families are divided into groups of about 27. The one-hour trip through the New Territories passes villages, fields and temples brightened by colored flags and commercial signs, final evidence of the decadent capitalist world before entering the dull, uniform blue and grey of China.

The train terminates at Lowu station, where passengers walk across the narrow bridge, the once impenetrable gateway to China. The red flag with yellow stars of China hangs higher than the red, white and blue of Britain's Union Jack, an arrangement clearly agreed upon by the two country's protocol officers. At the far end of the bridge, soldiers of the People's Liberation Army stand, like some kind of olive-drab Grenadier Guards, while eager tourists quickly contribute to the wealth of the Eastman Kodak film company.

Once inside the People's Republic, the segregation into groups becomes serious, and visitors must stay with their party for all bus rides and tours throughout the weekend. Almost my first act in China is to run afoul of these regulations by trying to get into the wrong railway car. A young tour guide asks to see my card, panics slightly because I am two cars down from Group Seven, my group, and leads me firmly but gently by the hand to my proper place, and tells me to wear my badge in future to avoid similar errors. Comrades in charge of tourism frown upon Western acts of asserting individuality such as not wearing an identification badge.

At precisely 1 p.m., to stirring martial music, the comfortable first-class train - each passenger firmly in his proper place - departs for the short run to China. And immediately the countryside is so Chinese, it is a visual cliche, like a setting for a movie based on a Pearl S Buck novel. Farmers in cone-shaped hats walk ankle-deep in the mud behind water buffalo, workers bicycle along the roads, women in baggy outfits bounce along with bamboo poles, loads hanging from each end, balanced on their shoulders, groups of geese and flocks of children scatter on either side of the road. Everywhere, peasants are planting rice, carrying vegetables or somehow engaged in preparing for that great Chinese passion - eating. The scene looks as if its director had carefully studied one of those huge Chinese wall murals before going to work.

At Canton, the stereotype jumps from rural to urban. Outside the huge station, we face a solid wall of people clad in the baggy blue jacket and pants of the Chinese worker. They are packed so tight that the air at the station exit is warmer, more humid than inside. I come to the scarcely-original conclusion that there are many people in China. Are they all here to meet friends, or to peer at the big, white-skinned, large-nosed gwai-los (foreigners, white ghosts)?

Everywhere over the next few days, curious Chinese gather wherever we stop, to stare blankly at the foreign devils. Old China hands say that one reason foreigners are not allowed to wander around freely in most cities is that they would cause a riot among curious Chinese craning to get a closer look. The experience is reminiscent of the scientist who put a monkey in a room to observe it, then peeked in the keyhole only to find the monkey peeking back at him. Have they brought us here to look at China, or so the Chinese can look at us, I wonder?

Canton, gateway to Hong Kong, has by far the most Western influence, and although there is a heavy schedule of visits to factories, monuments and the "Pavilion of Blood-cemented Friendship between the Chinese and Soviet Peoples," visitors can wander the streets on their own.

On my second day in the grim, rubble-strewn city, I escape the temptations of the Friendship Store, with its brocade and books, China and Mao badges, and take a random walk through the streets. These are uniformly dull, miles of two- and three-storied buildings seemingly stamped from the same pattern.

A camera-laden tourist wandering the back streets attracts considerable friendly attention, and very quickly becomes a Pied Piper to the street urchins. In an open doorway, I notice a small factory where workers are making test tubes and other laboratory equipment by hand, heating the glass tubes over a small burner and bending them. Perfect for a "China industrializes" shot, and I am invited in.

But the task is impossible. Whenever the camera gets close to one of the young girls, she squeals with embarrassment, and, despite shouts of encouragement from her fellow workers, flees her work bench. Soon the place is in turmoil, full of laughter and banter, but no production, most of the girls having left their benches to huddle in mock terror in the corner. Fearing the entry of a stern party cadre concerned that the monthly production figures of the Kwantung Province glassware factory might fall below the quota, I depart.

A phalanx of children blocks my path, but like Moses parting the water of the Red Sea, I cleave a path through the pack merely by pointing my mighty Olympus camera at them.

It is time for dinner, and one feature of the trip is a meal in one of Canton's best restaurants (we eat most of our meals in the cavernous dining room of the Tung Fang hotel, where tourists stay).

It is a feast, 12 courses of meat, vegetables, fish and prawns in combinations only the Chinese could dream up. Many would-be trenchermen fall by the wayside long before the last dishes are brought to the table. But if the Chinese make heavenly food, they make hellish liquor. Pigtailed waitresses in white smocks and Bruce Lee kung-fu shoes, no doubt motivated by the Chinese stereotype of Westerners as gross creatures with insatiable appetites, pour drinks with a reckless generosity. These include a reddish colored wine, like cheap sherry adulterated with sugar and rubbing alcohol, and a white, foul firewater tasting of sweat socks soaked in liquefied blue cheese. Fortunately, there is a seemingly endless supply of China's Tsingtao and Baiyun beer.

This big meal is the height of the nightlife, as determined late revelers gather at the restaurant on the top floor of the old wing of the Tung Fang hotel, where tired waitresses trying to close the place down and go home reluctantly sell drinks. Canton is not Sin City, and the fleshy pleasures of much of the Orient are absent in this moralistic society. (In fact, many tourists report a drop in carnal interests, perhaps the result of seeing all of the women in pig tails and the same baggy outfits). Reliable reports from refugees who make it to Hong Kong say there are prostitutes in China. These are called roadside chickens, or motors, but there have been no confirmed sighting of these rare birds by Western observers.

The highlight of the trip comes on the last day when we head out of the city for a people's commune, an hour away on a narrow asphalt road. The only other traffic we meet is bicycles, tractors and occasional trucks, a scene of pastoral calm marred by our driver's fascination with his horn.

The misty, overcast weather gives an eerie beauty to the countryside, where peasants behind their plows or bending over planting rice are reflected in the calm, muddy water.

The Huashan People's Commune, we are told, is of average size, consisting of 14,200 families divided into 26 production brigades. Do all communes have a demonstration board in the lecture hall complete with colored lights indicating new roads, irrigation canals and power lines? The pep talk by the head of the commune is surprisingly low key and easy on the propaganda, and we are taken on a tour of the machinery workshops and the hospital. At the hospital's old folk's home, an 88-year-old woman gives the system the biggest plug we have heard yet, telling us how bad it was before 1949.

As we get off our bus at the primary school, hundreds of children lined up in two orderly rows begin applauding. It is a moving experience. I am told later by an old China hand in Hong Kong that this is not a Chinese custom. The Chinese were taught to clap by the Russians, and they think that all Westerners like it. The kids keep up the applause as we pass in front of them and walk to the school. There, I realize I have left my film behind, so I head back to the bus. As soon as they see me, the children start applauding again. They keep it up as I run to the bus, enter the wrong one, exit to renewed applause, leap into the next bus, pick up my film and trot back to join my group, now disappearing behind the buildings. It is like running a gauntlet of hundreds of curious, peering black eyes.

"Now we know how Mao felt," remarks a caustic German.

In a one-room school, four-year-olds shout out their Mandarin lessons with all the gusto of a high school football team in training. In the sports building, we encounter the famous ping pong diplomacy. We watch the boys and girls playing at about 10 tables, then we are invited to play. The kids destroy the Westerners in every game. In the yard outside, children from all over the school complex run to the assembly yard and take their places in front of a stage, just like soldiers forming up on a parade ground.

A political demonstration? No. they all have ping pong paddles and, in unison, with great shouts they go through the motions of playing a game.

Our last official stop is a school room where about 20 children in bright costumes and heavy makeup stand outside the door and sing a song of greeting. It is the only flash of color we see in China outside the stage of the acrobatic and magic show. Inside, we cram into the desks, knees almost to our chins, and drink tea while the kids dance and sing to the squeak of the er hu and other traditional instruments - the token dance of praise to Chairman Hua Kuo Fung and Chairman Mao Tse Tung, as well as apolitical numbers such as The Swallows Return to the Meo people.

The show over, the children return to the front of the school to say goodbye to their guests, shyly offering their tiny hands to shake, a touching scene even to callous journalists convinced it is a public relations job for the People's Republic.

The whole new tourism policy seems to me to be a form of public relations exercise. While the country badly needs the hard foreign currency, as one tour guide explained it, "We want to make friends." And China, the xenophobic Gang of Four gone, feels confident enough to show itself off.

YUNNAN

Kunming to the Stone Forest

Spring 1987

I never touched the great scribe's pen; the Chinese muse will never sing for me. It wasn't the climb, although the thousand steep steps up the cliffside outside Kunming, capital of Yunnan Province, were frighteningly precipitous. But the narrow path to the top of Dragon Gate was as crowded as a Cantonese free market, with squealing children, smooth-cheeked young soldiers on leave and stolid, craggy peasants. Just ahead, a shrine in the rock wall contains the golden image of Kui Xing, the Patron God of Scholars, Wen Chang, the God of Literature.

So I turn away, a hundred steps short of the last overhanging terrace, to retreat past the Tower Which Reaches Heaven, the Cave of the Compassionate Clouds and the Cave of the Splendor of the Clouds. On this busy weekend afternoon, gasping pilgrims squeeze along the slippery-smooth, time-worn marble steps high on the mountain face, peasants picnic in little pagoda-like tea gardens and children try to lob coins into a stone phoenix nest high above an altar cut in the wall.

From 1781 to 1835, impoverished Taoist monk Wu Laiqing and his stone cutters hacked the steps out of this bare rock face. Along the way, they carved gods and grottoes, phoenixes, pavilions and these narrow corridors leading to the deity who helped students pass the Imperial Examinations -- or the current version.

No, I didn't touch the great literate's pen, as advised, but I don't want to write Chinese anyway, I rationalize. Instead, I pause by rows of snack stands to nibble on pickled turnips and tiny shrimps packed into flat cakes, to gaze at Lake Dianchi far below, and to contemplate the joys of travel way down south in China.

Climate, geography, distance from the capital and a rich mixture of some 26 minority peoples make Yunnan a unique tourist destination. The province was always removed from the mainstream of Chinese history, largely because it was once a three-month journey there from Peking. Its own rich history and culture provides ample diversion for the tourist wandering so far south.

This sunny March day, the capital, Kunming, earns its self-styled sobriquet, City of Eternal Spring. While far in the north, frozen tourists huddle along the Great Wall outside Peking, buying bulky fur hats for protection against icy winds, Kunming's air, scented with burning coal, is as soft and warm as in a tropical garden. Even Siberian seagulls winter in this balmy clime, locals boast.

Kunming, the former Yunnanfu, 900 kilometers from Burma and only 400 from Vietnam, reflects these Southeast Asian influences. Elephant trunk and bear's paw still tarnish some menus, but as the government passed a wildlife protection act last year, only simulated versions are now available. Or so we are told.

Two things bring home how near we are to the southern neighbors. Outside the Green Lake Hotel, minority people costumed like northern Thailand's hill tribesmen aggressively flog embroidered purses, belts and hats while a central government official looks away at this shameless, free enterprise hustling.

And a stroll through the municipal museum, with the great Red Soviet star on top, reveals the province's ethnic mix. There are Miao and Yao living on the border with Vietnam, and Jingbo women who wear heavy coin necklaces -- a coin for each of their past lovers. Some groups nail water buffalo skulls to house fronts, like the Torajahs in Sulawesi, Indonesia. The Bao people build stupas like the northern Thais, while the Jao's musical instruments and water pipes resemble those in Tibet.

Politically tied to Mother China to the north, Yunnan has had strong connections in modern times with southern neighbors. In 1910, French empire builders completed the Indo-China railway linking Kunming to Haiphong, Vietnam. The infamous 1,000 kilometer Burma Road, a mucky path through rugged mountains from Lashio, Burma, to Kunming along the southern branch of the old Silk Road, opened to motor vehicles in 1939.

When the Japanese cut off the road in 1942, American General Claire Lee Chennault's Flying Tigers airlifted supplies to the city over the 5,000 meter mountain passes of the "Hump." Although the Tigers flew into the city for many years, little American influence is now apparent. All I can find is a nondescript road the American flyers once frequented that an older resident recalls as "Yankee Street."

Kunming displays less English than more Westernized Guangzhou or Shanghai; Some street signs in Western script, a sign for a cooking school, and one that says, simply, "store."

The entrance to attractive Green Lake Park exhibits modern American influence in the form of large Mickey Mouse and Donald Duck signs. The spacious park, framed with classical, China plate-pattern weeping willows, is modern, urban China at play. Children zip around on the pavement in miniature electric cars that play Happy Birthday to You or on a more traditional dragon boat ride. On the lake, soldiers and young girls play flirtatious tag in rowboats, while all round, family groups and flocks of school girls admire the "Four Celebrated Blossoms" (camellia, magnolia, azalea and primrose) and soak in the warm spring sun.

A roadside "sugar artist" engenders early gambling habits in candy-craving children. They spin a roulette wheel to select the animal from the Chinese zodiac he will create for them. The lucky ones get a dragon, five times the size of others. For a few fen, the man dips a spoon into the molten, colored toffee, twirls it quickly around on his table as it cools to fashion the flat, skeletal outline of the chosen animal. Just as he hands over his creation, a gust of wind shatters the delicate dragon, scattering the pieces, tinkling like little temple bells.

The bells at the crowded Buddhist Bamboo Temple tinkle not just for the tourist but for the worshippers, mostly the elderly, bowing, lighting incense and praying. Despite the "No photography" signs, everyone inside is shooting posed family pictures, including commercial photographers with booths. A cheerful trio of gold-toothed, joss-waving ladies I photograph descends on me, demanding in harsh Yunnanese dialect that I send them copies. When some young soldiers pose atop a fence post, a screaming, indignant monk in mufti dashes from the temple to scatter the irreverent but sheepish PLA group.

Inside the temple, with its three fine gold Buddhas, stand the Five Hundred Lohans, "A pearl in the treasure house of Oriental sculpture." The story has it that in 1884, the abbot hired sculptor De Shen to adorn the temple. His amusing, nontraditional figures, drawn from local notables, are early Tiger Balm Gardens-style. The caricatures, somewhat like political cartoons, were perhaps too accurate. When the tableau was completed and revealed to the public, the artist disappeared forever.

If the economic health of a community can be judged by its marketplace, Yunnan is prosperous. In the thriving Muslim Market, men with faces brown and wrinkled as Yunnan's famous walnuts puff bamboo water pipes before heaps of dark local tobacco, slabs of dried beef, chickens in huge baskets and trussed-up turkeys. Country folk in baggy blue and brown, here to sell their produce, wander the narrow, cobbled streets wondering at big city life.

A woman squats on the ground wrapping duck eggs in brown mud and straw to make 100-year-old eggs. In the bird market, a patient vendor teaches her caged parrot to say "ni hao" (hello). Chefs cheerfully invite us into odoriferous, open-air cafes to lunch on bubbling soups and crackling gyoza-style dumplings. A showy noodle maker stretches, twirls and boils the white dough into long white strands, grandstanding for his foreign audience. In a nearby square, masseurs and masseuses in white coats and white, broad-brimmed hats, many of them blind, perform gentle massages, twisting limbs and kneading muscles in full public view.

Despite Kunming's appeal, some of Yunnan's greatest attractions are outside the capital. In the past two years, 10 regions have been opened to tourists, some on the international borders. But China is just too big, time does not allow for more adventurous exploration this time. With only a few days, I head to the prime tourist spot, the Lunan Stone Forest of bizarre but bewitching rock "trees" 120 kilometers to the southwest.

From the air, the dry countryside outside Kunming looks swollen like a fresh blood blister surrounded with bruise-colored greens and yellows. As our bus leaves the city and surrounding flooded rice paddies behind, we climb into red-dirt hills and fields of yellow rapeseed, green wheat and broadbeans.

This is rural, story-book China. Peasants work the fields with ancient hoes. The blazing holes in the ground we see from afar are kilns firing red bricks. Traditional, upcurving tile roofs top adobe or thatch and wattle huts. Boys chewing sugar cane drive horse carts or "walking tractors," and everywhere, there is road building, Chinese-style. Workers painstakingly, arduously break and fit together rocks. Even where it is prosperous, China has the enduring shabbiness of Mexico, with rubble and bricks and pipes and construction material all around. It is not all traditional, though. Japanese tourists in modern air-conditioned Hino buses race us for the Stone Forest.

Wavering, too-loud Taiwanese love songs -- another surprise to one still not accustomed to the "new" China -- float back from the tape deck, followed by a medley of Don't Cry for Me Argentina and The Mexican Hat Dance. Our guide, with a unique sense of humor, cackles cheerfully about the tiger that came into Kunming, just last year -- from where nobody knows -- killing two people and injuring three. He also entertains us with English jokes. Why does a bicycle need a kick stand? Because it is two tired. English is fast catching on in China.

Just outside the city, a small, roadside stone marks kilometer 0 of the Burma Road slanting off to the right, 1,000 kilometers to the border. A major WWII battle along this road that left hundreds of Imperial Japanese troops dead is now a pilgrimage spot for their descendants, but foreigners are only allowed to go as far as the ancient city of Dali.

Mid afternoon, we stop for tea and a saucer of the region's famous walnuts on a hill overlooking a small lake inhabited by a dragon. No one fishes there now, especially since the dragon ate six Americans from the Flying Tigers who were boating there many years ago.

Three hours out of Kunming, the approach to the Stone Forest has a festive, carnival air with colorful minority peoples crowding the road, decorated horses and buggies for hire and Bactrian camels on hand to pose for tourist photographs. It is at once both exotic and a Chinese Coney Island, Niagara Falls or Brighton. These geographical oddities have been amply commercialized; there is a Stone Forest Post and Telecommunications Building, Stone Forest Dining Room and a Stone Forest Store selling Stone Forest souvenirs.

Outside the Stone Forest Hotel compound, Sani minority women press cheap chinoiserie on all who wander out: pandas on velveteen pillows, deer-in-the-forest school of art bedspreads, and matched, black-velvet paintings to grace suburban American bungalows. A flock of flirtatious minority maidens follows us through the streets, pestering us in a strange tongue, proffering tea towels "two for one" and demanding "how much?" They offer to escort us through the forest, and duck playfully, squealing "no pic, no pic," when we try to photograph them. A particularly fair and flighty girl points at a pile of fresh horse dung on the ground, saying "pic, pic," and they scatter, bright and noisy as jungle birds.

In the fantastic limestone forest, we are like two-legged ants crawling though an immense, petrified sponge cake, through caves and up the twisted stone "trees." But the imaginative Chi-

44

nese see more than sponge here. To them, the shapes are warriors and maidens, peacocks, mushrooms and bamboo shoots. Even with the noisy Chinese families and intense Japanese, it is an eerie piece of aberrant nature, with a sense of both remoteness and the tourist bubble.

The forest caters to the Chinese love of posing for family snapshots in famous settings -- or at least aboard a Bactrian camel. Commercial photographers here provide period costumes (Ming, Ching, Ping?) for formal souvenir pictures, much like the "roaring twenties" and "gay nineties" outfits available in booths in North American fairs and festivals.

At sunset, we slip into part of the forest not yet opened to visitors, to catch the faint red glow of light on the fantastic rock shapes. In this light, it is like a badlands setting for a cowboy movie. The sun dies quickly, plunging the petrified forest into darkness. A silvery full moon hanging over a pagoda atop a tall rock "tree" sets a classic Chinese scene. Only one who has touched the great scribe's pen of could adequately describe its compelling beauty.

HONG KONG to SHANGHAI

Hogs on the Road

Spring, 1992

IT begins as a distant rumble, like rolling thunder from somewhere over the hills. The din grows to a threatening, deep-throated, hide-your-women-and-children roar, and a pack of leather-clad bikers comes raging through, like an invading horde on glittering metal steeds.

Chopsticks stop between bowl and mouth, hoes halt in mid swing, children run from schoolhouses, thousands stop along the road to stare at this strange, clamorous sight. The Hong Kong Harley-Davidson motorcycle club is on the road, and it is the strangest thing anyone has seen along the China coast since "foreign devils" were let into the country.

These are not the bad-ass outlaw bikers of legend, the "one percenters," as glamorized by Marlon Brando in The Wild Ones or Hunter Thompson in Hell's Angels, "The strange and terrible saga of outlaw gangs." This is the new Malcolm Forbes breed of bikers; executives, company directors, financial consultants and lawyers as at home at a seat in a boardroom as slouched low in the saddle of a raging, thundering Harley-Davidson.

The Harley Owners Group (HOG) is an organization of like-minded bikers, dedicated to Milwaukee iron. The Hong Kong branch is a cosmopolitan collection of bikers affluent enough to spend from $90,000 to $160,000 (US$12,000 to $21,000) for machines not built for the confines of city roads.

They hunger for the highway where these big bikes belong, to get out and ride free. So, after months of negotiating with Guangdong International Sports Tours, the HOGs have organized the first ever Hong Kong to Shanghai rally, eight days and 2,300 kilometers through northeast China over roads that probably haven't seen a foreign vehicle since before World War II.

It is a multinational biker gang of Hong Kong Chinese and American, German, British, Canadian, Swiss, Swedish, Dutch and Malaysian expatriates. Riders have come from Europe, the U.S. and South Africa. Two bikes have been air-freighted from the U.S. and one from Holland for this historic run.

At dawn, midweek in early October, the riders are out in an Esso service station near Hong Kong's Western District polishing the chrome, checking their machines and slapping on stickers from Esso, the trip sponsor. The smell of oil and exhaust and hot metal smothers the reek of Fragrant Harbor, and this could be a gas station in Middle Town America, with a bike gang gathering for a weekend run. Connie, the only woman rider, a Harley dealer who flew her Softail from Los Angeles for the run, is dabbing on lipstick before pulling on her helmet. Steve, Asia's Harley representative, is showing off the police bike complete with siren and flashing red and blue pursuit lights that he brought from Milwaukee to demonstrate to the Hong Kong police.

For executives and financiers, they are a bulky bunch. Peter is a six-foot-six German outfitted all in black, from boots to T-shirt to fringed leather jacket. Reed, the safety officer and lead rider, chapter chairman George, Peter, an aircraft engineer acting as the volunteer mechanic, and most of the other riders are above average size, especially for Asia. While corporate Hong Kong strides purposefully to work, the HOG riders blast out of the Esso station with roaring engines and squealing tires, bound for China and the free, ride-like-the-wind adventure of the open road.

Not exactly. Within sight of China, they face their first obstacle. The Hong Kong driver of the support truck carrying the bags, compressor, tools, spare parts and tires doesn't have a permit to enter China. The assemblage of 24 bikers, a half dozen riders, support cars, van and truck grinds to a halt, while the organizers sort out the bureaucratic problem. Finally, the truck is allowed to back up to the middle of the bridge and the Chinese truck that is to accompany them from here backs up to meet it, and they transfer all the gear across.

While the Hong Kong border guards are tense and officious, panicking at the sight of a camera, the mood changes across the border. It is like the circus had rolled into town, with friendly Chinese officials gawking at the bikes and posing next to them for photographs while the bikers cool off with Budweiser beer from a duty-free shack. One uniformed soldier asks the typical Chinese question, "How much do they cost?"

Now the born-to-ride-free bikers face an unpleasant reality. The Chinese will only let them ride in a convoy, with a police escort. Much later, only a few renegades will get to ride solo. The police hold back all the traffic through town while they assemble the convoy, with much shouting and instructions. Lead biker Reed blows his whistle so often, the other riders joke that he will start blowing the whistle to announce that he is blowing the whistle. After much confusion and shouting in English and Cantonese, the cavalcade departs.

For the entire length of China, the convoy screams through towns and villages with a wedge of police motorcyclists in front, then police a car with screaming sirens and flashing lights, followed by Harleys in full, window-rattling roar. These aren't just motorcycles, they're American Harley-Davidsons, the ultimate macho machines, bikes with soul and style. There are a dozen different models, Softails, Sportsters, Fat Boys and Electra Glide Classics, bikes more expensive, with bigger engines, than most Japanese family cars. The big, classic 80-cubic-inch V-twin engines give the bikes that power and the distinctive Harley roar, so different from the agitated sewing machine whine of lesser bikes. Although once disparaged as Hardly-Go Davidsons, these are HOGs, not rice burners (Japanese motorcycles). "I'd rather see my sister in a brothel than my brother on a Honda," says a diehard Harley slogan.

There is no thrill quite like the surge of power that comes from the slight twist of the hand throttle, and 700 pounds of menacing machinery almost lunging from under you and thundering away, with the satisfying rumble like a jet launched from an aircraft carrier. The club's stylists ride in the Harley highway slouch, copied from Marlon Brando or Lee Marvin in The Wild Ones, or maybe Peter Fonda in Easy Rider, depending on their age. They sit low in the saddle, arms loose and relaxed on those wide handlebars, legs forward, pointy-toed boots stretched way out resting on the highway pegs, giving a relaxed, ice-cool posture.

The style hasn't changed since the 1950s song Highway 101:
"He wore black denim trousers
and motorcycle boots
And a black leather jacket
with an eagle on the back.
On the muscle of his arm
was a red tattoo,
A picture of a heart
saying 'Mother I Love you.'
He had a hopped-up cycle
that took off like a gun.
That fool was the terror of Highway 101"

With all the confusion, it takes all day to make the 87 kilometers to Huizhou City, the first stop. Dinner is a banquet with local officials, with formal welcoming speeches and toasting with the fiery local liquor. At one table, Harley rep Steve and Peter, the mechanic, are deep in technical talk, of belt drives, gear boxes, drive trains and "How about them ramjet manifolds?"

At another table, a rider with a "Ladies of Harley" crest on her denim jacket is discussing the Hong Kong store selling Harley regalia. The Harley symbol, the all-American eagle, wings outspread, beak open fiercely, is worn on leather jackets and saddlebags, T-shirts, hats and rings and etched on bike parts. Hong Kong Chinese Rider Wilson goes whole hog with a Harley cap, sweatshirt and belt buckle. He claims to own HK$50,000 worth of Harley wear -- including his wife's underwear.

Another rider is reading a Los Angeles magazine article about the new American phenomenon, Rich Urban Bikers (RUBS). It says that Harleys are for people who like to look in the mirror, and he concedes he spends more time polishing the chrome than riding.

Some members are sensitive about the Hong Kong Hog's up-market image. David, an English engineer, complains, "In Hong Kong, they always ask 'How much does it cost, and do you get your amah (maid) to wash it for you?'" He has no amah.

Not everyone is enthralled with Harleys. The Dr., who is accompanying the rally in a support car, rode on the back of a Softail this afternoon. The laconic surgeon reports in an accent that is more Harley Street than Harley-Davidson, "Well, it's like riding the back of a motorbike, really." Yet he is eager to ride a bike for the final entrance into Shanghai, and a week later, back in Hong Kong, he is reported to be shopping for a Harley-Davidson, one of the converted.

From Huizhou, the bikers follow the coast north through old treaty ports, stopping at Shantou (Swatow), Xiamen (Amoy), Fuzhou (Foochow), Wenzhou (Wenchow), Ningbo (Ningpo) and Hangzhou (Hangchow). Beyond the crowded factories of the economic zone, the road winds through classic Chinese countryside, with traditional stone and mud houses with shingle roofs. Long-horned water buffalo spooked by the raging motorcycles are kept from running onto the road by the rope through their noses. Barefoot farmers work the fields with primitive wooden hoes, plows and ancient foot-powered irrigation pumps with crude wooden buckets.

It is white-knuckle biking through China's chaotic traffic. Roads are crowded with buses, bicycles, peddle rickshaws, three-wheeled walking tractors (oversized roto-tillers meant for the rice paddies). Farmers pull huge loads on two-wheeled carts, carry produce on bamboo poles on their shoulders or haul hay bales so big only their scrawny legs show underneath.

Teenagers fresh off the farm drive olive drab World War II

vintage trucks as though they were still in the empty fields, attuned to the speed of their water buffaloes. The many trucks turned over and abandoned in the ditches are grim reminders of how dangerous driving is in China, so the police escort clearing traffic ahead is grudgingly appreciated.

Fujian, the next province, is cleaner and greener than Guangzhou, with fields of sugar cane and lychee, banana and kumquat trees. For many miles, eucalyptus trees line the well-paved highway. Motorcyclists experience their surroundings more intensely than car riders, with the wind whistling past their faces and every bump in the road felt in the handlebars. Here, they inhale the smells of rural China: exhaust fumes, gas, oil, vegetation, wood smoke, manure and night soil.

Riding by Xiamen airport is like passing a baker's oven, as the temperature rises rapidly, there is a powerful smell of jet exhaust and aviation gas, then the roar of a jet engine as a Dragonair plane climbs into the darkening sky. Then, on the long bridge over the river, the temperature drops rapidly as a cool, stiff wind buffets the riders. It is a change of seasons in just minutes.

Minor breakdowns, flat tires and adjustments force frequent stops. A gang of motorcyclists in denims and jeans is a menacing sight, but none of these people has seen Marlon Brando or read Hunter Thompson, so curiosity prevails. Barefoot peasants leading cows to pasture or heading to work in the fields stop to stare at the gleaming bikes. A stern-faced traffic cop who has been difficult to deal with breaks into a huge smile when he is asked to pose aboard Dave's big orange and white Heritage.

Sportsters with 1 1/2 gallon gas tanks are city bikes requiring frequent refueling. It is a delicate operation; the riders get frantic whenever a local gas jockey splashes a few drops on the highly polished tanks or chrome. Many take the hoses themselves and very gently tip them into the tank, being exceedingly careful not to spill gas on their beloved metal steeds.

At rural gas stations, thousands appear from nowhere to gather outside protective steel fences to stare, as though we were zoo exhibits. One well organized station with a long red banner announcing "Warmly Welcome and see off the Members of Hong Kong Branch, Haley Dawson Motor Car Association Through Our Country," has set up a little table with cookies, candies and drinks for sale. Pretty young highway patrol women pose for photos like models at a motorcycle show.

Despite the strict schedule, the bikers run late, riding long after dark, the police car's flashing rooftop lights leading a half mile line of red taillights, like a string of Christmas decorations. On day two, after a number of tense near misses in the dark, the convoy rides in formation through Shantou City to line up in a row in front of the Shantou International Hotel. Police and staff stand guard over the HK$3 million worth of fine machinery, cordoned off with a red velvet rope like some gala Hollywood affair.

A bone-weary and saddle-sore bunch of riders gathers for dinner that night. David, a Hong Kong Chinese Harvard graduate, keeps bikes and sports cars in San Francisco, Vancouver and Hong Kong, and flies light aircraft. He is most passionate about biking. "It is three-dimensional, so you are more with the environment," says the property developer. "When you lean into the curve, you really feel it. Car driving is two dimensional."

"If you are on a motorcycle, you know what is going on, you are one with the machine," he adds. "With a Harley, you feel each bang of the cylinder, the tappets. You can feel the air sucking into the carburetor. A car is too complicated."

In the grey light of dawn, the bikers are outside before a growing audience polishing chrome, gunning their engines, the brack-brackbrack shattering the silence. Lightly touched breakfasts of strange Chinese concoctions sit uneasily in their stomachs and lunch is many miles and long hours away.

It is another clear morning, and the bikers never face rain the whole week. Peter, an executive with a major German corporation, says this is fortunate, because most of the riders lack experience driving on wet roads. "When it rains, a Hong Kong Harley rider takes his Porsche to work," he adds.

One of the ladies is caustic about bikes and bikers. "Nobody was cleaning their bikes yesterday morning when there was no one to see them," the Harley wife remarks.

"I came to see China," she adds, zipping up her leather jacket. "To me, a bike is just a big mess of metal. It is not a toy for boys but for middle-aged, middle-incomed men."

The crowd of onlookers held back behind the velvet rope has grown to hundreds as the bikers prepare for the dramatic departure. An old biker once described to me the technique, the style of swaggering out to his bike in front of the locals in any small town, which always attracts a crowd. "You pull on your jacket and gloves real slowly, deliberately, ignoring everyone. And when you look at the crowd, you look right through them, focus about three feet behind their eyes. It really spooks them."

After posing for a photograph before the big banners welcoming the Harley group, riders and passengers mount up, 24 big muscle bikes revving their engines, the deep-throated Harley rumble echoing along the street. The main street through town is blocked off, TV cameras are rolling, escort cars and bikes with flashing red lights start their wailing sirens. Reed blows his whistle for this grand motor cavalcade to take off before the thousands of spectators now lining the road - but a wisp of a desk clerk runs out of the hotel to accost him. He waves his hands, signaling cut your engines. Someone has not handed in a room key and she is not letting the procession go without it. They find the culprit and, somewhat anticlimactically, depart.

The showy bikes don't come through unscathed, though. Going through a small town with heavy traffic, a rustic driving a tractor hauling a huge load cuts across the road despite the police car almost sideswiping it, then runs down Reed in the lead bike. He goes down sprawling over the dirt road, kicking up a huge cloud of dust. Police have trouble keeping back the hundreds of onlookers that appear from every shop and house. The gleaming bike is scratched, the turn signals twisted off but Reed suffers only a bruised elbow, thanks to his red protective suit, which fellow riders call his Full Body Condom.

Fame precedes this unique cavalcade by midweek. Outside Wenzhou, TV and newspaper coverage and sponsor Esso's radio advertisements bring out tens of thousands of spectators. They line the road for many miles, laughing, some calling out "Halley, Halley," so we feel like royalty or rock stars. George, the chapter president, gets spooked by all the people, terrified a child will run across the road and be flattened by a bike. Outside the city, two World War II style motorcycles, with sidecars flying huge flags, and some 100 small bikes from the local motorcycle club join the cavalcade for the triumphant ride into the city.

Excitement builds with the entire populace out to see the parade, and we arrive very late to a gala reception, with blinding TV lights, strings of firecrackers exploding all around the bikes and great colored balls of fireworks shooting into the sky. It is like a victory parade and a near mob scene as the bikes roll into the compound. Inside, a banner greets the HOGs: "Warmly Welcome Halle Darvision Motor Car Hong Kong Branch Asso. to pass through Wenzhou."

Beyond Wenzhou, along the scenic coast where visitors seldom travel, the population thins and steep roads wind up into the mountains past terraced fields, waterfalls and little lakes where men fish from primitive wooden boats. "It's like riding through a painting," developer David says. Later, the road passes through a kind of Death Valley, with traditional graves sculpted into the side of the mountain as though scooped out with a giant melon spoon.

Despite the hectic pace, there is some time for sightseeing, and one morning, we attend a kung-fu demonstration. It is more acrobatic than martial, but it impresses one of the Chinese bikers. That night, out on the town, he fools around with exaggerated kung fu fighting stances, taunting one biker's girl friend, a tiny but supple dancer. The rider, with elaborate, showy gestures, dares her, "OK, come at me." A delicate, balletic foot lashes out, connecting with the open mouth, splitting the lip open. The biker is still spitting blood back at the hotel, where the doctor closes the cut with three stitches.

Zhejiang, the next province, is more industrial China, where the air smells of coal, factory smoke and hot tar. Steam trains belching black smoke chug by green rice paddies; trucks haul coal to grimy factories; and ancient, long, flat-bottomed boats with curved thatched roofs put-put by at a walking pace along canals that run all the way to Shanghai.

Somewhere north of Ningbo, the tightly organized convoy is stopped at a road construction site where asphalt degenerates to dirt and two lanes narrow into one. Trucks, tractors and buses backed up for miles in either direction block the convoy's van, truck and police escort, but the motorcycles squeeze past. It is total chaos of heat, dust and the oily smell of hot engines, as one by one the bikes spurt past the mess and regroup at the roadside. But TJ, a rebel, says "Let's ride," and zooms away from the pack.

TJ, a Chinese movie producer with long hair, a frizzy Ho Chi Minh beard and fringed leather vest, rides a big Electra Glide, a huge cruising Cadillac of motorcycles with padded armrests, running boards, windshield, radio and more lights than a Kowloon disco. He rejoices at being finally free on the road, weaving his powerful machine between tractors, bicycles and startled water buffalo. When he stops at a crossroads to ask directions to Hangzhou, Michael, an English financial consultant, roars up on his Sportster. The club brass has sent him ahead to find TJ.

"I'm supposed to tell you to stay here and wait for the rest," he says. They look at each other, and without a word, take off together, riding without the escort for miles, breaking every rule of the club and rejoicing in the best time of the trip. Finally, like truant schoolboys, they stop at a shack-sized store, climb off the bikes, and TJ orders drinks in Shanghainese. The proprietor sets a table and chairs out on the dirt yard. When the convoy finally catches up, the lost riders are somewhat sheepishly sipping from large green bottles circled by a curious audience of hundreds.

The ride is nearing the end, and some of the bikers are getting restive. At yet another banquet, this time in scenic Hangzhou's Huagang Hotel, local officials and chapter chiefs indulge in the Chinese custom of dueling toasts with a potent, clear local maotai. George, who speaks Mandarin, thanks the hosts, the police, the Chinese people, the hotel staff, and others. Joerg, known as "Miami," joins in with gusto. Miami is a Swiss watch company executive whose hair stands back as though he is permanently pointing into a wind tunnel. He faces a valiant, but losing battle with the maotai, and is waving his chopsticks around like conductors' batons.

A three-piece Chinese classical band begins playing traditional music on a small stage at the front of the room. Miami joins them, conducting with his chopsticks, and soon he has them playing a jaunty Oh Suzanna. Then Miami starts tumbling and doing handstands, his legs flying in the air as he hurls himself across stage, while the Chinese officials look on, straight faced. Later, the one-man Swiss acrobatic team is spotted wrapped in a towel wandering around the hotel corridors looking for his room.

Next morning, in the parking lot, Miami eyeballs another rider and moans, "You look like a piece of shit." He complains he is aching all over. "My skeletal is banging like an old Harley."

Eight days after leaving Hong Kong, at dusk on a Saturday, the HOGs reach a blue highway sign: Welcome to Shanghai. They have ridden an arduous 2,300 kilometers through country that few foreigners see. For the last time, they assemble the convoy and ride into China's largest city on a freeway cleared of traffic. Ahead waits a noisy reception at the Olympic Hotel, with a lion dance and children in theatrical makeup bearing bouquets for each rider. Then the riders will fly home and swap the leathers for business suits.

At twilight, just outside the city, an immense, roaring shape zooms by low overhead, lights flashing, as a jetliner settles into final approach to Shanghai international airport. It left Hong Kong just hours earlier.

THE YANGTZE

Slowly Down the River

August 1995

IT is damp, stifling and grey in the Ox Liver. Then the mist lifts as swiftly as a stage curtain to reveal the sun gleaming on awesome cliffs and high crags pressing in all around us. Cruising down the river, the mighty Yangtze, on a smoggy afternoon, we are once more dazzled by the fabled Three Gorges, even the disagreeably named Ox Liver and Horse Lungs. Our slow boat through China is nearing the end of what is perhaps China's foremost natural wonder.

For committed travelers, cruising the Yangtze is a must, ranking with seeing the Pyramids along the Nile, walking along the Great Wall or gazing at the Taj Mahal by moonlight. Known locally as Chang Jiang, the "Long River," this is China's Mississippi, an Asian Amazon, with tributaries navigable for 30,000 kilometers. We are on a four-day cruise down a mere 1,354-kilometer stretch from Chongqing to Wuhan. But it includes the most scenic stretch, 200 kilometers of the massive Three Gorges, Qutang, Wuxia and Xiling.

Since 1890, steamboats have navigated from Shanghai on the East China Sea, through the treacherous gorges, all the way up-river to Chongqing. Today, even aboard one of the large, luxury cruise ships, we can feel the surge of the silty brown water forcing us down river.

From the deck, we look down on small wooden fishing boats, gritty coal barges, grimy little cargo boats and giant local ferries with tiered decks, like giant, floating wedding cakes crowded with rural folk, many still in Mao blue, brown or grey. There is a certain urgency to seeing the Gorges. China has started building the Three Gorges Dam, the world's largest hydroelectric-dam project, to provide power for development and to reduce the risk of disastrous floods in the flatlands down river.

The controversial and unpopular dam will force more than a million people from their homes, and flood the Three Gorges and other scenic spots and villages along the river. So, in recent years, local Chinese tourists have rushed to see the revered Gorges while they exist, jamming the rails of the big, but basic, ships we pass on the way.

The modern boats built for overseas tourists such as Regal China Cruise's three Princesses are scale replicas of ocean cruise-ships, with bars, karaoke lounges, restaurants, barber shops, post offices, business centers and the mandatory souvenir shop. Like ocean cruisers, they have organized activities, with a decidedly Chinese flavor, with lessons in tai chi, flower arranging, mahjong and basic Mandarin.

"It's a bit like a holiday camp, isn't it?" remarks a rueful young American as the ship's PA system bellows its announcement of folk dancing in the lounge, sending truants slinking off to the Observation Deck bar.

The Yangtze is culturally important to China, dividing it between the northern noodle eaters and the southern rice eaters. So the best lesson of all is simply sitting on deck and watching China, ancient and modern, pass slowly by like a magnificent Chinese scroll painting slowly unrolling. Chongqing's grubby industrial suburbs gradually give way to scraggy mining areas with blackened figures loading coal onto baskets, then to agricultural China, with vegetable fields, grazing cows and tiny villages of rough stone houses.

We are soon reminded how dangerous the river is.

"My god, look," a passenger screams, and we run to the side just in time to see a body floating by, turning in the powerful eddies. It is probably a fisherman who fell overboard, or a farmer who slipped into the seething river. The passing corpse doesn't even attract a glance from the crew.

Everyone gathers on the front deck for Kuimen Pass, the entrance to Qutang, the first gorge. Eight kilometers long, it is the shortest, but narrowest, of the gorges. From the bottom of the chasm, it feels as though we are sailing through an immense crack in the earth's surface. It is often grey and misty along the river, driving photographers wild with frustration.

Here, the broad, turbulent Yangtze funnels between sheer limestone walls narrowing to 150 meters in places, the muddy water twisting and rushing through the channel at terrifying speeds, churning up dangerous whirlpools and eddies that could suck in small junks. So that explains the shortage of picturesque little wooden sampans on the river, I realize, as our steel-hulled ship delicately navigates the twisting course.

Early Western travelers called this stretch the Wind Box Gorge for the gales raging through the canyon. Now, as a steady blast whips at our clothes, we all zip up our jackets, but no one retreats inside.

The striking setting makes different impressions on the passengers. "How could anyone not want to do this?" shouts an awestruck American who has traveled the world, and is making his third trip down the Yangtze. He looks at the cliff walls pressing in on each side, head turning like someone watching a tennis match.

Yet a middle-aged woman sitting on a deck chair nearby remarks to another, "I love your hair that way."

"I got it done for 60 yuan in Chongqing."

"Oh, that's good. Do you know there is a hairdresser on board?"

At the narrowest part, where long, thin waterfalls slice down sheer cliffs closing in on both sides like a vice, the Gorges remind me of the Grand Canyon. But the ship is more comfortable than the raft I rode there, and we don't have to sleep on the riverbanks.

Soon, we leave the limestone cliffs overhanging the river for open, steep hillsides where villages cling to the slopes like Inca settlements in the Andes, lonely little places accessible only by river. Later, we pass Wise Grandmother's Spring in a rock crevice, then Rhinoceros Looking at the Moon Rock.

When we steam into the 40-kilometer Wuxia (Witches Gorge), lofty hills, high, dramatic, almost unnatural, loom out of the perpetual mist that hangs over the river. The effect is unearthly, but I am struck by how familiar it looks. Chinese painters and poets have celebrated the somber, forbidding beauty of these mystical gorges for 20 centuries. Although it is my first visit, I have seen these peaks in so many ancient Chinese brush paintings and countless artistic photographs in coffee table and travel books.

The 12 peaks are partially obscured by cloud and mist, as if seen through a silk screen. Here, the Chinese inclination for seeing things in rocks, and naming them, runs wild. The Climbing Dragon, Sage Spring, Facing Clouds, Fir Tree Cone and Congregated Immortals Peaks line the north side, Assembled Cranes, Misty Screen and Flying Phoenix the south. Goddess, or Observing the Clouds Peak, the most famous, resembles a maiden kneeling in front of an altar. Unimaginative dullards can only see rock. Straight ahead, Congregated Immortals Peak seems to block the channel, but somehow the captain edges the big boat around the narrow corner and we drift on down river.

Here, man's presence is even more precarious. A hazardous path cut into the rock runs along one side of the sheer canyon, long flights of steps lead to a few landing stages. A lonely temple sits high on a cliffside, and small pagodas perch on the rock faces. In places, with binoculars, we spot the dark mouth of a cave high up the mountainside, and I imagine a hermit monk meditating there, oblivious to this floating palace.

Even here in the middle of the gorge, farmers weed corn patches growing on the cliffside, and terraced slopes reach down to the water's edge. A series of large, plain pagodas at the tops of the cliffs are observation posts to monitor the water level and, a Chinese staff member explains, to control the dragons that rage along the river.

The Yangtze journey provides a look at life in little-known areas of China. One afternoon, we dock at the grimy, coal-sooted town of Badong, then ride a bus for two hours, lurching along a precipitous dirt road through a picturesque part of backwater Hubei province, which few foreigners can have seen. This mountain area is home of the Tujia minority people, basic farmers who plant their corn patches in rows of twos, live in mud-brick houses and carry their goods on their backs in woven bell-shaped baskets instead of Chinese-style yoke poles.

Our destination, the Shennong Stream, was opened to tourists only a few years ago. In the local version of whitewater rafting, we ride small wooden boats for hours down the clear, peaceful stream running through the forest, the banks rising high and green on both sides. A Tijua boatman steers from in front while two others with long poles keep us away from the rock walls. Sometimes we pass over water so shallow we scrape over smooth river stones. Our Chinese guide calls it "The sport of gliding in water."

In several places we can make out ancient wood coffins set outside caves high up the cliff, remnants of a mysterious ancient tribe. Along the way, guides point to shapes of the rocks. There is a panda, there an elephant face. Some see them, others only see rocks. It is the most peaceful, satisfying afternoon I have experienced in China. Then, suddenly, the Shennong pours into the Yangtze, the clear water swallowed by the muddy, the division as plain as a line drawn on paper.

Further along, at Zigui, a Sino-Stratford-on-Avon, we make a literary stop at a mountaintop temple to pay homage to Qu Yuan, the country's most famous patriotic poet. China's Shakespeare, who lived here during the Warring States Period (475-221 BC), wrote 25 poems, which have been translated into 10 languages. All along the river, we run into references to the bard of the Yangtze, although we find none of his works, aside from an ode to an orange.

A garish dragonboat barge is moored on the muddy bank, with two dragon boats tied alongside. These are now used for instant races, tourists splashing ineffectually to the beat of the boat drums. According to legend, the patriotic poet drowned himself in 278 BC to protest government corruption. Local people went out in boats, beating the river with paddles to scare the fish away and throwing rice dumplings to stop them from eating the dead poet. (Other legends have them racing their boats and beating drums in search of tragic Qu Yuan.) So started the Dragon Boat Festivals and races that are now popular worldwide.

High on the cliff, up steep steps and past a gauntlet of souvenir hawkers, sits the Qu Yuan Temple and a towering bronze statue of the poet. In the type of recycling of sacred palaces found all across China, this temple replaces the original, submerged since the massive Gezhou Dam, completed in 1971, raised the river. This incarnation, built in 1972, will also be flooded when the Three Gorges Dam project is completed, so the big brass statue will be moved to version three of the temple, further inland.

Inside the darkened temple, faded black-and-white photographs give a sense of how little this area has changed. The shots of crowds of local men at early Dragon Boat Festivals wearing broad, thatched hats and baggy costumes recall the works of the great Victorian-era photographers in China. But these were taken less than 20 years ago. Behind the temple, the good bard's tomb and red coffin behind a grilled enclosure overgrown with grass, feels somehow abandoned.

Xiling Gorge, the last and longest (76 kilometers), was also the most dangerous for early navigators and is still tricky even for modern ships. It is also the most exciting for sightseers. We slowly cruise past the Ox Liver and Horse Lungs, Yellow Ox, Bright Moon and Lantern Shadow Gorges. Finally, at Southern Crossing Pass, the end of the great Yangtze River Gorges, water rushes out of the narrows onto a broad, calmer river, and to a sudden change of scenery.

This flat, pastoral landscape reminiscent of Holland comes

to a sudden end when the river widens more and we reach the start of work on the Three Gorges Dam. Now we drift past an unsightly mega-construction site, with thousands of men and heavy equipment swarming around in a confusion of mountains of dirt and gravel and rock, the dusty scene running for miles along the bank. Enough material to build 44 Great Pyramids will be dumped into the river here, creating a dam more than a kilometer-and-a-half long and 90 meters high. It is an impressive, but depressing, sight.

Later, at the Gezhou Dam, for now China's largest, we enter a mammoth lock along with several other large cruiseships plus a few cargo boats. The gates close, the water level slowly drops, and the ships descend like plastic models in a bathtub when the plug is pulled. The gates open, and we float into a different world, a populated, flat, cultivated land.

Our short sojourn on the great river ends in Wuhan, capital of Hubei province. Even though we are still 1,125 kilometers from Shanghai and the ocean, this is a deep sea harbor. Once an international treaty port, Wuhan has a great maritime tradition. It was the starting point of the famous 18th-century Hankow Tea Races when sleek clipper ships sailed to London with their precious cargoes. And how could Britain have survived without its morning tea?

Despite the awe-inspiring experience of the Three Gorges, the visions of that massive earth-moving operation ends the cruise on a melancholy note. The great, new dam will provide electricity to build a better China, but the ancient country will lose part of its soul.

HONG KONG

KOWLOON
The Bare-faced Truth

MARCH 1998

"You have a big nose," Miss Lam announces. True, but I don't need a physiognomist to tell me that. And she has more bad news: I am actually a year older than I thought. According to Chinese tradition, the smiling soothsayer informs me, age is counted from conception, not birth.

And I am paying to hear all this.

This disconcerting information is being delivered in the boisterous, earthy, aromatic precincts of Hong Kong's Wong Tai Sin Temple, a conglomeration of Eastern religions located about a 20-minute subway ride from the city's deluxe hotels.

The business of worship starts right in the Wong Tai Sin Mass Transit Railway station, where a temple entrepreneur sells red packages of joss (incense) sticks to burn as offerings. At the approach to the temple, right at the subway exit, mendicants and mercenaries, who charge HK$10 (about $1.30) for joss sticks and $5 for pieces of red paper with auspicious gold Chinese script saying things such as "luck" or "wealth," converge on `all new arrivals.

Gold-painted plastic amulets dangle from hawker stalls, and

a profusion of bright, temple-red paper prayers, cards and packages of joss sticks clutter the shelves. Nearby, the appropriately named Sik Sik Yuen Clinic provides care to parishioners. The rich scent of incense and the smoke from burnt paper offerings hovers in the air along the stone steps lined with a bamboo thicket.

In the temple compound, worshippers gather around taps of blessed water, believed to cure many illnesses, while others light incense sticks, bow and set them in the sand in big brass urns. The rhythmic clickclickclick of people shaking bamboo cups with chim (oracle sticks) comes from the temple. While many worshipers kneel and pray, others gossip or take family snapshots and children run around playing. Wong Tai Sin, by far the busiest, most boisterous of Hong Kong's 600 temples, illustrates the Asian custom of combining piety with socializing, worship with sightseeing.

The temple and the district are named for Hong Kong's most popular Taoist deity. Built in 1921 and now dwarfed by high-rise housing estates, the compound is a classic example of traditional Chinese-style architecture with vermilion pillars, two-tiered golden roof, yellow lattice-work and an array of multicolored carvings. Under a green and gold pine ceiling, the deity Wong sits on a raised marble platform surrounded by carved and gilded ornaments, while several wishing ponds and a pagoda are dedicated to Buddha. Buddhist and Taoist gods are worshipped here, while Confucius is revered in the Confucius Hall.

To the left of the temple, the multi-tiered Fortune Telling and Oblation Arcade is probably the largest single collection of fortune tellers in Asia, with about 160 cubicles for freelance soothsayers, chim stick readers and palm and face readers. A woman waiting for customers spots the approaching foreigner, and leads me to another alley of stalls, to one that says "English." The cheery man behind the desk proffers a card written entirely in Chinese characters, and answers all my questions with a smile, and a price. I walk on.

Along the arcade, locals window-shop for the right oracle:

young couples anxious about their love, stockbrokers worrying about their future, gamblers looking for something to give them an edge, housewives and occasional tourists all looking for answers of some kind.

A few stalls away, I find Priscilla Lam, who speaks better English than most of the other seers and tellers. Diagrams of faces and hands written over with Chinese script decorate her cubicle, along with drawings of different types of chins, noses, eyes and lips, and photos of a minor guru in gown and beads, squatting cross-legged before a temple. A can of bamboo chim sticks sits on the counter along with a half-dozen porcelain statues of Tin Hau, the Goddess of the Sea, and a giant Chinese tea thermos.

There are several ways to look into the future in this celestial bazaar. Pay a deposit for a cupful of chim sticks, take them to the altar, kneel and shake the canister. Return with the first one to fall out, and the soothsayer will read and interpret the significance of it for HK $30 (about $4), and negotiable, especially for someone speaking a little Chinese, or on a slow day, to half that. "But that is just story telling," Lam sniffs, clearly favoring the more detailed (and expensive) palms-and-face package.

It is about $26 each for face and hand reading, or $40 for both, but Lam agrees to do both for $37. (I later hear that these psychics can be bargained down to $13 for just face or palm reading, but at that price, she would probably read stinginess in my character among my other failings.) So, opting for the full face and hands treatment, I squat before her on a little kitchen stool, like those used in the roadside tea shops.

In her gold necklace with a jade pendant, Lam, looking more like a Hong Kong office worker than a Gypsy palmist, has been reading the future for 10 years. She asks me my date of birth and where I was born, translates it into Hong Kong time, and consults a book to transpose the date from the Gregorian to the Chinese calendar.

"Chinese think when you are in the womb that counts as part of your life, so you are almost one when you are born," she says, writing down the date, and informing me that I am a Snake. In the Chinese zodiac, that is.

"We believe that the palm tells about 60 percent of your life, and the face 40 percent," Lam says, grabbing my two hands and staring at them intently. "You have a square face and square hands. Palms and face match. That is good." Finally, something positive.

"You do what you want." Meaning I am stubborn. "You are practical, don't trust things of the imagination." Not exactly desirable qualities for a writer.

"Your nose is very long," she continues. "Most negotiators have a long nose. They are very patient, they keep insisting on hearing what they want to hear." My eyes are deep, so I plan more than other people. My ears are close to the head, so I play safe and don't take chances. And I have thin lips. "This gives the impression of being sincere and honest," the chirpy diviner continues, without actually saying I possess these qualities.

"Your career line is strong. You can work all your life, without retiring." A lifetime of drudgery. "This is not a good year for you. Play it safe, other years will be better." And finally, the stock in trade for all fortune tellers; "You will lead a long life."

At this point, she starts to sound more like the American Medical Association. "Your face is hot, even though it is not summer. Take care of your high cholesterol. Your blood is too concentrated." Now she is like a school counselor. "Donate blood, then don't eat so much meat and oily food. Eat less chicken, pork and McDonald's and more green vegetables and fresh fruit." She continues: "As a writer, your spirit is important. Get fresh air. It is good for the brain and bright ideas."

And finally, with a last glance at my face, she announces firmly, "You will be fatter in the future." No one can accuse Cantonese fortune tellers of only telling you what you want to hear.

For my $37, I've been aged a year, had a character analysis and a frank, if not flattering, evaluation of my appearance, received health advice and been given a disquieting look into the future. It is, I suppose, quite a bargain.

THE NEW TERRITORIES

Island Hopping

January 1999

A herd of black cows grazing in the grassland seems an unlikely obstacle for a leisurely walk in Hong Kong, but there they were, a dozen ruminants chewing and mooing in the field ahead. The beasts were placid, though, calmly returning to their feeding on the appropriately named Grass Island (Tap Mun).

Many of Hong Kong's more than 260 outlying islands scattered around the South China Sea are tiny, unpopulated islets or mere rocky outcrops accessible only by private boat and known only to yachters and scuba divers. Others have substantial communities, an hour or less away by frequent ferry service from Central District. So weekends head to Cheung Chau and Peng Chau for the Chinese village atmosphere, to Lantau for beaches, hiking and to see the Big Buddha, or to Lamma, for the seafood served in basic, open-air waterfront restaurants.

More remote, sparsely inhabited islands such as Tap Mun, Ping Chau, Po Toi and Tung Lung Chau, which require more effort to reach, are unknown even to most Hong Kongers. These isolated places (none with vehicles) retain traditional rural Chinese culture, along with fine beaches, mountains and open spaces. And each island has its own character.

Po Toi

On an already hot Hong Kong mid-morning, a small, slightly battered blue-hulled ferry docks at the St. Stephen's Beach pier near Stanley, on the south side of Hong Kong Island. Savvy travelers board quickly and rush for the top deck or the stern on the main deck, competing for outside seats with former residents returning for a visit and with excitable Hong Kong teenagers.

Right on time at 10am, the ferry departs for tiny Po Toi, Hong Kong's southernmost island. In popular Stanley Bay (Chek Chue Wan), the ferry passes weekend windsurfers, sailors in small boats and sea kayakers before heading into the choppy open sea. On the four-mile (6.4 kilometer) journey, we follow the rugged southern coastline of sheer cliffs, then pass uninhabited islands and rocky outcrops. A crewman in a broad straw hat collects HK$38 for the return trip. The crew speaks only Cantonese, so foreign travelers have to point to the ticket for the 3pm, 4:30pm or 6pm return ferry.

The waters here can be rough, and not for landlubbers, but it is a short trip. Just 35 minutes after departing, the ferry enters Po Toi's picturesque, sheltered Tai Wan Bay, home to the island's 30 or so remaining residents. By mid-morning, sleek, flashy yachts and private pleasure junks - their hulls the shiny dark brown of roasted duck skin - are already anchored here, their passengers enjoying a seafood lunch at the beachfront restaurant.

The island is so rugged and remote, John LeCarre used it as a setting for a dramatic scene in his 1977 spy novel, An Honorable Schoolboy, but today it has well-marked and maintained hiking paths.

A short, paved path leads left from the jetty past a sandy beach with restaurants to a picturesque, seaside temple for Tin Hau, the Goddess of the Sea. We head in the other direction, along a longer, but easy, path running through bush and along the craggy coast past prehistoric rock carvings. Beyond that, it leads to such unusual, colorfully titled rock formations as Buddha's Palm Cliff, Monk's Rock and Tortoise Rock, and to a hilltop lighthouse. Those who like to go to extremes can walk on to Nam Kok Tsui, the southernmost point of Hong Kong. The rounded shapes of Chinese islands are visible on the horizon, and ghostly outlines of container ships sail past on the open South China Sea.

From this southernmost point, we return the hard way, climbing steep steps to the top of 188 meter-high Ngau Wu Mountain. From here, an alternate path back to the beach passes by Mo's Old House, supposedly haunted. "You're not going to Po Toi," apprehensive Hong Kongers said earlier, when we mentioned our plans. "That's the ghost island." Unlike the ornate haunted castles of movie sets, with their towers, turrets and dormers, Mo's is just an abandoned summer house built about 50 years ago, but never occupied. Yet this crumbing relic is the source of tales that the island is haunted.

Hikers and boaters alike end up in Po Toi's main attraction, the basic, open-air Ming Kee Seafood Restaurant, set on stilts on the beach near the pier. Passing the chaotic kitchen with its flaming gas stoves and a large, plain room with plastic chairs, concrete floor and plastic awning, we grab a table set out on the sand. Island chic includes waitresses in T-shirts, jeans and black rubber boots, hikers in T-shirts, shorts and bare feet, and elegant yachties in designer boating wear. Some stylish ladies are even decked out in fancy hats more suited for the Ascot races than a South China Sea outdoor diner.

For Hong Kongers, food counts, not decor, and the Ming Kee is known for its fine fare, especially seafood. Prawns, crabs, clams, scallops, lobster and fresh fish come steamed, fried, or with delicious sauces such as garlic and black bean, black pepper and chili, or ginger and onion. Carnivores indulge in stir-fried or sweet-and-sour chicken, or pork and beef dishes, vegetarians in seaweed soup and steamed vegetables and drinkers in cold beer or wine.

On this peaceful sunny afternoon, we sit with bare toes wiggling in the sand, and dine on fresh, succulent seafood. There is no accommodation on this island, so, as yachties weigh anchor we make sure we are at the pier for the last ferry back to Hong Kong Island. Haunted island or not, we do not want to spend the night sleeping on the beach.

Tung Lung Chau

The constant wind off the South China Sea has stripped much of Tung Lung Chau clean of its former dense bush covering, revealing rounded hills. The north end of this island at the southern tip of Clear Water Bay in the eastern New Territories is largely bare and open, allowing great views of the surrounding seas and approaching ships. Among the most rugged of Hong Kong's many islands, it is distinctive for its large, rocky outcrops and high, sheer cliffs.

From the ferry we turn right, joining passengers going to see their ancestral homes, shabby little buildings with some elderly folks working in the small gardens. The overgrown path leads through a forest, silent except for the quintessential sound of the Orient, the creaking of bamboo. At the end, we climb down a steep, rough path through waist-high thickets to the rocky shore. The ancient rock carving that we have come to see supposedly represents a dragon. In fact, it looks more like a child's scrawl etched deeply into the rock.

Returning back along the same path, we reach the north side of the island, where the golf course across the inlet is so close it appears that if someone teed off from there the ball could land at our feet.

Tung Lung was once a sort of Gibraltar, with its 18th-century Fat Tong Mun Fort guarding the sea passage between Hong Kong and Guangzhou. The Qing dynasty fort was built between 1719-1724 to fight off pirates preying on junks that sailed through the Fat Tong Mun channel into Hong Kong's sheltered waters. The fort, armed with eight cannon, and manned by a detachment of one officer and 25 men, was abandoned in 1810 when the garrison moved to Kowloon. Today, instead of pirates in junks, yachts, speedboats and coastal freighters now pass through the narrow channel.

The ruins were overgrown with vegetation when the Antiquities Advisory Office started excavation work in 1980. The partially restored fort on the edge of a cliff, with waves crashing against the rocky shore far below and spindrift whipping along the sea like shredded plastic bags, conveys an eerie sense of those dangerous early days.

The open-air Holiday Store on the main path sells drinks and basic food -- the "Hong Kong Ferry's school of cuisine," with baloney slices, luncheon meat or fried egg plopped on bowls of packaged instant noodles.

The ramshackle restaurant is like a beachcomber's hut, with a patchwork roof of canvas and a Marlborough cigarette awning stretched across bamboo poles. A few cats wander around between the rusty metal chairs set on a bare concrete slab floor. Large plastic water barrels, boards, bricks, driftwood, old life buoys and wood pallets clutter the dilapidated, but pleasant spot.

Dozens of squares of Styrofoam packing scribbled with messages or sketches are tacked to the rafters or nailed to the ceiling. Mostly in Chinese, they are mementos of individuals and groups who have visited the island. Police Adventure Training Unit, Outward Bound and various cadet groups have all trained on Tung Lung, and TVB has used it as a setting for some of its melodramas.

The restaurant appears to be the unofficial center for Hong Kong's dedicated rock climbers, and photos of climbers clambering up the sheer cliffs decorate the shop. On one wall, a photo shows the last Governor of Hong Kong, Chris Patten, looking slim and tanned, visiting Tung Lung Chau on May 30, 1993. It is unlikely that he dined at the Holiday Store.

Tap Mun

Despite the bovine distractions, Tap Mun, in Tolo Harbor, is mainly a fishing community. From the deck of the ferry approaching the dock, we see aged fishing boats, people working on the nearby fish-breeding rafts and a fishing village stretching along the shore. The island is also reputedly a smuggling center, and, sure enough, a grey hulled marine police launch patrols in the harbor like a street cop on the beat.

The east end of Tap Mun is gentle and scenic, ideal for easy hiking. Paths cross open, grassy slopes providing scenic views of small beaches, the open sea with passing yachts, fishing boats and freighters, and other small islands.

The west end of the island is more rugged, with paths penetrating thick bush, overgrown in places. It is like walking through a living green tunnel of vines, palms, grasses, cacti, creepers and crawlers. Sharp, prickly leaves, like pineapple stems, scratch and claw at our clothes. Finally, the path opens up, leading to an easy climb up to Wintz Hill (Mau Ping Shan) and the white pillar of the surveyor's cairn. From here there is a great, unobstructed 360-degree view of the surrounding sea and the pyramid shape of Sharp Peak (Nam She Tsim) on the mainland.

In Tap Mun village, fish wrapped tightly in paper and ribbons like mummies dry on fences and clotheslines, while others the size of tiny minnows glitter like silver coins in woven baskets. Tanka and Hoklo women wearing broad, woven hats pound dried shrimp into a powder.

Tap Mun's two-century-old Tin Hau Temple, the last one that fishermen and seamen can visit before heading out to the open sea, is one of the most popular in Hong Kong. The green-tiled temple to Taoism's Goddess of the Sea is equipped with traditional trappings of a huge bell, drum and portable altar for carrying the goddess. We are admiring the main temple when the sudden explosive crackle of firecrackers from the altar next door shatters our silent reveries, and the acrid scent of black powder mingles with the sweeter aroma of temple incense.

The fishing village's only real restaurant, the New Hong Ke, serves Chinese-style seafood and other dishes. The English menu lists steamed medium-sized prawns, fried prawns with chili, fried clams in ginger and spring onion sauce, and stir-fried garoupa, all at market price. Dishes are about HK$60 each, cheap by Hong Kong standards. Curiously, although it is bright and airy, the restaurant is enclosed, taking no advantage of its scenic seaside setting. One wall is covered with colored prints of people who have dined there, including two former governors David Wilson and the peripatetic Patten, a well-known Sino-trencherman and island-hopper, who visited twice.

Ping Chau

Only determined island lovers venture out to Ping Chau, the farthest outlying island from Hong Kong and the hardest to reach (about an hour by MTR, subway and commuter train from Central, and an hour and 45 minutes by ferry). Police boats looking for illegal immigrants regularly stop ferries to the island in Hong Kong's remote northeast, the closest one to mainland China. Daya Bay, with its nuclear plant, is just 12 kilometers from Ping Chau.

Like all of the ferries to the more remote islands, the boat is a beat up old craft, smelling of oil and old ropes. Once heavily populated, Ping Chau is now almost abandoned, except on summer weekends, when inhabitants return to run small restaurants and shops selling drinks and snacks to day-trippers, thousands of teenage campers and picnickers.

From the ferry, China is clearly visible a short distance away, and with binoculars I can pick out the new buildings sprouting along the Chinese coastline. A walking trail loops around the island, passing traditional stone houses and pleasant beaches washed by perhaps the clearest water in Hong Kong. Few hikers go beyond the barbecue pits, campsites and picnic facilities, so after a short walk, we leave the masses behind. At the southern end of the island stand two rocky outcrops, the Ping Chau "Watchtowers."

The eastern coast of the island must be one of the most peaceful spots in all of Hong Kong. Along this coast, unusual bedded sedimentary mudstones and siltstones are tilted, tiered slabs, like lopsided layers of earthenware plates. After circumnavigating the island, we return to a broad, sandy beach, and the crowds of weekenders.

HONG KONG

It is scorching hot in mid-summer, with no shade along many stretches of the path, so we are sweating and parched after our hike. Fortunately, this is a Chinese community, and the first place we get to, a little cafe overlooking the sea, has an ice chest full of cold Carl-zee-bahgahs (Carlsberg beer).

MACAU

GUIA COURSE

Racing for Glory

October 1992

THE high-octane aviation fuel that powers Grand Prix cars burns with such clear intensity, it is hard to tell if a crashed car, or driver, is in flames. Few drivers likely contemplate this chilling fact as they pop a celebratory cork and pose alongside lithe young Moet & Chandon "Hospitality Girls" on the winners' podium.

Avgas and Champagne are the essential ingredients in lightning-paced, grueling but glamorous Grand Prix racing. Outside of Japan, the sport comes to Asia just once a year. On the last weekend in November, racing drivers and bike riders, pit crews and international press all rendezvous in Macau, the Portuguese enclave across the Pearl River from Hong Kong. The Macau Formula 3 Grand Prix, one of the world's oldest continually running races, is the big weekend for the Hong Kong and Macau motoring set, with noise, speed, a dose of danger and a whiff of sex.

This "World Cup of F3" is a major international event, with the finest young drivers racing for prize money, glory and the coveted Super License which enables them to move up the ranks of professional racing to Formula 1. Former Grand Prix champions also return for another fling at fame, before 30,000 spectators and some 200 million TV viewers in 74 countries.

The Macau Grand Prix weekend is more than a race, though. It is an occasion for local auto aficionados to flaunt their high-priced cars and driving skills, and to carouse. November is party time in Macau.

Unlike full-time race tracks, Macau's Guia course, named for the city's trademark lighthouse, is a street circuit. High performance cars and motorcycles reach speeds of up to 160 miles per hour on streets where normally only plodding buses, cars, Mini Mokes and bicycles run. The Guia is a tough 3.8 mile course of tight turns, hairpins, long straight-aways, rises and dips. In the days running up to the big weekend, Macanese live with the angry hornet buzz of cars and bikes doing practice runs and time trials -- vvrroooom, vrrooooom, vrroooom.

Saturday morning, day one of the races, the press center, like a command post with faxes, telephones and typewriters, crackles with tension as the international motoring media sets up shop. Hordes of reporters, press badges dangling round their necks, watch heats on TV monitors while photographers in vivid red "Press on Course" bibs cradle lenses like truncated bazookas.

Down in the pits, where the air is sharp with the fumes of racing fuel, mechanics tinker with gleaming Suzukis, Yamahas, Kawasakis, Hondas and Ducatis all standing like rows of steel steeds ready to charge. On the hot tarmac, bikers sweat in full leather suits with thick knee pads like overgrown calluses, protection for legs that are inches from the concrete on high speed banks. Between races, riders peel the suits down to the waist, displaying tattoos and bike accident scars to fans, girlfriends and nubile groupies.

When the starting flag drops, riders on 500 cc and 750 cc monster bikes shoot off like bullets, racing down the Yacht Club Straight at explosive speed. Minutes later, the leaders, hunched low over handlebars, rocket past the stands in a blur, engines screaming. Then the control tower announces an accident, somewhere out of sight, and TV monitors show a shaky rider rising from the ground behind a screen of dust. The race stops, ambulances race out onto the course, bodies and bikes are hauled off, and the contest resumes.

After each race, the three jubilant winners mount the podium with the scantily-clad Moet and Chandon girls. Draped in leafy green victory wreaths, they shake up the bottle, pop the cork and spew Champagne all over each other, the girls and the fans crowded below. It is the racing fraternity's version of high fives.

While elated riders celebrate with Champagne showers, losers are in the pits making their excuses and other bikes are already racing in the next event.

Bikers and drivers are a different breed, track types say. Car racing has more status, and prize money, but bikers lead in the macho stakes. "You have to be crazy to do this on four wheels, let alone two," an awed enthusiast says. "But have you noticed that out of the first 10 leaders, five of them are Irish?"

When the leather-clad bikers wheel their mounts away, cars take over the pits. The drivers in fluorescent fireproof coveralls of dazzling white, yellow, red or orange look like walking billboards with sponsors' tags, crests and decals lining their arms like boy scout merit badges.

In this young man's sport, F3 drivers, many of whom have just graduated from racing go-karts, are particularly youthful. When two boys walked into a Montagut French Fashions racing team press conference earlier, I assumed they were models for teenaged sporting wear. Until the downy-cheeked youths were introduced as the racing team; baby-faced Paul Stewart, son of legendary racer Jackie, and square-jawed, serious David Coulthard, destined for glory on Macau's streets.

Unlike any neighborhood garage, the pit area is pristine, with enough spare engine parts, hoods, fenders, and wheels set out by each team to rebuild a car. No oil or grease stains mar the immaculate machines as mechanics, like technicians in their spiffy team uniforms, constantly wipe and polish the engine and body.

As I admire this loving handiwork, a cry comes up from a flock of Hong Kong photographers.

"Waaah!!!"

Two towering blond Camel cigarette models stroll by in high-cut dancer's leotards, showing that not all close shaves come on the racetrack. The Hospitality Girls throw the pit paparazzi into a photography feeding frenzy as bikers, mechanics, even other photographers jostle to pose with the long-legged beauties.

"Pit Poopsies" in bright, brief team costumes hold umbrellas over the drivers, pose for photographs and promenade around the pit area. The models add sparkle to Grand Prix racing, but only in France, Japan and Macau. Strutting their stuff this year are a Kawai Steel trio with yellow writing across pert blue bottoms; Golden Palace Hotel Macau girls in gold and green cheerleaders outfits; Art Beauty team models in green and white; and Montagut Girls in orange and blue. Outside the track, Camel girls in craftily frayed cutoffs and mustard-yellow tops sell souvenir posters.

Saturday is amateur day, with hobby drivers from the region racing their own cars. "These are guys who never get out of second gear in Hong Kong," a track cynic says. "They have to clear the debris off the track whenever these half-fast drivers race."

Mid-afternoon, drivers from the Gentlemen Racers Club, whose first qualification is the ability to afford a fast car, rev up their Porches, Ferraris, a Corvette and a rare Lamborghini Diablo for the Supercar Challenge. When the flag falls, 32 high-performance sports cars screech off the grid, tear down the straightaway hell-bent for the first bend -- and a roar comes from the crowd. A television camera at Lisboa Bend, where so many drivers come to grief, shows a pile-up of cars scattered around the track, their racing days ended. It looks more like a demolition derby than a sports car race.

"The Porsche dealer already has his calculator out counting his money from the repairs," chortles the track cynic.

As the Gentlemen finish their race, a Porsche chasing a Fer-

rari to the checkered flag, Classic Car Club of Hong Kong owners prepare their "unusual and exotic cars" in the pits. This is
a mixed group -- MGs, Volkswagens, Alfas, Triumphs and Lo-
tuses racing against a Ford Mustang, D-type Jaguar and a Ford
Cortina. Classic drivers pulling on their helmets and gloves are
paunchy, balding bulldogs, not the whippet-lean boys of the F3
circuit. Meanwhile, a Gentleman driver from the Supercar race
whines to his doting girlfriend about how someone had done
him wrong out on the track. He is near to tears of righteous in-
dignation.

What a motoring writer will later refer to as "the million dol-
lar carnage" continues, with an AC Cobra smashing into a wall,
several cars spinning out and a driver sent to the hospital. After
10 eventful laps, a Cathay Pacific flight engineer squeaks across
the finish line first with his classic green 1957 D-type Jaguar to
retain his title.

The amateur events finished, Saturday night is serious party
night with private celebrations, hospitality suites, cocktail recep-
tions and dinners in Macau's many hotels.

In a reception in the Mandarin Hotel, hors d'oeuvres and
drinks offered, several F3 drivers gather to sip sodas and mingle
with the fans. Personable Paul Stewart, a second-time visitor, reflects on the Macau Grand Prix. "Local fans may know less about
racing, but they are enthusiastic, because it is the one event of the
year here," he says. "It's exciting for us, too, because the competition is great with so many good drivers." Another driver is
explaining the medic's role to a circle of admirers: "If you're in an
accident, he's there to make sure that your heart works and you
brain works. That is it. He is an anesthetist."

When world champion bike racer, Texan "Revin' Kevin"
Schwantz -- who looks more a scrawny teenager just off his bicycle -- comes in, even the Formula 3 drivers are awestruck. Ignoring the party types, the young professionals gather together
like a bunch of kids hanging around a street corner talking about
their cars and bikes.

Next door, the Mandarina Duck Gentleman Sports Club awards ceremony is larger and more lavish, with oysters and roast beef, sushi and a more generous bar. Club members applaud and distribute trophies from today's competition, for first, second, third, best in the time trials, best improvement in the time trials and more. The driver from the pits, still scowling into his scotch over his injured pride, receives only a small trophy for participating.

In a large ballroom, the organizers, sponsors and local officials gather at Watson's lavish black tie dinner, with a live band playing and Champagne flowing. And all across Macau, bars are crowded with bike and car enthusiasts and visiting yachtsmen from the Grand Prix Regatta. A British reporter on the regular racing circuit observes between sips of complimentary wine, "This is the most fun meet of the year. It's a party for the organizers, for everyone except the drivers. In Europe's one day meets it is all tension. Here you get to meet the drivers, see them when they relax." But they are a clean-living bunch, as their profession demands.

At dawn Sunday, lights glow from the car park where the mechanics have been working through the night to get their charges ready for the race. The road outside the pits is a junkyard of novices' pranged-up cars with crushed fenders, battered bodywork and crumpled wheels.

Today, the professionals take over the track with the F3 and Guia races. Car racing is a family tradition, with names inscribed on some cars familiar to race fans of 20 years ago -- Stewart, Fittipaldi, Villeneuve. And there are so many Italian names, the lists of drivers resembles an exotic pasta menu -- Schiattarella, Gilardi, Ravaglia, Angelelli.

One Guia car bears a mystical inscription that is either Zen philosophy or a Japanese T-shirt slogan:

Born to infinity of

a critical plane:

A new dynamic relationship

bonding body, machine and nature.
Forging freedom, faith
love of the track.

In the midst of all the activity, a demure young lady in traditional Japanese kimono pitter-patters through the pits. A sizable Japanese film crew with cameras, tripods, huge reflectors and production assistants with clipboards, soundmen and boom men follows two "drivers" walking along, arguing. It is a Japanese movie being shot on location.

The actors, even more clean-cut than the real drivers, walk deliberately towards each other. They stand, staring steely-eyed for a long moment, then brush past each other. The shorter "driver," obviously the villain in this little drama, turns back to glare malevolently, with the kind of look normally found in Japanese Samurai comic books. Then the director, in a black beret, yells "Cut" in English.

Meanwhile, real life dramas take place all around, as pit crews work feverishly to prepare cars for the high-stakes race. It is a mechanical marvel as they dismantle the precious little cars like intricate puzzles, replace parts or entire engines, fit on new fiberglass body parts, and stick on decals like kids building models. The small, low-slung single seat F3s look like toys close up, and drivers have to remove the steering wheel to squeeze in. But when they start, the bracckk-bracckk-bracckk shakes the ground.

Throughout the afternoon, a crew with major problems works furiously to replace the engine as starting time approaches. Dripping sweat, they work silently, each man knowing his part, hands reaching for gleaming tools with the precision of a team of surgeons in an operating room -- except they use wrenches and screwdrivers instead of scalpel and forceps.

While they battle against time, a public relations director in the next pit sets up his clients, posing drivers, mechanics and pit girls around the car for publicity photographs and press releases. Nearby, news photographers taking pictures of drivers in a rickshaw have pounced on American biker, Richard Shaw, as a favorite subject.

Some journalists are interested in more than motoring matters, though. For days, a woman from a Hong Kong English-language newspaper prowls the pits trying to get the lowdown on the camp followers and the Hospitality Girls. Searching for the steamy, seamy side of the racing scene, she asks the models if they see the drivers after the races -- implying that they are fringe benefits. When she questions one particularly youthful driver if he goes out with the girls, he disarms her with, "Why, are you angling for a date?" She gets neither date nor dirt, and a story appears in the weekend paper about the clean-cut drivers.

Not all of the "girls" are as demure as the diminutive umbrella bearers, though. Two short, dyed blonde poopsies in Day-Glo lime bathing suits, hot pink jackets, crimson shoes and matching lips pose provocatively with anyone interested. One keeps adjusting her suit to hide the tattoo on her breast.

Races are best watched from hospitality suites in the Mandarin Oriental hotel across the street from the pits, with its complimentary bars and elaborate Asian buffets. There, privileged guests of race sponsors gather to eat, drink and watch cars screaming through Mandarin Bend below at maximum revs, and on TV monitors. Here, it is Champagne and caviar. Down in the stands, it is rice box lunches, hot dogs and beer.

The Guia Race for Group A touring cars is the most grueling contest, the professionals doing 30 laps in about 90 minutes. When Watson's driver Emanuele Pirro wins the big race, he takes the winners' stand and pours Watson's water over his head. These pros know on which side their sponsorship bread is buttered.

The atmosphere around the starting grids crackles like a high-tension wire as the important F3 event approaches. With the clock ticking down, the benighted Japanese crew desperately works on its troublesome car. Fortunately, the races are running almost an hour late, giving them a chance to make it.

The pensive young drivers pull on white balaclavas and sunglasses that make them look like sci-fi movie creatures, and squeeze into their cars while photographers and TV crews swarm over them, shoving cameras in their faces. Led by a $7 million Jaguar shipped over for the occasion, they take off for a practice lap, then line up on the starting grid.

Three Brazilian dancers, colored ribbons hanging from shorts and halters, jiggle onto the track, dancing, singing, playing guitars and bongo drums. They gyrate over to the two Brazilian cars, driving photographers wild. The bemused announcer looking down from the control tower says "There are some young ladies down there with bits of colored paper stuck to their, ah, persons." Meanwhile, team leaders hold intense, last-minute briefings with the drivers as crews check tire pressures and fuss over the cars.

Finally, the Macau governor and racing officials appear for the starting ceremony, along with jumping, head-shaking green, yellow, gold and red paper lions dancing on the track as firecrackers explode. With the smell of black powder and high-octane gas, it seems highly hazardous. Just as the speeches end, the beleaguered Japanese car finally starts, and lines up last on the grid. The mechanics, at least, have won their race against time.

The flag drops, the cars start in a great roar, charging for positions at the first bend like hybrid rabid beasts, so fast that road-level spectators feel the impact like a body blow. Young David Coulthard takes the lead and increases it convincingly, moving so far ahead that the TV cameras concentrate on the duels further back in the pack, to the dismay of his sponsors. The Scotsman wins the leg with a convincing nine seconds, making him impossible to beat in the second leg.

It is like a rock concert down at the award stand, with police holding back the pushing and shoving crowd and photographers fighting for a place in front. The scene gets nasty, with one tough old Dutch Vietnam vet raging at anyone who pushes in front of him: "What are you wankers doing, you don't even have a real camera, get outta there," his big foot lashing out at intruders.

Coulthard, who looks too young to drink, fumbles his magnum of Moet. There will obviously be more in his life. Then the cork pops, spewing out Champagne froth like great clumps of snow. The three winners spray the crowd in the traditional Grand Prix ceremony, and the racing part of the weekend is over.

That night brings to mind a comment from a Macau Grand Prix aficionado in the wood-paneled room of Hong Kong's Club Lusitano, weeks earlier: "This isn't about little cars running around a track. This is a social occasion."

Across Macau, alcohol proves as powerful a fuel as Avgas as races are rerun with ever greater skill at the awards ceremony in the Mandarin and the lavish final party in the Lisboa Hotel.

"Coming out of the hairpin, I blasted up through the gears, then down to Fisherman's Bend ...," says one driver.

"I was accelerating hard right up through San Francisco Hill when ... "

It is all the racing they can do until the little cars with the big engines come back for the next Grand Prix.

TAIWAN

TAIPEI

Snakes and Dragon Ladies

November, 1980

THE scrawny old man in baggy black pyjamas Brushes the Tail
of the Sparrow, Bails the Moon from the Bottom of the Sea and
Embraces the Tiger to Return to the Mountain. With slow motion
t'ai chi ch'uan Chinese shadow boxing movements, the wizened
warrior destroys imagined enemies while far below, Taipei, provisional capital of the Republic of China, awakes to another busy
work day. Two dragons leaping from the upswept roof of the
massive, Sino-Rococo Grand Hotel blink their bulging, 500-watt
eyes at the hundreds of Taiwanese surging up the wooded hill to
greet the dawn with t'ai chi, badminton, calisthenics or simply
a walk.

Having slept in to the decadently late hour of 5 a.m., I scurry
out of my little room, which is buried in the depths of the ornately decorated Grand Hotel, to join the crowds streaming up
the mountain. Skipping up the stone steps in my black kung fu
slippers, I am soon lost in a warren of paths, temples, clearings,
courts and exercise yards. All around, Taipeiers greet the day in
their own ways. Students in bright sweat suits jog up and down

the paths, do warm-up exercises and play volleyball or badminton.

In a clearing to my left, 10 swordsmen slowly eviscerate illusory foes in unison with crude aluminum blades. Old gentlemen in baggy pants do ballet type stretching exercises, hooking their legs against tree branches. An old woman, grey hair chopped straight across high on her neck, sits on a marker stone facing the rising sun her head nodding up and down rhythmically. To the right, early risers, matutinal regime complete, gather at a temple cafe to drink tea and eat congee (rice porridge).

In this clearing, five would-be warriors flail in unison in the age-old movements of temple boxing, kicking, punching and lunging - with restraint - at the air. As they move easily from Golden Cock Stands on One Leg to a graceful Arabesque, I wave goodbye to the kung fuers and scurry down the mountain. Colonel Chan, Kuomintang Army, retired, has promised to educate me in the culture and ways of the East.

Over SCREAM BLED EGGS, as the menu calls them, the colonel gives me a quick rundown on Taiwan. This Holland-sized island, a province of China, is, he insists, the custodian of Chinese heritage and the best place to observe the true Chinese way of life. It became a protectorate of the Chinese Empire in 1206, the year Mongolian conqueror Ghenghis Khan founded the Yuan Dynasty. Occupied by the Dutch, Spanish, French and Japanese, the island was restored to China after WWII. (Although the colonel doesn't mention it, this wasn't entirely suitable to the native Taiwanese who revolted in 1947. The Nationalist Chinese army put down the brief rebellion.) In 1949, as the Communists took over the mainland, Chiang Kai Shek moved to the island with two million supporters and set up his "provisional" capital of China. But the colonel promises the nationalists will return.

Meanwhile, the Nationalist Chinese brought the vast collection of art treasures of the Imperial Collection in China with them to Taipei, founding the National Palace Museum. This is our first destination, and my first lesson in Chinese culture. Jumping into a Yueloong taxi, we swing out into the broad, straight "American-style" streets.

I am sure even the colonel will agree that Taipei is not a pretty city with its dull streets, grayness and traffic. You have to look closely to see the beauty and the life, but it is there in the ancient city gates, grand and small temples, and the bustling street life.

Colonel Chan explains that Hong Kong tourists come here because of the open countryside, a break from the congestion of their city and for the culture. Americans and Europeans come for the food, and for the culture. Japanese tourists, well, the Japanese developed a taste for the sulfur baths and accompanying rituals during WWII.

Around us, modern cars and buses pass, while slinky, Terry and the Pirates comic strip Dragon Lady vamps in high suede spike-heeled boots ride by on the backs of Hondas, reminders of how much more wealthy and sophisticated this city is than when I first saw it more than 10 years earlier. Taiwan has the second-highest standard of living in Asia, and it shows in the dress of most of the people.

At the museum with the statue of Sun Yat-sen, father of modern China, the colonel wangles me an official photographer's arm band - number 009. Museum guide Miss Celilia Hu explains that the museum, founded in Peking in 1925, houses more than a quarter of a million objects. Most of the collection is stored in a tunnel behind the museum, and even though exhibits change every three months, it takes 10 years to show the entire collection.

No superlatives could adequately describe this impressive museum of the world's oldest civilization, a must-see for anyone interested in Chinese culture. Certainly, one day is inadequate to take it all in, and as we jog down the rows of exhibits of bronzes, jade, pottery lacquer ware, enamel ware, carvings, religious implements and paintings, I pause to note only the most unusual.

Look at this Shang bronze wine vessel with the Tao-tieh in relief. The Tao-tieh is an ogre, a cross between a horned lion and a griffin, sometimes called a "glutton for a literal translation of the name. Imagine waking up after too many draughts of the bronze wine cup facing that grotesque creature and the word "glutton" ringing in your head. Perhaps the design was meant to encourage temperance. Early Chinese artists relied heavily on imagination rather than copying nature, Miss Hu explains. I hope this little beauty springs only from imagination, and perhaps a few too many pulls from the bronze wine jug: an owl head figure in marble with ram's horn, monkey's eyes, eagle's beak, wings of a coiled serpent, elephant legs, human eyebrows and ears and body covered with fish scales. This night guardian of an emperor's tomb can walk, swim and fly.

But on to more pleasing exhibits, such as a jade battle ax with entwined serpents or 48-piece jade screen. On another floor, we see traditional Chinese paintings with the familiar jagged peaks, gnarled trees and lowering clouds and a carved ivory stand surmounted by 21 concentric balls each one carved in fine openwork design so you can revolve them separately.

We also see a bamboo carving of the eight immortals of the Sung Dynasty, and an ivory food container that took 100 years to carve. And finally the most valuable piece of pottery in the world, to my eyes a not-exceptional blue on white effort with the ubiquitous dragon.

Thanking Miss Hu and, reluctantly, handing back my 009 arm band, I join Colonel Chan on the steps of the museum and head to the airport. On the way, he talks about the favorite Chinese topic, food. Taiwan, he claims, offers the greatest Chinese food, in all its varieties, in the world. (Hong Kong residents might argue and Pekingers might claim they get the best northern food). While serving dog is now illegal in Taiwan, food stalls in an old section of the city offer "fragrant meat." Tonight, Chan promises, we will sample tiger and dragon soup (which I learn later is snake and a kind of wild mountain cat.)

First we attend the changing of the guard at the National Revolutionary Martyr's Shrine. Black-clad schoolgirls pose alongside ramrod-stiff marines in crisp G.I. Joe uniforms, white belts, gloves and scarves, the intricate moon door reflected in their stainless steel helmets. The navy, army, air force and marines take turns providing the honor guard for the shrine to both military and civilian martyrs.

Actually, two guards corps stride into the shrine precincts together: the formal Marine guard, marching with brisk precision, and a ragtag mob of young students doing their best to imitate the military maneuvers. By the time the guard has officially changed, the orange glow on the intricate red and green drum tower has faded to a dull grey and lights are coming on over the city.

On our way to Huahsi, or Snake, Street we pass a temple celebrating its 240th birthday. The streets around the temple are alive with people, lights and color. The Chinese celebrate religious occasions with considerably less restraint than Westerners. Votaries burn joss sticks and offer crackers, algae cakes, cookies and sweets at the altar, then hurry outside to shop in the adjacent streets at stalls lit by the harsh glare of bare bulbs. Black-and-yellow-robed monks hurry past the 12-foot-high floral wreaths, and, in a corner of the temple, a trio of dreamy-eyed ancients saw away on unrecognizable stringed instruments. Is the strange squawking emanating from the overhead speakers a distortion by the antiquated amplifier or an accurate reproduction of the trio's efforts?

Down on Snake Street, that great street, rows of snake and herbal medicine shops vie for the attention of an all-male crowd apparently all fearful of encroaching impotence. Colonel Chan explains that the snake soup and the blood and bile mixtures are good for the eyesight and general health, but I see no women in thick glasses here. We know what is really troubling these men, don't we Colonel?

One tout has hustled a particularly large crowd with his spiel, playing with a Taiwan cobra which sways its hooded head and darts its tongue at the spectators.

Keeping up a constant patter, the snake man feels along the

belly of the reptile, finds the right spot, and with a flash of garden-size shears, rips out the heart and gall bladder which he tosses aside, and drains the blood into a glass. Then, with a sound like the opening of a long zipper, he tears the snake out of its skin with his scissors and hangs the wriggling body from a rope near a dozen other skinned snakes. He pierces the gall bladder, drains the vile green bile into the glass of blood, adds powerful white Chinese wine, and offers it up for sale. Three drunken German tourists buy the potent brew, and to the noisy approval of the crowd, drink it between them. In a corner of the table, the snake heart is still beating 10 minutes later.

The snake man produces a tray with bowls of Tiger and Dragon soup, pops a pill in each one, and leads the way inside the restaurant. The potion is rather bland and a little tough, like barnyard rooster stew, but the colonel assures me I will be warm and "strong" all winter.

Our declining libidos thus fortified, we head for one of Taipei's popular Mongolian barbecue restaurants to feed our bodies. The smoky hall is already packed when we arrive, just in time to get the last table with gas heated hotpot with high chimney in the center. We grab a bowl line up with other diners at the kitchen, and file past a groaning board of beef, mutton, chicken, pork and venison, frozen and thinly sliced. Ghenghis Khan conquered half the world on this grub. Next come the sliced tomatoes, bean sprouts, green peppers, two kinds of onions.

Now we come to the sauces, everyone mixing to taste the soya sauce, shrimp oil, lemon water, liquid sugar, chopped chili, chopped garlic, sesame oil and liquid ginger. At the end of the line, four tough looking cooks surround a four foot diameter griddle heated by an immense charcoal fire. Reaching out of the cloud of smoke and steam, they grab the bowls, slap the contents on the hot metal surface, mix it around with three foot chopsticks and swirl the barbecued meat and vegetables back in the bowl. Above the hubbub of the diners and the sizzle of the stove, I imagine shaggy ponies whinnying as they graze on the steppes outside a felt walled yurt.

Back at our table, we mix up a "hotpot stew" in another bowl. This time, it is cabbage, bean curd, rice noodles, more mutton and egg white, all poured into the trough of water in the tabletop stove. Almond-eyed, amber-skinned, raven-tressed maidens flit between the tables serving Taiwan beer and shoshi, a foul, fiery Chinese wine. The shoshi burns its way down with the red meat and vegetables.

Finally, gorged, we struggle to the door with loud belches and grunts, and instead of mounting our ponies and riding off into the inky black Asian heartland like the Mongols, we taxi back to the hotel.

Half-an-hour later, Colonel Chan deposits me outside the Carnival Hotel on Nanking East Road, but flushed by the Tiger and Dragon soup, the red meat and the wine, I am unable to sleep. I prowl Taipei's streets impressed by the tonsorial fastidiousness of the locals. Every second doorway has a barber pole in front of it. Finally, tempted by the whispered invitation of "massage, massage" of young ladies in the doorways, I peer in. Young men stretched out on rows of barber chairs are getting massaged. An actual massage in a massage parlor? What has this ancient civilization degenerated to?

Shattered by this revelation, I retreat to my chamber to seek serenity and to dream of almond-eyed Mongolian beauties.

QUEMOY

War, then Peace

Spring 1997

FOR a tiny place that was one of the world's major battlefields a few decades ago, and which has only been open to foreign tourists for about a year, Quemoy is remarkably casual. About 20 minutes after arriving on the 55-minute flight from Taipei, my wife and I have checked into the River Kinmen Hotel, and are in Kincheng village at the motor-scooter rental shop.

The grinning owner shoves a Chinese form at me, and says his only three words of English: "Name. Number. Money."

What number does he want? Passport? Credit card? International Driver's License? I write down my Hong Kong telephone number and give him the equivalent of about $20 in Taiwanese dollars. He hands me the keys to an almost new burgundy scooter of the type that gigolos ride in Italian movies, and leaves us to it, with no instructions, no helmets.

But these scooters are simple, with no clutch, no gears, no shifting, just gas and brake controls. The light traffic in the few blocks of town presents no problem, then we are out on the open road, exulting in the born-to-be-wild, wind-in-your-hair riding -- even though we can only reach about 35 miles an hour. The pleasant, pine-covered island with its fine, empty roads is perfect for motorcycle riding.

But Quemoy (Kinmen, or Golden Gate, to the Mainland Chinese), an archipelago of 12 islands covering 58 square miles, is much more than a scenic tropical getaway. Once, the world's black-and-white TV sets were tuned to daily news reports from this outpost just off the coast of mainland China. In an attempt to wrest the island from Taiwan, the Communist army launched a massive artillery barrage on Quemoy on August 23, 1958.

Over the next 44 days, half a million shells fell on the island. Taiwan's forces, equipped by the U.S., retaliated with their own artillery and air offensive, severely damaging mainland forces. In October, China announced an "even-day cease-fire" program, and for the next 20 years the two sides traded artillery fire only on alternate days (with Sundays a day of rest). Instead of artillery shells, they fired canisters containing propaganda leaflets.

The volume of the war of words increased to karaoke-like levels, however, with the mainland broadcasting its propaganda to Quemoy, while Taiwan retaliated with four 30,000-watt loudspeakers on Quemoy blasting out anti-Communist messages and rock songs across the narrow strait. As well, over many years, when the wind was right, Nationalist forces on Quemoy launched thousands of helium balloons toward the mainland carrying pocket calculators, digital wristwatches and other products of Taiwan's capitalist factories (including, it is rumored, see-through silk lingerie) to demoralize the mainland Chinese. As far as I know, no one has determined the effectiveness of silk panties as a propaganda weapon. All of this ended in 1991, with the general relaxation of tension. What was one of the world's major battlefields a few decades ago gradually opened up to local, then international tourism.

So the island is a repository of fascinating military sites and memorabilia as well as natural beauty. Decades of large-scale reforestation, with each soldier stationed there responsible for the growth of one tree, has succeeded in the greening of Quemoy, turning it into what residents, (with an obvious eye on tourism), call a "park on the sea." And with the captive labor of all those soldiers based on the island, it is as trim and clean as a military base.

As we scooter across the island, we happen on soldiers everywhere in mottled, camouflage uniforms, like Chinese male Spice Girls. It is the most militarized place I've seen, with armed guards standing by sandbag emplacements, anti-aircraft guns mounted on the roundabouts, and jeeps and army trucks draped with netting. Yet the atmosphere seems unthreatening, like a military theme park, and there appears to be no restriction as to where we can go, except into the bases.

Navigating with our Chinese map, we reach the northeast-ernmost point of the island, and the Mashan Observation Station, the closest point to China. Despite not speaking a word of English, two bespectacled armed soldiers standing guard at the camp entrance make it clear that we can't enter now. The station is closed for lunch.

Shortly before 1:30pm, several Taiwanese teenagers show up on scooters, then a tour bus disgorges excitable, amiable rustics.

At precisely 1:30pm, the soldiers let us pass, and we enter a tunnel, which goes a long, long way, arrow-straight towards the beach. At the end, the tunnel opens into a blue-painted room, with narrow slits at eye-level, looking out to China, visible just beyond the narrow strait. We all take turns peering through one of the five mounted binoculars to what was once called the Bamboo Curtain. It is eerie, seeing this once forbidden zone, just over a mile away, and imagining the deadly artillery duel. Perhaps it is the only bit of their former homeland that many of these Taiwanese will ever see.

Continuing on, and frequently getting lost in the maze of roads, we find the August 23 Artillery War Museum. Like the entire island, this is now a swords-to-plowshares endeavor. Set in a pleasant park with a lake, it displays an F-86 jet fighter, a 155mm cannon and an amphibious landing craft, all now backdrops for tourist photographs. Laughing youths strike heroic poses before the pieces, hoist their girlfriends into the intake of the jet, and click off souvenir snapshots for the folks back home.

Inside, the museum displays grainy black-and-white photographs of Quemoy's military past. There is considerable media content here, with a display of news clippings and pictures depicting war correspondents with PRESS on their helmets and TV newsmen with an antique hand-held newsreel camera. Another shows mainly American correspondents gathered under a makeshift Quemoy Press Club sign. A display of English, French and Spanish clippings includes a U.S. News and World Report story: "The Reds are the real losers in the Quemoy war."

At the northwest point of the island, we happen on the Kuningtou Military History Museum, near the site where local forces repelled a major Communist amphibious assault in 1949 (10 years before the deadly artillery duel). Displays here are mainly huge, heroic battle-on-the-beach paintings, some basic mock-ups of the battle zone, plus weapons such as American M5 A1 tanks, known here as Kinmen Bears.

With dark (and the cocktail hour) fast approaching, we return to the River Kinmen Hotel, and reluctantly hand the desk clerk the scooter key to return to the rental office. I feel like a Hell's Angel robbed of his Harley.

In this spotless, friendly hotel, once again we face communication problems as the restaurant menu is only in Chinese. But a woman from a party of ebullient locals comes to our rescue. She explains the menu through the practical expedient of darting over to nearby tables to spirit away dishes from under the chopsticks of diners, to show us what is available. With her recommendations, we feast on lemon chicken, chili prawns, fish grilled with garlic, steamed vegetables, rice and chilled Taiwan beer.

People able to withstand the world's greatest artillery barrage are not stymied by the problems of a pair of hungry foreigners.

ISLA FORMOSA

Hard-boiled, Naturally

Spring 1997

HIKERS coming down the mossy stone path out of the thick forest welcome us with cheery greetings: "Ni hao, Ni hao?" ("How are you" in Mandarin). Hiking is a social activity in Taiwan, and all along the way we encounter friendly groups of climbers with walking sticks, tinkling bells on belts and backpacks, carrying umbrellas and wearing sporty khaki outdoor hats.

Walking the trails of Yangmingshan National Park, a 30-minute drive northeast of Taipei, we can appreciate why the Portuguese called this Isla Formosa (Beautiful Island). On rugged Taiwan, weekend escapes from the capital are only a taxi, train or subway ride away.

Even though this is the closest getaway to the capital, locals seem pleased, and mystified, to find foreigners here. "How you find Yangmingshan?" ask those with a modicum of English. Easy. We took a cab from downtown Taipei.

Like travel all over Taiwan, getting around the park can be a challenge. At the visitor center, park rangers try to help, but speak little or no English. Finally we buy a map in Chinese (English maps are out of stock) and, with much sign language, work out basic directions for a suitable half-day hike. At the canteen, we buy bottles of water and lichee juice and packets of biscuits and set off up the mountain.

From the center, we follow a broad, paved stone path up to a junction, where a map and directional sign are posted on a board. Taiwanese parks are well marked -- unfortunately, only in Chinese characters. So we stand there attempting to match the squiggly symbols on the sign to those on our map, until another hiker comes along and points the way.

As we continue up through the sweet gum trees, green maples and flowering cherry trees, we encounter more hikers. One elderly Taiwanese walking with his cronies wears a red ball cap that says, appropriately, Top Climber. "Very good healthy," a spry septuagenarian assures us as his wife nods approvingly at our efforts.

Foliage changes within the park, and we pass through pine and acacia forests planted during large-scale afforestation programs early in the century. With the clear air and the scent of pines, we could be in the middle of British Columbia, Canada, except for those pesky Chinese signs.

A couple walking down the hill carrying a bag of cuttings stops to chat. When I look at the fernlike plants and smell them, the woman says they are used for making tea. "Good for the throat, and for a cold," she explains. In her best English, she adds that their proper name is "Under the Stone Plant," and shows how they grow under the paving stones along the path.

The higher we climb, the fewer hikers we encounter. When no one is around, all we can hear is the throaty warbling of the bulbuls and babblers and the scraping of our boots on the ancient mossy stones. Little lizards skitter along the path, birds rustle in the bush and the wind sways the cherry trees. It is a rare, and welcoming, sound of silence so seldom heard in Asia.

At another intersection, as we struggle once more with the map, trying to make sense of the mysterious Chinese characters, a hiker coming down a path to the right says, "Chihsing Park. There," pointing back the way he came. The sign indicates it is just a few hundred yards away, so we follow the path. A few minutes later we break out of the woods to an open hanging valley with a panoramic view of the city spread around the Tamsui River more than 3,000 feet below. Families gather in groups, sitting on the benches, playing, reading papers and barbecuing chicken wings around Chinese-style pagodas and gazebos with upturned tiled roofs.

We pause awhile in the afternoon sun, nibbling biscuits and enjoying the expansive view. The lichee juice we bought earlier is delicious, thick, sweet and pulpy, like eating a succulent fruit dessert.

A turnoff from the park leads down to a small mountain lake, a fumarole we can see steaming in the distance, and a highway back to Taipei. But it is still early, so we continue up to the peak. The path becomes very steep, and it is hard going, straight up stairways of stone. You should be moderately fit to climb to Mt. Chihsing, but we've allowed plenty of time, so stop on the way to enjoy the views and catch our breath. Here above the tree line, it seems as though we can see all of Isla Formosa.

The last stiff section is like climbing a staircase, a steady slog up that finally takes us to the top of 3,739-foot Mt. Chihsing (the park's highest peak). Weather is unpredictable up here, with rain, wind and clouds common, so a weatherproof jacket is useful. But our luck holds. The sky, which has been changing all day, clears now, and from the top of this volcanic cone we have magnificent views of Taipei to the south, the mountains all around, the sea coast and Taiwan Strait to the north.

It is all downhill from here, the path zigzagging a long way down, through pine trees, pampas grass and dense thickets of young bamboo. Soon we start to catch the distinctive smell of sulfur, like fizzling matches. Further down, we walk on paving stones through fumaroles, great patches of parched, blackened earth belching and billowing steam, like agitated tea kettles. Some steaming fumaroles have the telltale yellow sulfur coloring around the charred area, others unnatural green crystals, like a color created in a scientific experiment gone wrong. Further down, the side of the mountain looks as though it has just been bombed, and we can feel the heat of the volcano under our soles.

Finally, the path leads to the visitor's center, where families with babes in arms, young women in mini skirts and high heels, and young men in trendy city duds walk the few meters from the parking lot to admire the giant stinking and steaming Hsiaoyukeng fumarole.

The water here is apparently hot enough to boil an egg. There is no need for that, though. After our brisk hike, we head back to Taipei, with its big-city action and the world's best Chinese food, just a half-hour taxi ride away.

Great Gorge

Far below us, jade-green waters froth over smooth marble rocks like lime juice poured over opaque ice cubes. The sheer walls of Taroko Gorge rise steep and high on either side, while the road clings to the cliff and punches through the solid marble in a series of tunnels. For sheer physical drama, this massive chunk of jagged marble, a deep split in the earth's surface, rates right up with the world's great natural wonders.

The Taroko Gorge in central Taiwan is one of this scenic island's major tourist attractions. Yet until this summer, it had been a one-day excursion for most foreigners, who flew into Hualien on the east coast, toured the nearby gorge by car, then flew back the same evening. With the opening in mid-1997 of the Grand Formosa Taroko Gorge, the first international-standard hotel in Taroko National Park, longer visits are now easily arranged.

So, at 8:20 one morning, we board an express train at Taipei's cavernous railway station and rattle through the city. We are the only Westerners on board. Beyond the urban sprawl, we are treated to scenes of age-old China. Scalloped Chinese graves are cut into the hillsides, brown rivers flow down from the green hills through rice paddies where brightly colored rectangular flags snap and flutter in the breeze. Fantastic, orange-roofed temples with ornate, dragon-shaped ridges and overwrought, Sino-psychedelic embellishments glitter in the sun. An hour out, we reach the coast and run alongside the Pacific Ocean, with ancient, bare wooden boats hauled up on stony beaches.

At Hualien, there is a mass rush off the train and on to waiting tour buses. (Outside of Taipei, there is little English spoken, so it is best to have everything pre-arranged.) A driver in a Grand Formosa hotel vest waits in front of a van with a large, hand-printed sign saying "Harchant" in the window.

The stretch of rural land between mountain and sea that we now drive through appears to have two major crops: vegetables and stone. Roadside stalls display piles of produce such as sweet potatoes, potatoes, squash, corn and jumbo-sized yellow bananas. Others sell locally quarried and hand-crafted polished boulders and stones, marbleware and dark green Taiwan jade.

A half-hour after leaving the station, we reach a long lineup of ponderous double-decker tour buses at the park entrance. Our driver blithely sails past, waving his ID card at the park officer, and we beat the crowd into the gorge. Soon afterwards, we pass the Eternal Spring Shrine, with a waterfall pouring out the front like a tongue lapping out of a red and white mask. A trail winds up the steep mountain face to a small Zen monastery, Kuanyin Cave (for the Buddhist Goddess of Mercy), a jade tower and a bell tower.

For 12 miles, the road clings to the cliffside and burrows through a series of tunnels cut into the solid white marble. With the jagged rocks and tunnels with huge round windows cut out of the walls to provide light and ventilation, it is like driving through immense chunks of Swiss cheese. Some cliff walls are bare, with swirly marble cake patterns, others blanketed with vegetation.

Double-decker buses squeeze through impossibly narrow spaces of the Tunnel of Nine Turns, and the canyon closes in so much in places it seems like the opposite walls are almost close enough to touch. At the Swallow Grotto, we stop to walk along and peer though the rock "windows" down the heart-stopping sheer drop of the crevice of jagged marble and granite. Far below, the Liwu River cascades over boulders on the river bottom like variegated blobs of melted wax. It is as though Salvador Dali designed Taroko. Further on, marble lions guard the entrance to the Bridge of Motherly Devotion with, of course, white marble railings. Atop a rocky outcrop here, a green-tile-roofed gazebo built for contemplating the wonders of nature is now a photo prop for tourists.

Tienhsiang, at the end of the gorge, is a mini hamlet of a few snack shops selling ominous-looking bubbling stews, a cubby-hole of a bus station office, some homes and several churches with hostel accommodation. A half-dozen souvenir stores display mainly tasteless marble lamp stands, paper weights, book-ends, vases, tableware and chessboards, as well as plastic toys, Chinese back-scratchers and other garish souvenirs.

The spanking new hotel Grand Formosa Taroko Gorge is tastefully set next to the Liwu River, not far from the hillside Hsiang-Te Buddhist Temple. Just three stories, the hotel blends harmoniously into the background. Rooms are comfortable, with the best overlooking the river. Desk clerks speak little English here, but with prebooking this presents no real problem.

Of seven hikes in the Taroko Gorge National Park, to natural wonders or to isolated aboriginal villages, the most accessible from the hotel is the 1.3-mile walk to Paiyang Falls. It is already late afternoon, so we set off up the main road where, about 300 yards away, a tunnel cuts straight through the big mountain. It is long and dark, except for the light at the end, but paved and easy walking. On the other side, we enter what seems a new, unexplored world. A broad path leads across a bridge, a sensational but easy, walk high above a rushing river and through a series of dark, twisting tunnels (one nearly 1,250 feet long) where a small flashlight proves useful. After about 20 minutes, we can hear the roar of falls ahead, like the distant rumble of ocean surf.

Finally, exiting a last long tunnel, we see it - a long silver stream running through lush foliage down the opposite mountainside. Crossing a small suspension bridge over the roaring rapids to a viewing platform is like walking on a long and particularly bouncy trampoline. Two young Chinese girls from Toronto studying Chinese in Taipei, ask us take to take their pictures as they stick their heads through the struts of the suspension bridge. When they leave, we have the entire river valley to ourselves. After savoring the solitude and the views, we walk back to the hotel, making it easily before dark.

By the time we are ready for dinner, the dining room is closed, so we settle in the lobby lounge, overlooking the interior courtyard with its ornamental pool, fountains and flowers. In this new hotel, the service is cheerful, friendly and strikingly inefficient, but the lounge is the only action in town. The electronically operated, computer-programmed piano goes through a cycle of Moon River, Baby Elephant Walk, the theme from the Sting, Lara's Theme from Dr. Zhivago and Tie a Yellow Ribbon.

But don't shoot the player piano. It is the only entertainment here, outside of watching satellite TV in your room or sitting out on your private balcony listening to the soothing sound of the river running through the gorge.

Short Hops, Subway Stops

The spring, 1997, opening of a MRT new subway line to the north brought a number of intriguing getaways to within easy reach of Taipei.

Gates of Hell: The Japanese, great connoisseurs of hot springs and medicinal waters, built resorts around Peitou, eight miles north of central Taipei, during their occupation until the end of World War II. Japanese military officers and businessmen once used the resorts to entertain temporary lady friends. Now, public sulfur pools such as Hell's Valley are more family-oriented, with locals gathering to observe the huge, steaming pools, and boil eggs in the 200-degree Fahrenheit sulfurous waters.

Taipei has swallowed up Peitou, which is on the newest subway line, but the area retains an air of a Japanese holiday resort with public saunas, hotels and inns, some dating back to the occupation.

The best of these, the In-Son-Ger (the Whispering Pine Inn), is an authentic rural Japanese-style inn, although high buildings now tower over it. Entrance to the low, unobtrusive tile-roof building is past pools of golden carp, splashing waterfalls, stone lanterns and bonsai trees. Simple, traditional rooms with wood paneling, shoji (rice paper) screens and tatami (woven mat) floors are made more comfortable with Western beds and chairs with backs. The inn has its own steaming, sulfuric sunken pool for soaking away all your cares.

Old China

When Hollywood wanted a typical Chinese seaside setting for Steve McQueen's The Sand Pebbles (1966), they used Tamsui, a fishing village on the north coast of Taiwan. The village is now the last stop on the new MRT subway line, just over a half-hour from Taipei.

This authentic Chinese port, with its busy narrow streets and all signs in Chinese script is more functional than merely recreational. A riverside promenade lined with ancient broad-beamed wooden boats with the traditional good luck eyes painted on the prows leads to a ferry pier, with its carnival atmosphere. Food stalls sell snacks such as grilled octopus and candied plum tomatoes. A trio of shiny tomatoes, like snooker balls skewered on a bamboo stick, is less than $1. The coating tastes remarkably like a North American county-fair candy apple. However, the fruit is not quite to Western tastes.

The town's historical attractions include a kind of Anglo-English college campus, with red-brick buildings and students in school uniforms. Nearby, the Spanish-built Fort Santo Domingo (Fort of the Red-haired Barbarians to the locals), built in 1629, recalls the glory days when Tamsui was the main link between Taiwan and the West.

Queen Nefertiti for a Day

Bizarre lava and sandstone shapes sprouting from the beach form a kind of natural sculpture exhibition at Yehliu (Wild Willows), near the northern harbor city of Keelung. A long hawker alley selling every imaginable kind of pressed, diced, cubed, sliced, shredded, raw, salted and preserved fish and seaweed leads to the weird geological formations.

Time and tides, and wind and rain, have shaped the formations into Mushroom Rock, Cinderella's Shoe, Beehive Rock and, the most famous, Queen's Rock, a natural bust of the ancient Egyptian monarch Nefertiti.

Few visitors venture beyond the beach. They miss the best part, a flat stone path leading through sea grasses and windswept trees to the end of the promontory, with expansive views of the ocean and freighters lying at anchor waiting to get into Keelung harbor.

From a pagoda there, you can see the sun go down like thunder over the Republic of China 'cross the bay.

TIBET

LHASA

Yak Butter and Tea on the Roof of the World

November 1994

IN the 17th century, the first outsiders to reach Lhasa, Tibet's Forbidden City, observed pious pilgrims with spinning prayer wheels prostrating themselves full-length before temples, thousands of red-robed, red-cowled lamas, and yak-butter-greased peasants who "eat their meat raw and never wash their hands or face."

When I first deplaned from a Civil Aviation Authority of China (CAAC) Boeing in Lhasa in the early 1980s, I saw the same lamas, pilgrims and peasants who eat raw yak and spin prayer wheels for salvation. Only the few battered green Chinese army trucks, the four-wheel drives and the air strip seemed new.

Visitors who now arrive at a new terminal see a large city with entire suburbs of new concrete buildings and an extensive Chinese influence. Tibet has changed more in the past decade than in the previous thousand years. Yet in important ways it is the same exotic place those 17th-century explorers observed.

With an average altitude of more than 5,000 meters, the Roof of the World is the world's highest region, and among the most isolated, boxed in by immense mountain ranges on three sides. Flying in from Chengdu, China, or Kathmandu, Nepal, it is obvious why this country remained isolated for so long. Jagged, snow-capped peaks of the immense Himalayas poke through the clouds, as though tearing at the aircraft's underbelly.

Tibetans are still cheerful, humorous people open to foreigners. Tibet's' Tantric Buddhism, or Lamaism, is a sometimes ghoulish, bizarre religion of human-skull cups and skull-encrusted crowns, human-bone trumpets, copulating icons and rumored cannibalism.

Until the British invaded Lhasa under Colonel Francis Younghusband in 1904, the only wheel seen in the country was the prayer wheel. Now, jetliners arrive regularly, and satellite dishes receive international television broadcasts -- when not banned by the Chinese government.

Tibet's harsh, stunning scenery seen on the new 68 mile (96 kilometer) highway from Gonggar airport to Lhasa is age-old. Prayer flags flap from all corners of low, square, mud-brick huts, herdsmen drive skittish, shaggy yaks which look and move like musk oxen, and fields of brilliant yellow mustard ripen in the crisp air. Women winnowing barley in the fields toss the golden grain into the air from woven baskets and sing to summon the wind to blow the husks away.

A yak-skin coracle (small, round boat) twirls in the eddies of the cloudy, jade-green Tsangpo River, which thousands of miles downriver becomes the Brahmaputra, India's largest waterway, emptying into the Bay of Bengal.

On my first visit, it was a grueling bone-jarring, head-bashing, four-hour, four-wheel-drive ride over a bumpy dirt road by Chinese jeep. Now, our modern minibus zips along a paved highway, getting us to Lhasa in an easy hour-and-a half.

This mysterious Holy City that eluded outside travelers for centuries opened to tourism in the 1980s. Each year, only a few thousand adventurous tourists come, attracted by the Tibetan lamaist form of Buddhism and the dramatic mountain setting.

The biggest change for tourists has been the improved accommodation. On my last visit, we stayed in the aptly named Number 3 Guest House, a grubby barracks-like place with lumpy, dirty beds and no hot water. The government was building the city's first real hotel that would vastly improve life in Lhasa for visitors. On that early trip, a gracious, elderly American Chinese lady joked that the coffee shop in the new hotel would be called "Yak in the Box" (a parody on the U.S. fast food chain, Jack in the Box). After the greasy, almost unpalatable food we had been eating the whole trip (at that time, the worst Chinese food in Asia was in China), she sounded almost wistful.

Now, the Holiday Inn Lhasa's coffee shop, the Hard Yak Cafe, serves giant yak burgers; its bar, Altitudes (the world's highest), stocks local and imported drinks; and the hotel offers the comforts of an international establishment.

Despite the rapid changes, Tibetans remain friendly, although still given to staring, especially outside Lhasa. These ardent Buddhists are decidedly pious. As we drive through the broad streets of New Lhasa, a dozy grandma, seeing our bus bearing down on her, gives her prayer wheel a few quick extra spins as she scrambles to safety.

Everywhere, in the temples and the streets, we hear the murmured chant, "Om mani padme hom." Frequent recitation of the incantation, "Hail, Jewel in the Lotus," helps the faithful achieve enlightenment and reach the Western Paradise of Great Bliss. The words are carved in stones, written on prayer flags and inscribed on prayer wheels. In this Tibetan dial-a-prayer, the wielder gains spiritual merit with each clockwise twirl.

Ten years ago, Lhasa was a mud hut city with only a few small Tibetan shops offering basic goods or plates of tasty momo (dumplings stuffed with ground pork) with chili sauce. Now it is like a shabby, modern Chinese city with straight, paved streets and shops and restaurants with large Chinese script signs.

Karaoke bars and discos are also new. Riding a pedicab one afternoon, I spot The Bar of West. It is a garish place with flocked red velvet wallpaper rubbed smooth, a three-foot-high blowup Coca-Cola bottle, fake plastic dart boards hung on a purple curtain, green globe bulbs glowing against purple plastic wall brackets and a green patterned linoleum floor. The battered pool table is worn to a shiny moldy green, and dusty tins of Five Star Beijing China beer and Pabst Blue Ribbon are stacked behind the bar, tended by bored, sullen girls.

The square in front of the 1,200-year-old Jokhang Temple in the heart of old Lhasa, which was a muddy rubble when I last visited, has been paved over. However, the streets around this Holy See of Tibetan Buddhism are as lively and chaotic as ever, with locals in heavy regional costumes and unusual headgear buying and selling everything from religious articles to food and kitchenware.

A strange swishing sound comes from pilgrims slowly making the inner circuit clockwise around the temple. Along Barkhor Bazaar, or Free Market Street, these devout people wearing crude shoes or pieces of cardboard on their hands stand, clap, stretch out full-length, foreheads touching the ground, stand up and repeat the action. Slowly they slide along the road, like giant snails in their bulky leather overcoats.

Inside the ancient temple, rustics with matted hair, wild-looking women with turquoise beads woven into their hair, ancient ladies with faces leathery as sheep-skin coats, twirl small silver prayer wheels or giant, yak-sized golden ones.

A solid line of devotees shuffles down steep stone steps and through the crowded warren of dark winding corridors, the blackened, uneven stone floors sticky with yak butter spilled over the centuries. At each of the 24 shrines to various Buddhist deities, they pour yak butter from brass goblets, tin tea kettles, plastic jars or thermoses into basin-like lamps with dozens of flickering wicks. The lamps throw a dim yellow light on fantastic, bizarre murals and statues. Chanting and clutching prayer beads, the flock pushes forward to throw ceremonial silk or gauze scarves on the gilded Buddhas and to receive blessings. The musty atmosphere here in the nether regions of the temple is eerie, otherworldly, the cloying air pungent with the smoke of yak butter candles, burning juniper, incense and unwashed bodies.

From the roof of the temple overlooking the square we can see a stark new reality of Tibet. Even here in the old city, office and apartment blocks are replacing the traditional Tibetan low-rise stone buildings with elaborately-carved wooden eaves, as China colonizes and modernizes the country.

Not far away, prayer flags hang like lamas' laundry outside the awe-inspiring Potala Palace, Tibet's Holy See, with "Golden domes like tongues of fire" as an early foreign correspondent described it. The magnificent mountaintop 13-story Potala Palace with its gleaming gold rooftop stands against the clear blue sky, a symbol of old Tibet. The world's highest palace was the Dalai Lama's Holy Citadel before he fled to exile in India in 1959. Now, only a few of the 1,000 rooms with 10,000 shrines and 200,000 images are open to the public.

Tourists ride minibuses to the back entrance while Tibetan pilgrims from across the nation climb the steep steps to the front entrance. Together, they form solid lines winding up stairs and along the corridors. Tibet's Tantric Buddhism, or Lamaism, features elements of demonology from the ancient, animistic Bon creed. Detailed murals of demons, gods, heavens and hells cover walls of temples and monasteries everywhere. In some places, protector gods are so fierce, the lamas cover their faces with multicolored scarves to save laymen from nightmares. Elsewhere, happier Buddhist deities are entwined with svelte, naked women.

Gaping lamas lurk in the shadows here, slyly offering to sell bronze Buddhas. Here, as in other temples across Lhasa, workers are busy renovating -- and installing electric lights, which I fear will destroy the spiritual aura.

Numerous ornate temples and isolated monasteries perch on mountains surrounding Lhasa, testimony to the Tibetan piety. One day, I join a group of visitors in a minibus for a long, scenic drive along dusty roads.

On this brilliant morning, with bright summer sun lighting a chilly autumn landscape, we pass through barren valleys hemmed in by rugged, dusty hills. Along the way, our Chinese guide points out a holy mountain where sky burial takes place. Tibetans bury their dead in five ways: in a tomb pagoda, for Dalai Lamas; water burial (in the river for the fish to eat) for the sick or children; earth burial for criminals; fire burial (cremation) for leading lamas; and sky burial for others.

In sky burial, an undertaker lama called a joba takes a body to the sacred mountain, chops it to pieces and whistles for vultures to come and feast. Some witnesses contend the lama samples a morsel himself, others that he merely drinks a cup of blood. The bones are ground into fertilizer, I'm told, or carved into religious objects or musical instruments.

"Most Tibetans enjoy sky burial," our guide says.

After several hours, Tsurpu monastery suddenly appears, monk's-robe purple against the mountain at the end of a rocky canyon. Monks, women in Tibetan floor-length black gowns with striped aprons, and a few calves wander the dusty courtyard oblivious to the cold wind that sends us scurrying for shelter behind the walls.

Inside the main hall, rows of monks, men and boys, chant, beat drums with curved sticks, bang cymbals. Pointing out animal skulls hanging from the rafters, our guide explains that this is the Gelugpa (Black Hat) Buddhist Sect, which uses blood in its ceremonies.

Like the Tibetans, we have come for an audience with the living child Buddha, the 17th incarnation of the Karmapa, and the only spiritual leader now living in Tibet. Buying a kata, the traditional white scarf offering, I line up with the pilgrims slowly moving to a dais in a small room. There, a jaded-looking boy of about 10 sits, tapping each passing pilgrim lightly on the head with a short rope on a stick. A lama then gives each supplicant a piece of red yarn to wrap around their neck or wrist.

As we reach the front, the English woman ahead of me puts some shiny pens with holograms on the pile of offerings. I fold the scarf as instructed and drop it alongside. Then the boy gently touches me on the head, and I am out of the chamber. For a non-believer, it is merely a curious experience, but seeing the rapture it brings to these pious people is touching.

On another morning, we set out for Ganden, one of Lhasa's three famous monasteries, and the most spectacularly located. Leaving the main road east of Lhasa, we climb a series of switch-backs leading high up to the hilltop, with stunning views of the river valley far below.

Up here at 4,300 meters, I notice my hands have turned pur-ple, I'm gasping and giddy after a few steps, my head pounds and morning coffee gurgles unpleasantly in my stomach. Alti-tude sickness strikes most lowlanders in Tibet, with headaches, dizziness, slight nausea and shortness of breath. For most, it lasts only a few days, and the hotel provides oxygen bags in every room, but the going is slow at first.

The constant refrain everywhere along Tibet's roads, as guides point out temple ruins, is: "It was destroyed in the Cultural Rev-olution." During that era starting in 1966 when Mao's young Red Guard vandals went on a rampage across Tibet, this magnificent site suffered more than most, being almost leveled.

Ganden is being reconstructed, and already a hamlet of holy buildings sits atop the peak, where monks again live and wor-ship. A herd of saddled yaks with red wool braided in their manes stands outside a temple as though part of an ancient caravan.

Alone, I wander around the buildings, and find a dimly lit hall. Inside, the monks are chanting and the air is rich with the now-familiar smell of yak butter. The temple may be new, but the spirit is as old as Tibet itself.

LHASA to GYANTSE

Looking for Younghusband

November 1995

DUST devils swirl down a single potholed street lined with shabby one-story buildings. Along the roadside, rough-looking merchants trade hides and furs. The place has a vague feeling of the Wild West, of a one-horse town. But Gyantse, Tibet, is instead the Wild East, a one-yak town.

This dingy little burgh, this wind-blown village, played a major role in modern Tibetan history. The turn of the century was the era of the so-called "Great Game," the furtive struggle between Britain and Russia for control of Central Asia. By 1902, the Tsarist Empire was rapidly expanding eastward, and Lord Curzon, Viceroy of India, feared Russian expansion into Tibet - - and perhaps further. In a letter to London in 1902, he vowed to "frustrate this little game while there is yet time."

So, in 1904, the colonial government in India launched an expedition that has been called "one of the most contentious episodes in British imperial history."

That year, Major Francis Younghusband led a force of more than a thousand British, Sikh and Gurkha troops from India, through Sikkim to The Roof of the World. The invading army marched over the Himalayas with 10,000 coolies, 7,000 mules, 4,000 yaks and six camels hauling two Maxim guns and four artillery pieces, as well as massive supplies. Correspondents from the Daily Mail and Reuters, and a gentleman from The Times (of London) accompanied the invasion force, as did a small signals unit that laid a telegraph line as the army advanced.

Although Younghusband's expedition eventually reached

Lhasa, the capital known for centuries as the Forbidden City, the original destination was Gyantse, one of Tibet's four main cities. Here in this town, with its massive hilltop jong (fort), the invaders defeated the Tibetans in a crucial battle that changed the medieval kingdom forever.

Historical events, and the airplanes, have opened Tibet to outsiders in the past decade or so. Most tourists visit only Lhasa, taking day trips to the surrounding sites. But the Chinese government has opened most of the Tibetan interior to individual travelers in recent years. So, in Lhasa I arrange a car with a guide, Tsering, and a driver, to travel to the spot where Tibet and the world clashed so dramatically. We travel in the opposite direction, from Younghusband's destination, the capital, towards Sikkim and India.

For the entire three-day journey, my dragoman sits in front of the Chinese jeep talking nonstop to the driver in Tibetan. Tsering's worth as a guide is questionable. Earlier in Lhasa, when I asked him to identify a tree in temple grounds, he informed me, "It is an ordinary tree."

And in a temple's strange and spooky room of the protector gods, I wondered what the skulls painted on the rafter symbolized.

"They are painted skulls," Tsering notified me solemnly.

But this early morning, with the sharp, high-altitude sun, ice blue skies, hard, clear light on the surrounding mountains and the gold roofs and wine dark walls of temples, I am content to merely observe the Tibetan countryside as Tsering drones on.

Leaving Lhasa, we follow the Tsang Po River, which runs into the great Brahmaputra. The swiftly flowing river, broad in places, narrow in others, will no doubt soon be discovered by whitewater rafters looking for a new thrill. For now, locals still cross in yak-skin boats, like huge leather baskets, to camp on sandy mid-stream islands.

Rustics in native dress lead donkeys and wives down the dusty roads, and peasants work the fields along valleys between barren, dusty hills. Small herds of black yaks, which look and move like musk oxen, graze unattended. Some sport red decorations woven into their shaggy hair.

Tsering pauses long enough to point out an area high on a hilltop, where Tibetans practice sky burial, hacking up corpses and leaving them to the vultures.

These brown, dry mountains are deeply eroded, and the sun, so strong and direct in this thin air, leaves dark shadows like knife cuts in the valleys walls. We pass a truck which has gone off a bridge into the river, then another which went into the ditch, a grim comment on local driving skills.

Leaving the river, we pass a massive power development community (the "electric city" Tsering calls it) and begin the long, long, steep corkscrew climb up the mountain. Tsering points out a line crisscrossing up a mountain opposite us. It is the old trail that he rode along when going to school in Darjeeling, India, via Sikkim, in 1948. It was an arduous four-day mule ride to the Sikkim border then, but it was the only way to travel until the Chinese opened this road in 1951.

After the long climb, the top of the Khambala Pass (4,900 meters) comes very suddenly, revealing a breathtaking view of jagged, snow-topped mountains far in the distance, like the iced teeth of a crosscut saw. Far below, Yamdrok Yamtso, one of Tibet's largest and holiest lakes, spreads out, a hard, cobalt blue that appears artificial, as though someone had colored the lake with fountain pen ink.

Here at the peak, pilgrims stop on their journey to place rocks on a mound, burn incense and hang prayer flags. Old and faded pennants flutter from between two low mounds of rocks, and Tsering and I agree that it is too bad that we didn't prepare for our journey by bringing flags and incense.

On the mountain peak above, the white snowball-like dome of a Chinese radar facility sits like a giant, mislaid ping pong ball -- there to observe other countries' planes, Tsering says.

From here, the road descends gradually to the lake, a popular site for day trip picnics from Lhasa. The Tibetan villages along the road are clusters of traditional low, mud-block buildings in good repair, prayer flags flapping from the flat roofs. On the far side of the lake, we stop by a lone tent set up in the middle of this bleak valley. It is Tibet's version of a truck stop cafe, where men are cooking soup and mo-mos, tasty Tibetan meat dumplings.

In this unlikely place, I encounter a band of a dozen elderly Americans from Hawaii, all dressed in the latest brightly colored outdoor gear, vivid reds, blues and oranges among the brown rocks. After trekking in Sikkim, they came overland from Nepal, en route to Lhasa. They are delighted to hear that the Holiday Inn hotel there has hot showers and a good restaurant and bar. We chat while Tsering eats both of our lunches -- I have no appetite at this altitude -- then go on our separate ways. The road now follows the lake and turns onto a dry, dusty valley floor past hillside forts destroyed in the Cultural Revolution, like so many in Tibet.

The jeep now climbs gradually to the Karo La Pass, just 75 kilometers from Gyantse, the last and highest on this route at 5,045 meters. Near the top, I get out to look at a glacier, which almost reaches down to the road. That must have been the same ice that Younghusband's soldiers scrambled across in 1904, as they fought the last battle before marching on Lhasa.

"The battle for the Karo Pass was to make military history," as Peter Hopkirk notes in his excellent account of the event, Trespassers on the Roof of the World. "So far as is known, it was fought at a greater altitude than any other engagement before or since."

The Sikhs and Gurkhas overran a six-foot stone wall built across the pass, and the way was open to Lhasa. Even now, in late fall, it is too chilly to stay out long, and I shudder at the misery the soldiers from the Indian plains must have experienced when they passed this way.

As we descend into the next valley, we encounter one of the strangest artifacts of that early 20th-century expedition. Telephone poles made of mud, in places with wires still strung from the short crossbars, stretch off into the distance - a strange remnant of the Empire from Britain's brief period in Tibet.

The resourceful British signals unit accompanying the Younghusband expedition built this line as the army advanced, connecting the expedition to Darjeeling. One pole has 1910 daubed on it in red paint, obviously a memento of a later scrawler. More modern wooden poles now in use run parallel to the original line, going on and on across the windswept, dusty valley.

Tsering points out some mud walls he says are relics of British houses. We climb a hill to one, a kind of solid mud tower with no windows or doors. Tsering says it is a house.

"But it is solid," I note.

"Yes, maybe it is a toilet."

It is harvest time in Tibet; the fields are golden with wheat and farmers are threshing and singing as they hold the reins and whip the horses running round and round over the golden sheaves. This ancient scene, too, must be exactly as the Younghusband expedition saw it.

Travelers in the 1930s reported that this road was no more than a number of mule tracks about a foot wide twisting over the rocks and between the boulders. Now it is a paved highway.

Although one of Tibet's leading towns, Gyantse is a bleak place in a scenic setting. It has a forlorn, empty, end-of-the-world feeling. The fort looms in the background like a Tibetan haunted castle.

We first check in at the police station, an unfinished building with a small generator to supply the communications radio and a big pile of yak dung patties to fuel the little tin stove in the middle of the room. The woman officer in civilian clothes scratches out something in crude letters on a sheet of paper -- our permit to visit this area -- and Tsering hands over some ragged bills.

English traveler Robert Byron, who referred to Tibet as Asia Magna, was perhaps the first writer, and the first real "tourist," to travel to Tibet after the Younghusband expedition (although numerous military and political officials preceded him). The adventurous Byron, who wrote of the trip in First Russia, Then Tibet, came in the early 1930s, when it took him eight days to fly from London to India on Imperial Airways' new Air Mail service. His mother's only request was that he not bring back a Buddha.

But in those days, he could only travel from India, through Sikkim, and was only allowed as far as Gyantse, where a British commercial agent was posted after the 1904 invasion. Lhasa was still the Forbidden City. Today, we can only travel from the other direction, from Lhasa, and can proceed no further south.

Just south of Gyantse, the road branches south to forbidden Sikkim, down the valley from where Younghusband (and later Byron) came. I talk a reluctant Tsering and the driver into going on a short way down the valley.

Just south, a fort set high on a hill to the right guards the valley. From here, the Tibetans with their ineffectual matchlocks could only look down helplessly on the invaders. After about 10 kilometers, we stop at a small monastery. It is eerie, as squatting monks chant in the dark, cold chamber, and are served their meal of tsampa (roast barley flour) and yak butter tea. As so often in Tibet, there is a sense of timelessness.

A short distance down the valley, near a village called Guru, was site of the first fatal meeting of Tibet's medieval army and a modern one., on March 31, 1904. The Tibetans were armed only with swords, matchlocks and a talisman -- a piece of paper with the Dalai Lama's personal seal -- which the lamas promised would make them bulletproof. But magic was no match for modern arms, and in four minutes the invaders destroyed the Tibetan army. As Hopkirk notes, the medieval army disintegrated before 20th-century firepower. Daily Mail reporter Edmund Candler, who was injured in the battle, later recalled the devastated Tibetans leaving the scene.

"They were bewildered. The impossible had happened. Prayers and charms and mantras, and the holiest of their holy men, had failed them... They walked with bowed heads, as if they had been disillusioned by the gods."

I'd like to go further toward the border, toward the scene of the later battle of Red Idol Gorge just 20 miles from Gyantse, but my nervous companions refuse, returning to the town for the night. Our hotel, the Gyantse, is a new, large and typical Chinese hostelry with a cold, barren feel, and the smell of wet concrete.

Dinner, tour-group style like in China years ago, consists of a challenging mush of overcooked, soggy noodles in a soup (the Chinese don't appreciate al dente), spicy cucumbers which are edible, a heavy bun, and two plates of greasy indeterminate meat -- probably yak. When Byron was here, socializing with the Tibetan gentry, he noted Tibetan food is preferable to any that is found in Greece (where he had traveled extensively). Today, this is barely believable.

The bedroom is large, and grubby, with an ancient thermos holding some hot water, roughly painted walls and thick, heavy, dirty quilts. At this altitude, sleep is difficult, and accompanied by disturbing dreams of strange Tibetan gods.

Eager to leave the hotel, I wake on a very cold dawn as the sun rises and slowly washes down the hilltop fort, casting a fresh, clean light on the mountains.

The Palkhor Cholde monastery, like a purple shawl against the mountain, is the town's main attraction. More interested in history than religion, I go to see the citadel, squatting on a rocky hill which sticks up several hundred feet like the end of a French loaf in the middle of the town. Tsering and I walk up, both puffing and panting, as this is higher than Lhasa. The fort is not normally open to visitors. A large rock blocks a big red door at the entrance, but some workmen remove it to open it for us.

Inside, a persistent self-appointed guide pesters me, "Dalai Lama pitch kutchi kutchi" (give me a Dalai Lama picture, please). In most Tibetan monasteries, camera-conscious lamas, like vultures in red cloaks, ask for up 40 yuan to photograph their temples. The men renovating this fort, doing hard labor with pick and shovel, earn six yuan a day.

Two backpackers coming down from the fort say that the workers locked them in earlier until they gave them pictures of the Dalai Lama. According to the none-too-reliable Tsering, the Dalai Lama pictures sold in the marketplace don't count, as they are Chinese imitations.

It is a steep, hard climb up to the run-down fort, now reduced to rubble. Along the battlements, it is so windy and dusty, it feels like we are being blown away. When Robert Byron arrived in the early 1930s, he found people living here. Now the thousands of rooms are all in a shambles.

Some rooms are papered with sheets of blackened paper with scribbling on them, probably prayers in Sanskrit. Others have painted Buddha images, historical murals or thousands of little clay Buddhas all in a row before an altar. A worker shows us a room with three Buddha statues that seem in good repair. In other rooms, rows of sacred writing have been gouged out, victims of the Cultural Revolution.

Finally, working our way up through the three-dimensional maze, we reach the roof. Leaving Tsering panting and smoking a cigarette, I climb up a series of rickety ladders, higher and higher, to the last little place, like a pigeon coop on the top. I stand there awhile, alone, looking out at the great view of the town and the valley below, and try to imagine how the Tibetans felt as the British approached. I can see down the valley where Francis Younghusband and his troops marched up from Sikkim. The troops could have turned right, toward Lhasa, and missed the fort, with its ineffectual cannons, but they couldn't leave it in the hands of the Tibetans.

The surrender of the jong was to have a crushing effect on Tibetan morale. An ancient superstition said that if the great fortress ever fell into the hands of an invader, further resistance would be pointless. In fact, the whole expedition proved largely pointless. After the signing of a token treaty, the Anglo-Tibetan Convention, the army departed just seven weeks after entering Lhasa. And for 80 years, the city once more became off-limits to foreigners.

But all that was still in the future, as the armies struggled over this now-deserted bastion. From here, Younghusband's invading army marched on to Lhasa. And I, more comfortably, ride back in the jeep.

MONGOLIA

ULAN BATOR TO KARAKORUM

In the Steppes of Genghis Khan

June 1994

GENGHIS Khan died falling off his horse. The greatest cavalry general in history, my boyhood hero, perished like a dude ranch drugstore cowboy.

The shattering disclosure of the exalted general's death in 1227 comes to me from a young Mongolian woman, as we stand out on the ocean-like plains just outside Karakorum, his ancient capital. In the 13th century, the Khan and his cavalry rode their shaggy ponies out of the windswept North Asian steppes, all the way west to Europe and south to China, creating the vast, but short-lived, Mongol empire.

Now, in the late 20th century, it is difficult to reach the great warrior's former capital, now just a few crumbled piles of stone. It is worth the effort. Mongol Airlines (MIAT) flies from Beijing to Ulan Bator, the capital, but it seems more appropriate to ride the iron horse to the great Khan's homeland.

Beijing is the start of one branch of the legendary Trans-Siberian railway to Moscow. Early on departure morning at the station platform, roadwise backpackers and hordes of returning Mongols descend on food carts to stock up on quarts of beer, water, juice, bread and other supplies for the long trek north. Occasionally, dull explosions of full beer bottles dropping from boxes to shatter on the concrete platform punctuate the morning hubbub.

This is no luxury Orient Express, but a serious form of transportation. As the train edges out of the Chinese capital and gains speed, rattling past the grim suburbs, the Mongols dress down for comfort, changing into track suits and shorts, and start drinking breakfast. Before they have downed their first beer, the train is rolling through green hills, past the Great Wall, immense stone ramparts built to keep the ancestors of these modern Mongols' out of the Middle Kingdom. In places, the ancient fortifications snake almost down to the tracks.

Green grass gives way to brown, then to sand sprouting a few scrubby trees as the train chugs across Inner Mongolia and into the Gobi Desert. Already, there is a sense of the great northern void, of entering a wild and unknown frontier. Throughout the long, hot day, empty beer bottles flung through the open windows shatter on the rocky ground with sharp tinkles.

By next morning, we are deep in the vast, unpopulated Mongolian steppes, the feeling of space almost intimidating, especially to travelers from Asia's crowded southern cities. Late afternoon of the second day, we wind around low, grassy hills and into Ulan Bator's outskirts of semipermanent gers (or yurts), traditional dome-shaped tents laid out in compounds enclosed by wooden snow fences.

With the arrival of the Trans-Siberian, the little Ulan Bator station bustles with excitement and activity, more like an isolated village stop than an international terminus. Ancient trucks and battered buses pick up locals, while tourists depart in minivans and private cars operating as taxis.

Ulan Bator (also known as Ulaanbaatar) is no Paris of the plains. The broad boulevards and concrete block architecture of Mongolia's only city, home to a quarter of the nation's population, preserve the grimness of Soviet years. Boxy, forbidding grey stone or cement government buildings line the central Sukh-baatar Square (twice the size of Red Square, with the same over-whelming gracelessness).

While most of the accommodation is quite basic, the city now has a number of three and four-star hotels. The best are the Geng-his Khan, Ulaanbaatar, Bayangol and the Edelweiss.

Still, some architectural treasures in a style generously dubbed "St. Petersburg" grace the capital, especially some classical pub-lic buildings and museums.

And country folk in for a brief visit brighten up the drab capi-tal. In the square, young city slickers with ancient cameras pho-tograph rustics outfitted in dels, the traditional long Mongolian coat split along the side like cheong-sams to allow horseback rid-ing. Men pose before the equestrian statue of Sukhbaatar (the national liberator), their children with giant stuffed bears and camels. These stiffly posed souvenir photos will later decorate yurts all across the steppes.

The country comes right into this city, where cows graze on the parliament lawn and a Mongolian cowboy galloping by on a hairy horse nearly bowls me over outside the External Affairs of-fice. As I jump back, I feel an unpleasantly organic squishing un-derfoot. Cow pies and road apples (horse droppings), not speed-ing cars, are pedestrian traffic hazards in the Mongolian capital.

Ulan Bator's sights display a strange melange of many out-side influences. The Summer Palace is Chinese, with Indian and Tibetan influences, a Pan-Asian assembly with elaborate roofli-nes, a multitude of Buddhas, intricate ornamentation, vivid colors and profuse gold embellishment. The small, plain wood Winter Palace, several stories high with the characteristic peaked roof of snowy countries, seems Sino-Siberian.

The Gandan Lamasery, once home to 100,000 monks, is Ti-bet North. In the 1930s, Communist zealots destroyed thousands of Buddhist monasteries across Mongolia. In recent years, these holy places have reopened to eager congregations, so once again praying worshippers prostrate on reclining boards and red-robed lamas in heavy boots, Seven Dwarfs hats and coats with extra-long sleeves chant to a background of clashing cymbals and blaring trumpets.

The entertaining, but unusual, cultural presentation at the State Drama Theater shows both Chinese and Russian Cossack influences. Especially phenomenal is the costumed man in brightly rouged face doing throat singing, a bizarre chanting, making a sound like a Jew's harp deep in his throat that sounds as though it is rolling down from the dark, lonely hills.

The local diet, however, is pure Mongolian, based on red meat and "white food," such as mare's milk, koumiss, hard cheeses and dried curds. Restaurant meals consist of greasy mutton, chicken or beef with rice, potatoes and cabbage, and few fresh vegetables.

Mongolians reason that things that grow in the ground are meant for animals to eat. A local woman sharing my table one evening complains of traveling to the United States, where they fed her vegetables and salads. "What do they think I am, a goat?" she demands. Yet these red-meat-and-cholesterol-fed Mongolians are in more robust good health than most pallid tofu-and-bean-sprout vegetarians.

Through the pure good fortune of being in Ulan Bator in mid-July during Naadam, the Mongolian Olympics of "Three Manly Games" (archery, horse racing and wrestling), I see these rugged people in action. On the first day, all the might of the Mongolian military parades in the massive square for the opening ceremonies. Alongside modern cavalry, troops of mounted soldiers in ancient Mongol uniforms of furry hats and dome helmets, carrying bows and quivers of arrows, ride their shaggy little ponies in formation down the main street. It is easy to imagine these fierce soldiers riding out of the hills, standing high in their stirrups to shoot their whistling arrows, terrifying peasants all across Europe.

In these Manly Games, women compete in archery and the jockeys are boys and girls from six to 12 years old. Only wrestling is all male, fought by combatants wearing strange jackets that cover the backs and shoulders and leave chests bare - for a reason that would delight modern feminists. Long ago, legend has it, a mystery wrestler easily defeated all other contenders. But when they found out it was a woman, they vowed it would never happen again -- and that is why Mongolian traditional wrestlers wear the abbreviated, vest-like jacket.

In the fields outside town, locals set up the most basic of bars: crates of Mongolian beer sold off the back of battered farm trucks. Mounted horsemen crowd around, standing high on their stirrups to exchange tattered tugriks (the local currency) for crates of beer, which they balance on the saddle as they ride off.

The real Mongolia of nomadic herdsmen is found on the rolling grasslands just outside the capital. To visit the ancient capital, I join a tour group on a hard-sprung, Russian-built bus for the bone-jarring, 12-hour, 420-kilometer ride southwest to Hujirt, just an hour's flight from Ulan Bator. Soon after leaving the city, the road ends and Mongolia truly starts. Here is space to match the North American Prairies, the South American pampas, the African veldt.

This is the Mongolia of my fantasies, the wide open, Big Sky, Marlborough Man country of Asia. All day we bounce in Russian buses over rough roads across scenic open country that stretches to the heavens, with only a few white yurts sprouting like wild mushrooms on the hills.

Late in the afternoon, we stop at a nomad camp, where colts and goats and robust healthy children with rosy apple cheeks frisk among the domed felt tents. Invited inside a ger, we experience Mongolian hospitality in the form of chewy chunks of cheese as hard as nougat and great bowls of koumiss (fermented mare's milk). The foul beverage, like vinegary milk, is perhaps palatable to those who like buttermilk or smelly bean curd, but is not for sensitive city stomachs. However, it is impolite to decline the hospitality, so we choke down a few sips.

Outside, cowboys mounted on horses with distinctive, high

saddles, snare milking mares with lassos on the end of long poles while teens hang around on their little ponies as natural as big city boys on bicycles or skateboards.

Back on the rocky road we bounce on, the long Mongolian night falls and the rolling hills turn the dark green of the horsemen's velour robes. Finally, after midnight, we reach Hujirt -- just a 50-minute flight from our starting point.

Set up for tourists, Hujirt is a camp of rows of yurts, like a Mongolian trailer park. After the long ride, the tents are surprisingly comfortable, pleasantly scented with wood smoke from the heavy iron stove in the center and with wide bench beds along the side that we collapse into with groans of appreciation.

Next morning, on the way to Karakorum, Mongolia hits us with another of its surprises -- hundreds of worshippers in local costume on horseback, truck, bus and old East European motorcycles are flocking through the hills to worship at Chankh monastery.

Nearby, crowds gather at tents set up in a field for a festival. On the other side of the tent, just past the priests chanting around a mound of snow white cheese, mounted horsemen have guaranteed seats for the sporting events. It is a mini-Naadam, with several wrestling matches going on at once in the field before us. Wrestlers with huge boots and open jackets go through the opening ceremony, slapping their thighs and performing the stylized, arms-outstretched falcon and eagle dances.

Squatting on the ground with locals, I try to learn the intricacies of Mongolian wrestling, which looks like one drunk helping another drunk home, but not so graceful. With the tripping, pushing, shoving, it is like slow-motion sumo wrestling, with no ring.

Later, after a few more bruising hours in the bus crossing the rough terrain, we finally spot the 108 stupas of the 16th-century Erdene Zuu Monastery, once the center of Mongolian Buddhism. Built from the ruins of Karakorum, it is like a small Potala Palace on the plains, with sharp, upturned rooftops and ornate, Tibetan-style ornamentation.

Touts at the door to the former walled city sell crude carvings -- for U.S. dollars only. Inside, livestock graze in the long grass of the big, peaceful square, the stupas sticking up like white pickets along the surrounding walls.

A fetching young nun unlocks several temples to show us the various paintings, Buddha statues and artifacts. Inside a candlelit temple, chanting monks in heavy, rust-red robes, pointy-toed leather boots and flap-eared hats resemble Tibetan holy men in Lhasa lamaseries. Later, the winsome young nun corners me near the altar, whispering, "Change money?" offering a usurious rate here in the temple of God.

As we talk about the glories of the ancient capital, she shatters my lifelong illusions, telling me, in her schoolgirl English, about the death of the national hero, Genghis Khan. Leading me a short distance across the road, she points out the last vestiges of the glorious Mongol Empire that stretched from Siberia to Western Europe, the remnants of his great capital Karakorum: one broken statue of a tortoise, abandoned in a field of gopher holes.

Standing in that rocky field under the wide blue sky, I spot a group of horsemen far across the fields, riding wild and free across the vast steppe. Like a posse from an old Western movie, they stand high in the stirrups and lean far forward, their horses' manes flowing in the wind. It is a dramatic vision of natural grace and freedom. While the great Mongol Empire no longer exists in stone monuments, it is still alive in the spirit of its horsemen.

THAILAND

THAI HIGHWAYS

From Palm to Pine

February 1997

COOL tropical breezes blow off the porcelain-blue Andaman Sea. A small thatched roof shades the midday sun, and sand, soft as icing sugar, tickles my bare feet. Nearby, village boys scamper up a gracefully curving palm tree to kick down big green nuts full of thirst-quenching coconut water. Beyond, the empty white beach curves to the horizon. A waiter hurries across the sand balancing a tray of iced Singha beer, spicy Thai seafood soup and grilled prawns.

As an old friend used to say, "I've been in tougher situations."

Cruising down the broad, paved Friendship Highway, the speedometer needle edging well past 120 kilometers per hour, the radio pulling in a Bangkok easy listening station, northern Thailand's mountains rising ahead, it is bliss on wheels.

Until a roadblock appears across the shimmering concrete ahead, and a posse of ominous highway patrolmen waves me down. A tough-looking officer in tightly tailored brown uniform and dark sunglasses leans into the window demanding, "Do you speak Thai?" Ah, no.

"You break Thai law." I was doing 140 kilometers per hour in a 120 kilometers per hour zone. But it is a typical Thai experience, punctuated by smiles and good humor. The now cheerful motor-cycle cop fines me 200 baht on the spot, but gives me a receipt, so it is probably legitimate and not a donation to the policeman's benevolent fund. It is the only major hitch on an eight-day, 3,300 kilometer driving trip around Thailand, a country about the size of France.

Driving holidays are destined to become popular in Asia, with its newfound love of automobiles, increased leisure time and a rapidly growing network of excellent highways equal to those in North America and Europe. On my own road trek around Thailand, I follow a route to the royal palaces, historic and contemporary, on the assumption that the royals would know the best of their own country.

My excursion starts at the Avis car rental office on Bangkok's Wireless Road, where I outline my itinerary for the agent. I'll head straight south to Hua Hin, back up to Ayutthaya, then around in a great loop to the east and north to Nakhon Ratchasima (Korat), Sakhon Nakhon, Udon Thani, Chiang Mai and Chiang Rai, almost at the Burmese border.

"Wow, you're covering all of Thailand," says the astonished agent, who suggests I get lots of sleep, and buy some music tapes. "Put on some calypso, just sit back and cruise along, enjoy yourself," he recommends.

With that advice, I ease into Bangkok's notorious traffic, go around the block twice, and finally get onto the freeway, just a half block away. Then, excited and eager, the Mitsubishi Lancer GLX's air-con blasting a cooling breeze on this scorching day, I head south to Hua Hin on one of "the Great Drives of Asia."

More than an hour later, in that great parking lot called the Bangkok Expressway, I have only done 24 kilometers, and I am crawling along at a water buffalo pace in a choking exhaust haze.

The first good piece of advice I got was "Don't drive in Bangkok." It is a bad start, but finally I escape the gridlock, and, once outside the city, it is a breeze speeding down Highway 4 at a steady 120 kilometers per hour. When I told friends about this drive to Thailand, some recoiled. "You're driving in Thailand?" They were incredulous, as though I were crazy. Others reacted enviously: "You're driving in Thailand!" On this first morning out, I find that -- other than in the roadside hell of Bangkok -- the second reaction was right. The Thais are generally skillful and polite drivers, not overly aggressive; the roads are excellent, though not always well marked; and the friendly police try to be helpful, although the only English most of them speak is: "Do you speak Thai?"

Just south of Cha-Am, on the sunny Gulf of Thailand coast, I spot a sign pointing to the turnoff to Phra Ratchaniwet Marukkhathayawan Palace. But here I run smack into what may be termed the "two-kilometer defense." When I try to turn in, the soldiers at the gate wave me away, telling me to go two kilometers down the highway. Five kilometers away, following a fence along an army camp, I find another post with two more soldiers. They point me two kilometers back the way I came. Driving back past the original guards, I drive almost back to Cha-Am, and a police station. The officer there tells me to go two kilometers back the way I have been. Finally, back at the original gate, the two soldiers cheerfully wave me down the dirt road to the palace. "Two kilometers."

This sprawling seaside summer palace of King Mongkutklao, or Rama IV, was reassembled here in 1923 from an earlier palace at Khai Luang. Elevated covered walkways link the complex of golden teak buildings set on concrete stilts with empty spaces underneath, like traditional Thai homes. The royal chambers feature Western plumbing (a bidet reflects a French influence) and a four-poster canopy bed. This peaceful late afternoon, with the bird song and the scent of jasmine, the empty shuttered buildings tinted sky blue feel like an oversized summer cottage, out of season.

The summer resort was only used for two years, before being abandoned. Current monarch King Bhumibol Adylyadej and Queen Sirikit now summer in Klai Kangwon (Far From Worries Palace), built in 1926 just three kilometers from the Hua Hin railway station, 232 kilometers south of Bangkok. The contemporary palace is closed to visitors, although the grounds can be visited with special permission from the Royal Household Office when the royals are not in residence.

Hua Hin, Thailand's first seaside resort, remains a slow-paced tourist town of low wooden houses, fishing piers, peddle rickshaws, and peddlers with ancient mechanical ice shavers and soft drink syrups making Thai-style snow-cones. German, Swiss, French and Australian restaurants and bars, even a Kiwi Corner, pamper today's international tourists.

More than any other hotel, the elegant seaside Sofitel Central Hua Hin evokes the age of old "Siam," when this area was a resort for Thailand's gentry. When I last stayed here several decades ago, it had deteriorated to the atmospheric, but crumbling Railway Hotel that even budget travelers could afford. Sofitel tastefully renovated and expanded the low-rise heritage building, with the new wing retaining the breezy, open-air style. Teak floors and furnishings, crystal chandeliers, ceiling fans and well-worn marble hark back to a pre-synthetic era. Every room has a large terrace where vintage planters' chairs with elongated legs, a holdover from the original hotel, provide restful perches for sundowners. This hotel stood in as the Hotel Le Phnom in the movie The Killing Fields, shot here in 1983, an event recalled by a photo of the film crew hanging in the lobby.

Over cappuccino in the Museum Coffee & Tea Corner, adorned with faded photographs and hotel memorabilia, a local tells me of Hua Hin's many attractions. Besides the beach with its ocean activities, there is the nearby Sam Roi Yot National Park, with wildlife and interesting caves, scenic waterfalls, the River Kwai only hours away by road, and Phetchaburi, a historic city of temples and palaces.

There, the next morning, I track down the now abandoned Phra Ram Nivesan, (also called the Ban Puen Palace or Phra Ramrajunives Mansion) on the bank of the Phetchaburi River. Alone in the vast, empty rooms with few furnishings, padding around in stocking feet on the cool marble floors in the dim interior, I am struck by the abandoned, 19th-century mood. A German engineer, Carl Dohing, designed the building like a mansion in Europe where the king once stayed, and photos of royals from Austria touring the area in 1910 decorate the halls. As I leave, several Thai girls arrive, their voices echoing around the corridors.

From here, I skirt Bangkok heading north, driving through flat delta rice paddy country, past modern housing developments (in Greek or Tudor style) and along the muddy construction site of a new ring road. Ayutthaya, 76 kilometers north of Bangkok, was the Thai capital from 1350 to 1767. Slowed by the construction and confusion surrounding Bangkok, I arrive at Bang Pa-In -- the most colorful and best known of the royal palaces -- a half-hour after closing time. But the military guards exhibit the most endearing aspect of Thai bureaucracy - flexibility. I can't go in the main gate, but they let me past the police post to take a picture, and I have the run of the place for as long as I want.

This summer palace complex, dating back to 1632, is like a theme park of architectural styles -- a mix of classical Greek, Italian, Victorian, Imperial Chinese, even Swiss Cottage. With the fretwork and filigree, the overall result is partly Asian Carpenter's Gothic. Cherubs and traditional Greek-style statuary, women with lyres, even a stone gent in lederhosen, line a bridge crossing a pond from which a lavish classic Thai pavilion rises, island-like. But summers were too hot here for the royals. So, with the introduction of air travel in the 1920s, they summered in palaces in the cool northern mountains near Chiang Mai and Chiang Rai.

Day four, I leave Highway 1, the fast main expressway crowded with trucks, buses and pickups speeding north, for Highway

2. The fine Friendship Highway that the Americans built during the Vietnam War slowly leaves behind the industrial south for the rural, open northeast region the Thais call Issan. It is here, beguiled by the two parallel strips of white concrete stretching across the green hills, rising and dipping to the contours of the earth, that I run into the police block.

So, 200 baht lighter, I check into the grand Royal Princess Hotel in Nakhon Ratchasima (also called Korat). The luxurious Princess (I am consistent here in my pursuit of the royals) illustrates Thailand's rapid recent development. A decade ago, towns like this had only small, basic local hotels.

That evening, the hotel's eager young Thai assistant manager shows me around historic Korat, with its ancient wall and moat. We end up strolling the night bazaar, a cleaner, less-frenzied version of Hong Kong's Temple Street Night Market, the air scented with charcoal-grilled chicken, chilies and garlic.

"The streets are narrow and the cars are wide here," my guide notes. "If you come back in two years, it will be like Bangkok." I fear he may be right.

While southern Thailand offers beaches and culture, the north has mountains and its own distinct culture. North of Korat I drive 12 kilometers off the highway to visit the Khmer ruins in Phimae. Although the restored temple complex is limited to a small area within a walled compound, the eerie stone carvings and towers evoke Cambodia's mysterious Angkor Wat, especially on this blistering day with no other visitors in sight.

As I drive deeper into the Issan district, the terrain and the people change. Women in broad straw hats work the fields and walk along the road carrying thatched baskets, men in Cambodian-type sarongs and headscarves carry ominous machete-like farm tools, and peasants appear in Vietnamese-style cone hats. Further north, young water buffalo sauntering across the road present different driving hazards.

As the highway twists up into the cool, forested mountains of Phu Phan National Park, for the first time in five days I turn off the air-conditioning and crank down the windows to breathe the fresh mountain air. These slow, winding roads are a welcome relief from the freeways and traffic of the south.

Before Sakhon Nakhon, I turn off the road and a soldier waves me on toward the Phu Phing Palace in the park. The king and queen stay here while working with the local people on such projects as promoting handicrafts. I follow a twisting path through the parklike mountain grounds, passing gaggles of college girls returning to their tour buses. The palace, several expansive, comfortable modern buildings set among the trees, could be a group of grand houses in a North American suburb, only larger.

That evening, driving straight west into a ruby red sunset shimmering over the rice paddies, I ruefully recall the firmest advice I was given: "Don't drive at night." It is a harrowing experience, especially at dusk, with farm vehicles with no lights returning from the fields, and cars and trucks not switching their lights on until it is completely dark. In the pitch black, I swerve away from the dark shape of a bicycle peddling down the road without even reflectors, coming within inches of smashing the heedless cyclist into the ditch. So I roll down the window to a wonderful, earthy smell of fields, burning foliage and buffalo dung, and slow to tractor speed, resigned to a late arrival in Udon Thani.

Of the various routes available beyond that city, near the Friendship Bridge leading to Laos, I was warned to avoid the 203 through the mountains past Phu Rua National Park. Highway 203 proved a joy to drive, an excellent highway with little traffic wending through the scenic mountains. It is more spacious here than in the south, the rice paddies interspersed with tracts of rain forest. In the hamlets, women sit out on elevated platforms with their produce for sale spread out before them.

All along these northern highways, ornate gold, red, green and orange temples sparkle in the forest like multicolored sequins on the green baize of a pool table. At a small, gilded monastery, I meet three monks. The eldest, who speaks good English, says: "This is the best part of Thailand. It has the best air, the best climate." The worldly cleric knows that in Canada, we drive on the other side of the road. He urges me to drive carefully.

One of his preteen acolytes speaks up. "He says he has never seen a foreigner driving around Thailand," the elder monk explains. The bald-pated boy adds something else, and I push for a translation.

"He says foreigners are different. He says you are ... fat." I decline the invitation to address his English class and continue on down the road.

Later, at a basic roadside store/restaurant, I stop for lunch. The delicious noodle soup with slices of pork, served in a Chinese-style bowl with chopsticks, is a bargain at just 10 baht.

With time to spare, I turn off the highway, plotting a relaxing, roundabout route to Phitsanulok. Only a few motorbikes and a pickup truck bus share this potholed secondary road, where the going is slow. And suddenly, traffic stops completely. Ahead, a swift stream flows over the road. It is the heavy flooding I had read about in the Bangkok newspapers, with accompanying photos of cars, buses and trucks abandoned in midstream.

Indecisive motorcycle drivers sit around their machines; a dugout canoe ferries a few passengers with their bags; a farm truck loads several bikes on the back to drive across; and a few bus passengers wade through the thigh-high water. But it is the end of the road for me. Returning to Highway 12, the main east-west artery, I drive straight into the setting sun, reaching Phitsanulok just before the dreaded dusk.

Next morning, the hotel desk clerk assures me that all roads to Chiang Mai are washed out, information reinforced by the pump jockey at the gas station. A highway patrolman who doesn't speak English seems more optimistic, so I turn the Mitsubishi north again. In fact, the going is ideal along a smooth highway that I have all to myself in places. Approaching Chiang Mai, I reach the kind of winding, scenic mountain road that sports car drivers love to get their hands, or wheels, on. But all the traffic here is small Japanese pickup trucks: Isuzu, Datsu, Mitsubishi, Toyota, Nissan.

Chiang Mai is a prime tourist area with handicraft villages, elephant camps, river rafting, trekking, hill tribe visits, dazzling temples -- and a royal palace. Fifteen kilometers from the town along a road twisting up through bamboo forest and lush greenery, I reach the hilltop Phu Ping Royal Palace set in Doi Suthep Pui National Park.

A sign at the entrance says, "Dress properly, no firearms, and don't pick the flowers." Up here in the cool mountain air, the gardens and greenery are northern climate -- azaleas, roses, fuchsia, impatiens, hydrangeas and clover. The spacious mountain resort is part modern, part traditional Thai. The finest buildings are whitewashed, with varnished doors and pillars, glazed bronze and green tiles shimmering in the sun, and roofs with chofa (sky tassel), curved finials poking up from the rafters like crooked fingers testing the wind.

The royal family had a good eye for real estate. Where they went, others followed, and now mountain resorts in the area accommodate less-regal tourists.

The best of these resorts is the luxurious Regent Chiang Mai, where I wash off the dust of the road in a giant soak tub, an iced Mekong (Thai whisky) soda in hand. Every suite here has a sala (open pavilion), overlooking its private rice paddies, framed by misty mountains. The carefully laid-out and landscaped grounds simulate a traditional Thai farm village, with pools, waterfalls and rice paddies. The lavish teak pavilions are created in the local style, and interior decoration includes traditional Thai artwork and silks, wood carvings, antique furniture, handicrafts, celadon ceramics and silverware. The long day's drive ends in the open-air Elephant Bar, then the Sala Mae Rim restaurant with a zingy tom yung kung (prawn and lemongrass soup), red chicken curry, spicy beef with basil, and tall, cold Singha beers.

From here I take a side trip to the last, northernmost palace at Doi Tung. Outside Chiang Mai, I happen on an auspicious sign, a half-dozen elephants, jumbo, pewter-grey pachyderms ambling down the road, the mahouts squatting on them wearing ball caps backwards, American style. As I am on the trail of royal palaces, this symbol of the royal family seems appropriate.

Beyond Chiang Rai, the highway narrows, and signs in English disappear. Guessing at a turn off, I head up a narrow road climbing a steep mountain in the Nang Non (Sleeping Lady) range. Lost, I ask a passing farmer for the "king house," as they call it. He points up the road.

Like Phu Phing, the Doi Tung Royal Villa is a working palace, a headquarters for the royal family's work among six hill tribe villages in the area. Here, in the infamous Golden Triangle, where the borders of Thailand, Laos and Burma meet, the recently deceased Princess Mother established reforestation projects to replace opium fields.

But the palace is also a tourist site, complete with jewelry boutique, hill tribe souvenir shops and an arts and crafts center near the entrance. The palace itself, with a stunning view of the valley stretched out far below, consists of a cluster of large Western suburbia-style buildings and several new villas in traditional architecture, with glazed-tiles and cross beams extending from the peak of the A-frame roofs. It is like an upmarket mountain resort, part Alpine, part Thai.

The setting is spectacular: spacious well-maintained grounds with terraced gardens, hanging baskets and flowers spilling out of planters everywhere. In this mountain region, tall, straight pines and other temperate climate conifers grow. My 3,367 kilometer drive has taken me from the Bight of Bangkok almost to the Burmese border, from palm to pine.

KOH SAMUI

Beaches and Buddhas

February 2001

AT 10am on Koh Samui's Chaweng Beach, the cheerful hawkers and hustlers are already out. Ambulatory chefs carrying mobile kitchens of tiny braziers suspended from shoulder poles sell grilled chicken, corn and bananas. A henna tattooist applies his art to a pale, bare arm, a masseuse whacks and kneads meaty backs and thighs, stretching, pulling and pummeling the flesh.

On this sunny morning in the Gulf of Thailand, Germans sprawled on beach chairs are sipping their first beers of the day, French women whip off bikini tops, exposing sun-bronzed breasts, Hong Kongers discuss lunch and Australian girls get their hair braided and beaded, Bo Derek/Rastafarian style.

Twenty years ago, Koh Samui was an island of coconut plantations, fishermen and a small wandering tribe of adventurous backpackers searching for the perfect beach. Just over a decade ago, only a few bungalows provided basic accommodation. Now, the island is one of Thailand's major tourist destinations, with resorts lining beaches such as seven-kilometer-long Chaweng, the main tourist center, as well as Lamai, Maenam, Bophut and others.

The resorts come in all different styles, sizes and price ranges, some traditional tropical low-rises, others larger, more modern. Along Chaweng, one resort displays a pair of statues of huge faces on its beachfront, another bizarre fake palm sculptures, others driftwood sculptures.

Scenic Chaweng bustles with action as a steady stream of commerce passes the holidayers, although the hustle is low-key and friendly. Signs proclaim "Beer is yum" and advertise "Thai massage, foot massage, skin your feet." With the soles of my feet intact, I wander down the long stretch of fine sand. The foreign visitors here are near naked, while the Thais are clothed in big floppy straw hats, sunglasses, long-sleeve shirts and long pants, and shawls over their shoulders, exposing the minimum of skin to the searing sun.

A henna tattooist approaches me, displaying a book of designs that these epidermal artists copy, largely geometric patterns or illustrations of birds and butterflies.

"It is good for dancing," he assures me, as I try to hide behind my paperback novel.

"I don't dance," I reply.

"It's good for boomfing. You boomfing?" he asks, turning to a page with mildly pornographic designs illustrating couples "boomfing."

At night, Chaweng is a lively, neon strip of restaurants, cybercafes, bamboo hut bars and clubs for dancing, and perhaps boomfing as well. The scent of fried garlic and chilies wafts from numerous small open-air cafes serving tasty Thai food - coconut chicken soup, spicy fish curry, fried noodles with shrimp, beef with garlic and chili, pork with basil, and garlic fried rice. The menu in a restaurant overlooking a small lake lists "Jesty Thai" dishes, and that is no joke. Italian, German, Mideast, Japanese, Korean restaurants, even a Gringo's Mex-Tex (run by a Canadian) all cater to international tastes.

But there is more to Samui than this intense beach-and-town scene. Small Japanese pickup-truck buses, called song-taew, circle the island. So, leaving behind the aromas of suntan lotion, the sea and fried garlic, I hit the road to explore the island.

With coconut plantations covering most of Koh Samui, it lacks the natural, jungle-clad appearance of many Thai islands. With such a supply, roadside vendors sell fresh, green coconuts for just 15 baht each. The clear coconut water is deliciously chilled, the slippery white flesh smooth as silk.

Even the island's south end, away from the main resort beaches, is being developed with small restaurants, resorts and craft shops. And the resourceful locals now display monkeys, once used to harvest coconuts, in coconut-picking performances, along with elephant shows and rides.

Nathon, the island's main town, bustles around the pier, where boats arriving from Surat Thani on the mainland dock. Unlike Chaweng, it has a reason for existing aside from catering to tourists. A few solid concrete four-story buildings front the harbor, but on the quiet side streets, pleasant, slightly seedy two-story teak shophouses recall a Thailand before the tourist boom.

At the north end of the island, away from the swimming beaches, fishermen unload nets from wood-hulled fishing trawlers draped with colorful bunting, while small boys play with Styrofoam boats. Squatting before ramshackle huts, they mend nets and sort the catch.

Outside Bophut village, I encounter a bizarre sight for Southeast Asia: a miniature Eiffel Tower topped with a satellite dish. Bophut is a small French enclave, with notices advertising balades (hikes), a large sign boasting "Recommande par le guide du Routard" (a French guidebook), and an Ecole Francaise de Plongee (scuba-diving school) along the main street. In front of a small restaurant, several men play boules, the game from southern France and Italy, throwing the big, silvery balls onto the uneven, sandy road, where they wobble and roll erratically. The players, imbued with a tropical torpor, don't seem to mind much.

It is quieter than Chaweng, but with enough bars, clubs and restaurants to suit all but the most ardent party animal. Leaving La Sirene and Les Gourmets restaurants for a later date, we stop at the Happy Elephant. Our terrace tables overlook the long, empty beach, with not a single hawker in sight. The late lunch of Thai noodles with shrimp, beef with green curry sauce and chicken with cashews is exquisite, and reason enough to visit this island.

Past Bophut, on the island's northeast corner, Samui's main visitor attraction is set on a small peninsula. Here, the giant 15-meter-high Golden Buddha (Phra Yai) sits serenely atop a small outcropping, the former island of Koh Fan.

Among the T-shirt and soft drink shops, the monks and nuns have set up an ingenious, automated alms-giving device next to a sign, "Please offer rice for doing merit for yourself and your dearly departed ones." To gain merit, visitors deposit a 10 baht coin and uncooked rice kernels shoot out of a spout into a big pewter bowl. Adjacent to this, monks begging bowls go around on a conveyor belt, like in some Japanese sushi restaurants. After buying the rice, merit-seekers scoop it into the passing bowls (to be deposited back to be resold, again and again, in a form of Buddhist rebirth). Small golden statues of standing or lying Buddhas decorate the small sanctuary.

Under a shade tree, a coin-operated fortune-telling box is less interactive: put a coin in and some twirling lights come on and halos on Buddha statues begin to flash, like in a carnival sideshow. In the same courtyard, visitors are writing their names and addresses on red bricks with felt pens ("donation, any amount" the sign says). An orderly pile of bricks daubed with names of visitors from everywhere from Scotland to Hong Kong sits in a corner, presumably to be used to build future temples.

The entrepreneurial nuns also rent long-sleeved shirts, skirts and pants for those inappropriately attired, but many farangs (foreigners) simply just ignore decorum and approach the Buddha in brief shorts and T-shirts. Gingerly, we walk up the steps baked hot in the tropical sun and hard on tender city feet. It is worth the small climb to the golden statue. The reward is a fine view of the sea with fishing boats setting out, chirping of songbirds and a sense of peace far removed from the tourist bustle.

Leaving the somewhat gaudy spiritual site, I spot a billboard: "There is a local saying, 'Whoever comes to Koh Samui must visit Phara Yai on Koh Phan or else it's just like he has not reached the island.'" And I think of those still roasting on Chaweng beach.

When we return to Chaweng, the French women are a little more leathery and the Germans are launching into evening beers. The Australian girls, a covey of pink-skinned Bob Marleys, flaunt their braided hair and the Hong Kongers are talking about what to have for dinner.

VIETNAM

SAIGON

At Peace on a Cyclo

Fall 1992

IN Saigon, it always comes back to the war. I was sitting on the patio-sized rooftop of the Rhythm and Booze bar, trying to gulp down iced 333 beers before the steamy night air could turn them as tepid as Mekong River water, when the congenial proprietor brought out his scrapbook. A younger version of the middle-aged Vietnamese beamed out from the "Bao Chi" press card pasted to the front.

Hoang Van Cuong was a UPI photographer. His faded, almost sepia-tone war photographs recall a generation of turmoil. Flipping through the pages is like reliving newspaper war reports of the Americans' defeat. There are journalists in bell bottoms and 60's long hair scrambling aboard a bus with protective grills over the window, fleeing Saigon. Tanks bashing down the gates of the presidential palace on that fateful day 17 years ago. Barefoot soldiers in pith helmets and battle fatigues smoking cigarettes around President Nguyen Van Thieu's empty chair in his abandoned office, A famous photo of the war shows a fat, balding American on a helicopter punching a small Vietnamese trying to get aboard. And one of my favorite, taken by a friend, Dutch photographer Hu van Es, shows an ant-like line of desperate people climbing up from a rooftop to a waiting helicopter.

The Vietnamese don't dwell on the war, unless they can profit from it. They show no rancor against the nation that dropped so many tons of explosives on them, and are anxious to have the rich Americans back. Everywhere in Vietnam, eyes light up in delight at the sight of foreigners. This isn't just affection, but an eagerness to hustle them, without the horrors of napalm, bullets and bombs.

"This time the Americans will really pay," an eager Saigonese businessman told me. The aggressive yet friendly hustle on every level, from bureaucrat to street hawker, is part of the Vietnam experience for Western visitors.

But ghosts of the "American War" haunt the country, even for those who only lived through "Nam" vicariously, through newspapers and TV newscasts. I was settled back in a Cathay Pacific L1011 Tristar dipping into the caviar trough as the smiling hostess replenished my glass of Krug Grande Cuvee, thinking how much better this was than arriving in a grim C-130 troop plane, when the announcement came.

"Ladies and gentlemen, we will soon be landing at Tan Son Nhut airport." The name hit like a blow to the midriff, evoking visions of exploding mortars and aircraft going up in huge orange balls of flame. The wrecks have been moved, but the moldering stucco aircraft shelters remain from the dangerous days of the mid '70s. Other Vietnamese names I would hear over the next few days are as powerfully evocative: Da Nang, Cam Ranh Bay, Khe San, Ban Me Thuot.

Outside the Saigon terminal, hotel, restaurant, bar and nightclub touts press their cards into my hand. Flipping through them later, I find a Canadian Hotel and a Toronto karaoke club, reminders of later realities, of refugees fleeing by boat to the West, and returning as successful investors.

A nostalgia for a world I never knew took me to the Rex Hotel, formerly the U.S. Army bachelor officer quarters and site of the infamous Five O'Clock Follies. Here, U.S. Army spokesmen briefed the press with military and bureaucratic double-talk: kill ratios, body counts, ordinance expenditures, sorties flown, structures destroyed, enemy contacts made.

The modest Rex, now one of Saigon's top hotels, is agreeably dated, its dark wood interior embellished with intricately carved ornamentation. My dark, musty room is just like the one where, in Apocalypse Now, Martin Sheen went one-on-one with a mirror, and lost. American officers stayed in these rooms during the war, on frenetic leave from the horrors of the jungle.

Correspondents such as Peter Arnett, Morley Safer and Neil Davis reported the last days of the war from the rooftop bar, as bombs exploded and clouds of smoke rose from the city suburbs behind them. The old wartime hangout is now a garish restaurant/bar, with deer topiary and bonsai trees, deer and elephant statues, and crass, white plaster maidens, in natural and futuristic socialist-hero styles.

Piercing jungle skrawks come from mynahs in bamboo cages, tropical fish swim listlessly in large, tiled, crown-shaped tanks. A huge, slowly twirling yellow and silver crown outlined in tiny twinkling lights and a giant, flashing red Rex sign give the venerable venue a gaudy, carnival feel. Still, the view over the flat city is pleasant, and good steaks are less than $5.

Outside the hotel, persistent beggars, money changers, postcard and T-shirt salesmen, and especially drivers of cyclos (three wheel bicycle taxis, with the seat in front) pester guests relentlessly whenever they walk out the door. A tenacious urchin follows me down the street waving a library of international magazines and newspapers. The miniature media mogul has publications from Asia, the U.S., Europe and Britain; the Asian Wall Street Journal, the International Herald Tribune, the Far Eastern Economic Review, Singapore Straits Times, Le Figaro, Le Monde and Der Speigel.

I brush him away. He persists. Where did I come from? Hong

Kong. He immediately whips out a South China Morning Post. I could appreciate the grumpy foreigner I saw whose T-shirt read "Don't Hassle Me."

A block away, I lunch on excellent, crisp baguettes and mutton stew with white beans in a cheap cafe on Le Loi Boulevard. The bill says it is Givral's, and I realize with another jolt that this is where Graham Greene set an opening scene of his classic Vietnam novel, The Quiet American.

The colonial Continental Hotel across the street was a favorite meeting place of the expat community in both French and American colonial eras. Greene whiled away many gin-soaked hours on the open-air terrace (then known as the Continental Shelf), looking out on the broad street at the delicate young Vietnamese ladies in cone hats peddling their tiny bikes, filmy ao dai dresses fluttering around them. They've closed in the verandah, turning it into a posh, but affordable restaurant, but the view of street, and the bicyclers, is largely unchanged. And they still serve the strong, black filtered coffee with rich condensed milk, which tastes almost like chocolate, and is said to be the best in Asia.

Later, a U.S. greenback buys me an hour's ride on a cyclo. We roll along the tree-lined boulevards and hot, sunny side streets as the driver, angling for a tip, relates his tale of woe, including years in re-education camps. Saigon, with its French colonial architectural heritage, is among Asia's most attractive cities. Blocks of low stucco buildings with small balconies and shuttered windows that survived the war now slowly decay from neglect.

Sitting out front like that is relaxing on the quiet boulevards, more stimulating at intersections, exposed to the chaotic traffic. Women ride small motorbikes wearing long, elbow-length formal gloves and big floppy hats, farmers push carts piled high with bananas, bicycles, cyclos and motorcycles drive all over the road, weaving in and out, moving around each other, coming near to collisions.

After cruising the suburbs, the driver stops for tea at a roadside stand, outside the Exhibition House of Aggressive War

Crimes, better known as the Museum of American War Crimes. Housed in the former U.S. Information Service building, it is a junkyard of war machines scattered around the lawn: an attack helicopter, jet fighter, Cessna spotter plane, tanks, flame throwers and anti-aircraft guns. Several rooms display small arms, photographs of the war, and displays of the "crimes" of American and later Chinese invaders.

We cycle past the former U.S. Embassy, a big, ugly square block now overrun with jungle and rubble, so familiar from photographs of helicopters lifting off, evacuating the last of the Americans. Across the street, grizzled ladies in cone hats and black pyjamas squat by the road, selling cigarettes and raffle tickets.

Passing the red brick, twin-spired Notre Dame Basilica, we cross a broad street -- and there it is, the Presidential Palace. Communist tanks rolled up this street on the morning of April 30, 1975, smashed down those front gates, and ended decades of war.

The driver drops me off at the gate, we tussle over the price, and he peddles off happily with a few dollars. Entry to what is now called the Reunification Palace is 1,000 dong for Vietnamese 5,000 dong for foreigners. This is the officially sanctioned economic apartheid that is practiced throughout Vietnam for everything from train tickets to coconuts.

Hundreds of dragonflies hover like Huey helicopters in the hot summer morning, Western classical music plays from unseen speakers as I walk up to the front steps. Looking back, I vividly recall the news footage of the tanks crashing through the gates, taken from here by Australian cameraman Neil Davis. In the last years of the war, President Thieu and his wife lived in this tawdry palace with its austere reception room and gaudy conference hall.

On the fourth floor is the famous pole where the victorious soldiers unfurled the Viet Cong flag. A floor below is the pathetic family play room, with a small, pleated pink Naugahyde bar with four bar stools, a card table, a small dance floor and a games room with billiards, ping-pong and chess. Billions of dollars and tens of thousands of lives were wasted to keep the president secure in this 1950s-style rec room.

Well, good evening, Vietnam. Once the liveliest city in Southeast Asia, irrepressible Saigon is regaining its glitter and sizzle. My evening foray into the city streets takes me down busy Dong Khoi, once Ru Catinate, then Tu Do (Freedom), to Maxim. The old-style supper club is a holdover from the earlier days, with a dated song-and-dance floor show on the circular stage in the grand, Moulin Rouge-style room.

The nine-piece band playing corny big band music, to a backdrop of scenic photos of Chinese gardens and city skylines by night, switches to Japanese songs with the arrival of a group of visiting businessmen. A slightly suggestive fake Thai temple dance follows, with the lady dancer in a very brief, glittering gold costume and tall temple hat. They say that time stopped in Saigon in 1975. In Maxim, it never got beyond the 50s.

Tu Do, the street of the tarts, is reviving, though. You can't keep good hustlers down. Bars such as the Senorita Dolce Vita, Hard Rock Cafe, Yellow Umbrella and Good Morning Vietnam operate in the area where once hundreds of GIs roamed. In a small "cafe," I let two bar girls hustle me for a "Saigon tea" for 8,000 dong, fulfilling that aspect of the war experience at least. The girls have mellowed, though, with not so much of the old, aggressive "You number 10 cheap shit Joe."

In the late evening, young girls in ao dai or blue jeans cruise the streets riding motorcycles or as cyclo passengers, presented like tasty morsels in Saigon's version of the bicycle ice cream vendor. Greene wrote lovingly of these delicate girls, who "twitter and sing on your pillow."

Vietnam, hot damn.

On adjacent Dong Du Street, I find what I've been looking for, the Apocalypse Now bar, named for the classic Vietnam movie. The basic, storefront place represents so well the Vietnamese penchant for exploiting the war without holding a grudge. "Lift the Embargo" and "Apocalypse Now" T-shirts for sale hang on the minimalist black walls, and a wild-eyed Marlon Brando glares down from a giant movie poster. Sixties rock music and the low prices attract expatriates and budget travelers from the nearby Saigon Hotel.

I find Yana here, a friend of some of the Hong Kong Foreign Correspondent Club's old-timers. Yana was part of the Vietnam media pack that included correspondent John Steinbeck Junior, son of the novelist, and photographer Dana Stone. She lived a while with Sean Flynn, son of Errol, a glamorous war photographer who disappeared on a motorcycle into Cambodia one day in 1970.

Yana now works for foreign correspondents who have begun returning to Vietnam, arranging cars, guiding, translating. She looks like a latter-day, elderly flower child with her hippie bag full of memories. But she remembers the conflict, and the old correspondents, well. Would I like to see her old war pictures?

MEKONG RIVER

Between Heaven and Hell

Spring 1997

IN Vietnam, it seems, heaven and hell are never far apart. A day's journey out of Saigon (officially Ho Chi Minh City, but only bureaucrats and politicians call it that) provides visions of an odd, but endearing temple to enlightenment, as well as a man-made netherworld.

The journey itself is an experience somewhere between heaven and hell. Vietnam's better hotels and travel agents provide cars, drivers and guides for day trips, but rough-looking taxi drivers, many former Army of the Republic of Vietnam soldiers, loiter across from the Rex, cajoling passing tourists. Unfortunately, a fast-talking street tout talked me into hiring his freelance vehicle. Standing on the burning sidewalk, I haggle with one, deftly beating him down from US$50 to $35 for a day's jaunt into the countryside.

His car, an ancient, clapped-out little Renault, is painted the flat, thick, Easter-egg blue of a Saigon tart's eye make-up. With its broken seat and bad shocks, it is painfully uncomfortable as the driver erratically weaves with blaring horn through the chaotic traffic of bicycles, bicyclettes, motorcycles, pedestrians and children everywhere.

Just a few kilometers out on Route 22, and I know I have made a mistake. The battered Renault with a hole in its bare metal floor and no side windows is cramped and sweltering as we weave along the crowded, potholed roads.

In mangled French, my volatile driver insists his vintage vehicle is superior to the comfortable, air-conditioned Japanese models cruising past us. Still, the excursion to two of the Mekong Delta's more unusual attractions, one a haven of peace, the other a memorial of war, is worth the ordeal.

In rural Vietnam, women in black pyjamas and classic woven cone hats squat at the side of the road selling long, golden baguettes, packs of cigarettes, car and bicycle parts, fruit and vegetables or fresh young coconuts for drinking. Water buffalo work the rice paddies, and ancient, wood-hulled supply barges drift slowly down placid rivers.

Even away from the city, traffic never lets up in this crowded country. Although prosperity has brought new Japanese vehicles to the highways, immense, battered museum-piece American trucks, remnants from the war years, haul huge logs, families of four or five wobble along on small motorbikes and plodding oxen pull creaking two-wheeled wooden wagons. And everywhere, countless bicycles.

Several hours in this rolling oven, 100 kilometers northwest of Saigon, near the Cambodian border, we reach the town of Tay Ninh, site of the Cao Dai religion's major house of worship. The elaborate Great Cathedral, the most prominent structure in a complex of pastel yellow buildings in Sino-Vietnamese style with European elements, looks like a holy place designed by a 1960s acid head.

I've never seen anything quite like it. More garish and ornate than even a Taoist/Confucian temple, it is like a religious theme park, with gaudy adornments, splashes of bright color and multicolored dragons entwined around pink pillars. A busy mural depicts French author Victor Hugo, Chinese revolutionary leader Sun Yat-sen and Vietnamese poet and prophet Nguyen Binh Khiem, while statuary of Jesus Christ, Lao Tse, Confucius and Buddha completes the ensemble. A great, luminous sphere, the Divine Eye, hangs over the altar overlooking worshippers.

Through good fortune rather than planning, I arrive on time to witness midday prayers. At the great door (women and men must use different entrances), a member of the congregation summons me upstairs where a dozen foreigners observe the service. The atmosphere is vaguely medieval with the priests' outlandish costumes and murmured prayers.

Seen from the balcony, it is like a scene from some fantasy adventure movie as hundreds of squatting supplicants in white, and priests clad in brilliant red, yellow and blue ceremonial robes form a geometric pattern on the stone floor below us. In the cool of the huge temple, voices chant while an orchestra all in white plays eerie, sacred music with skrawky er-hu (Chinese-style) stringed instruments.

As I observe this mysterious scene, a sweet, tiny old nun with a doll-like face approaches and attempts to explain the basics of this strange creed in hesitant English. Then she hands me a piece of paper, hand-written in English, outlining the founding of this strange theology, which amalgamates ideas from many different religions and beliefs, East and West.

Founded in the 1920s by Vietnamese government official Ngo Van Chieu, Cao Daisim is a bizarre synthesis of all existing religions, including elements of Buddhism, Confucianism, Taoism, Hinduism, Vietnamese spiritualism, Christianity, Judaism, Islam, even animism spiritual seances and occult rites. Its eclectic ecclesiastics have communicated with, and sanctify, such a mixed group of improbable spirits as Joan of Arc, William Shakespeare, Louis Pasteur, Victor Hugo, Sun Yat-sen, Adolf Hitler, Winston Churchill and Vladimir Ilyich Lenin.

Despite the bizarre setting in what may be Asia's strangest holy place, the chanting and music imbue the ceremony with a mysterious sense of serenity. It is as moving as any cathedral or temple I have seen.

Outside in the hot sun, as I sip a soft drink bought from a bicycle hawker wearing a cone hat and pyjamas, my pestiferous driver urges me to move on, even though I have paid him for the whole day.

Returning home along the same crowded highway, about 36 kilometers outside Saigon the driver, with a predetermined itinerary for Western tourists, detours to Cu Chi district. As we bump along in the flat delta country, he points to the rice paddies, exclaiming "VC, VC, VC" (Viet Cong). "Boom-boom. B52 bombers," he shouts with elaborate gestures, taking his hand off the horn for the first time today.

The Cu Chi tunnels are the most accessible part of the infamous, elaborate tunnel network the Viet Cong built over decades of war. Communist guerrillas started digging the tunnels in 1948. Later, they became a refuge from the constant bombing and operations of American troops in the Iron Triangle and War Zone C. The ornate tunnel system was a logistic center as well as a Viet Cong hideout and, in 1968, the staging area for the deadly Tet Offensive against Saigon.

As my irksome driver parks and squats in the shade of a tree, lighting up a cigarette, a small man who resembles a VC guerrilla in his camouflage uniform bicycles up to meet me. Like it or not, he is my guide.

The ex-soldier leads me down an embankment to a big, empty building, like a classroom inside, and escorts me around a series of photographs and diagrams showing the intricate underground systems. He explains, in halting English, the self evident pictures along the wall showing soldiers living in the caves and a diagram of the intricate system.

The 250-kilometer complex eventually spread like a spider's web under an area from the Cambodian border to within 32 kilometers of Saigon. The underground passageways joined villages and linked dormitories, kitchens, conference rooms and classrooms, hospitals and schools, ammunition dumps, escape hatches and propaganda lecture halls where cadres from the north passed on the word of Comrade Ho. But despite the facilities, life in these dark tunnels must have been a form of hell.

Outside the building, the guide leads me to a clearing in the jungle to show me a bombed-out tank lying in the undergrowth, a vicious bamboo trap with stakes at the bottom of a pit, and a nail trap sprouting wicked, sole-destroying hooked spikes. Then, kicking a few leaves aside, he reveals a small gap in the ground about the size of a coffee-table book, he pauses for dramatic effect as I determine that I can barely get one foot into it. Then, lifting the cover, my tiny guide (a full-grown Vietnamese perhaps half my body weight) sits on the edge of the tiny hole in the ground, holds his arms over his head, and slithers into it, disappearing like a snake.

I follow him into the heart of darkness. This 50-meter stretch of tunnel has been enlarged for Western-sized physiques so I can crawl awkwardly after him for a short way through the hot, sweaty and claustrophobic tunnel, and immediately appreciate the VC's appalling living conditions.

Then my guide, who might have been one of the tunnel rats, crawls into an even smaller shaft, with no light at the end of the tunnel. The cave gets smaller, hotter, dirtier, until we turn a corner and face total blackness. "Fifty meters more," mumbles the disembodied voice ahead. But this is far enough for this large foreign body, and I already have my notes from underground, so I scuttle back clumsily, surfacing into the tropical sunlight sweaty and dirty like a bedraggled ground hog. There are snakes, spiders and cockroaches down there.

Brushing off the yellow dirt, I pay the guide 12,000 dong (about US$1) and he gives me a receipt on a rough brown sheet, like European toilet paper. Then the souvenirs come out: a lighter made from two M16 shells, an anti-aircraft shell lamp, some American GI dog tags.

As I fight off the souvenir salesmen, shots ring out from a nearby rifle range where would-be soldiers-of-fortune squeeze off a few rounds of an AK-47 or M-16. At about a U.S. buck a bullet, this real life shooting gallery is expensive.

Instead, I repair to a thatched-roof shack for a quick three-pack of canned 333 beer. It is necessary, as a matter of face, to drink in Vietnam, or risk being tagged "Papa limp flag" (as a teetotal friend was once maligned). This is another endearing aspect of the exuberant spirit of the people that makes Vietnam so enjoyable to visit.

I am washing away the cave dust with a 9,000 dong beer, when a group of backpackers arrive. They pooled their money and spent only $20 for the day for their more comfortable vehicle. And they wangle the beer down to 8,000 dong. I've been had twice in one day.

But once more my driver is agitating to move on, so we head back to the big city. For an hour-and-a-half, we bump along the rough, dusty road in the French wreck, back to Saigon, and a shower. It was a great trip, one that I would do again. But next time, I'll get a proper car and driver.

CENTRAL VIETNAM

The Way to Hue

August 1994

WHEN our so-called guide asks, as we approached Vietnam's legendary imperial city, "Why you come to Hue?" we know we are on our own.

Too late, we realize that the driver and guide we hired in Danang for a day's outing to one of Vietnam's most famous sights have never been to Hue. We will have to rely on our guidebook and map.

Our hapless quest started in the country's northern gateway, Hanoi, an exceptionally gracious city considering its recent war-torn history. The Vietnamese capital is suspended in an age between the jetliners flying in to Noi Bai airport and the oxcarts and bicycles that clutter the long, dusty road through the shambling suburbs to the city center.

A city of lakes, parks, tree-lined streets and colonial buildings in various stages of deterioration, Hanoi is the only major world capital where the leisurely cyclo-pousse (peddle rickshaws) provide the main public transportation -- and a relaxing way to explore. The streets will inevitably become as busy and traffic-congested as Saigon's, but there is still time to savor the easy tempo before the invasion of the Hondas.

For now, in this unhurried city, citizens still linger for hours out on the sidewalks sipping coffee. The miniature, child-sized bamboo chairs are Southeast Asian, the delicious, slightly chocolaty coffee, served in demitasse cups with condensed milk, a legacy of the former French colonialists.

The sign at one such cafe catering to foreigners, the Home

Away From Home across the street from the Ministry of Defense Guest House, promises "Cold beer, superb coffee and good friends! English sometimes spoken!" It is a forewarning of our problems.

Local English takes even more intriguing turns. Sitting out one afternoon at the Giang Vo Lake Floating Restaurant and Bar (a makeshift raft on pontoons), while cooling breezes ripple the water, we study the menu with quiet trepidation: "Frog stir-fried with little water, duck simmered with 8 Chinese medicines, beef fired by skaking the sancepan, boneless tig's trotters farced with mushroom and hopch totch, beef processed and roasted with five spies, fried snake pies, beef testicle stir fried with hotch-potch."

Much of Hanoi's outdoor amusement revolves around several lakes, with city-center Hoan Kiem as lively as Mexico City's Chapultepec Park. Hawkers sell parachute-nylon hammocks, woven plates painted with comic faces, lacquerware bowls and plates, tortoise-shell work, silverware boxes and jewelry. Instant entrepreneurs set up bicycle hand pumps or weighing scales, selling their services for a few dong (the local currency). Professional photographers with ancient cameras snap stiff portraits with a temple background. One at a time, several girls in flowing white or yellow ao dais, the women's national dress, pose under the trees. The models take turns wearing the only pair of high-heel shoes.

The locals are friendly, but aggressive and on the make. When my somewhat smaller companion and I hire two pedicabs, my driver tries to hustle some extra dong. "Madame small, sir very big," he argues. "Three Vietnamese, sir, same-same. Sir 100 kilos."

There will be no gratuity for you, my good man, I mutter, climbing aboard. But he proves a congenial enough guide, and the leisurely roll through the quiet streets proves a soul-soothing experience.

Still, the remnants of ancient Vietnam we seek are a long day's rail journey to the south. Because the train arrives in Hue in the middle of the night, we decide to take it on to Danang, and backtrack by road to the ancient capital the following day. So at 8am on a chilly Hanoi winter day we are aboard The Reunification Express as it departs on the million dong (about U.S. $50 each) ride. The train is shabby, but passable, and with only four to a compartment provides space to stretch out at night.

Grubby industrial Hanoi crowded with the masses, mostly traveling on two wheels, soon passes into rural Vietnam. It is the classic, unchanged, Southeast Asia of cone hats and water buffalo, of villagers knee-deep in mud making bricks and women ankle-deep in paddy fields planting shoots of rice. This is not all a carefree Eden, though. The pretty, perfect circular ponds are craters from bombs aimed at these railway tracks long ago.

At frequent intervals, a train attendant comes by with buckets of chilled soft drinks and cans of Ba-ba-ba (333 beer) that we buy to go with our baguettes and runny French "Vache Qui Rit" cheese.

"A loaf of bread, a 333 and thee," I toast my lady.

Sometime in the night, we cross the old DMZ (Demilitarized Zone) and enter the former South Vietnam. It is still dark out when the train attendant announces "Danang," and collects the bedding. Gritty-eyed and yawning we step out on the platform, where a few pedicab drivers wait in the shadows. Dawn breaks as we glide quietly through the streets to the hotel.

Da Nang (Tourane to the French before 1954), in the densely populated central coastal lowlands, was the center of the Cham civilization long before the American military built a major base here. Renting a motorbike for US$7 for the day from a passing teenager, we set off on it to explore the environs.

Eleven kilometers from downtown Danang, China Beach, of U.S. military R & R and later TV war soap fame, and the site of Vietnam's international surfing championships last year, is a long and lonely stretch of sand and sea inhabited only by beach urchins peddling seashell souvenirs.

A pack of aggressive waifs hound foreigners around nearby Marble Mountain, five marble hillocks pocked with natural caves used as Buddhist sanctuaries. One persistent, precocious miss hawking crudely carved elephant paperweights tags along as we climb the steep steps of Thuy Son, the largest "mountain," pointing out rock formations and bullet holes in ancient temple gates. At the top, she looks out at the view of China Beach and the surrounding hills, and informs us, "Americans always say: 'Totally awesome.'"

Hue, about 80 kilometers (50 miles) northwest over mountain roads, is too far for the clapped-out little rental bike. So, avoiding the roadside hustlers offering us their run-down cars, we play it safe by commissioning one through the hotel. The receptionist explains that although the driver doesn't speak English, his friend, who does, will go along as a guide.

At dawn, our confidence is shaken when a shabby, barefoot man leads us to his old beater, which smells of gas and leaks exhaust fumes through a hole in the floor. His middle-aged companion introduces himself as Mr. Tan. "I am a student," he announces, a suggestion belied by his disheveled appearance.

But it is a fine morning, with a soft, yellow light reflecting on the rice paddies where farm boys splash and play on their water buffalo. Rows of ducks waddle across the roads, old women carry huge bundles of wood or produce balanced on shoulder poles. Girls in colorful pyjamas outfits, long black hair streaming from woven hats, flutter through the fields like flocks of tropical birds.

National Highway 1 soon leaves the plains for one of Vietnam's most scenic drives, a steep, winding road up Deo Hai Van, the Pass of the Ocean Clouds. At the summit, we pause at the Cafe in the Clouds for strong coffee served in tiny aluminum cups. From this 496-meter peak, it seems we can see all the way back to Danang and forward on to Hue.

Outside Hue, our old clunker weaves precariously through two-wheeled and four-legged traffic hazards, nearly running over peasants wobbling along on rickety bikes. Two bicycles with a hammock slung on a bamboo pole between them to make a basic ambulance are reminders that roadside medical service here may not be up to international standards.

Only now, approaching Hue, do we realize that this is our escorts' first visit here. The historic city was the imperial capital of Vietnam from 1802 until the French took control in 1883, and the provincial capital of South Vietnam from 1954 until reunification in 1975. But I don't think Mr. Tan knows this.

Although severely damaged in the decisive Tet Offensive (1968), much of the imperial relics outside town remain intact. Our companions grin at us vacantly when we ask about the sights so, map in hand, we direct them along a dirt road to the 19th-century Thien Mu Pagoda. Indifferent to the charms of one of Vietnam's most famous buildings, our Danang escorts merely glance up at the towering symbol of Hue, then return to the gasoline-reeking car to light up cigarettes.

The 21-meter-high octagonal pagoda overlooks the Perfume River, where boats marked "Tour ist" unload visitors from Hue. They've come to see the bronze Buddhas, the ancient stele set on the back of a massive marble turtle and the giant bell supposedly audible 10 kilometers away, and to chat with the monks tending the extensive gardens.

In this haven of peace, we happen on a bizarre reminder of more brutal days, the little blue Austin car that took monk Thich Quang to Saigon in 1963 to stage his famous self-immolation in political protest. The car is now parked in a shed, with a copy of one of the most famous photographs of the war -- the flaming bonze with the Austin in the background.

Back outside, we wake our driver and direct him to the extensive citadel in the town center, scene of bloody battles during the Tet Offensive. The US$3.50 entrance fee for foreigners is a sizable sum in Vietnam. Local officials have already learned to get the guests.

Not much of this fee seems to have been spent renovating the expansive, walled ruins surrounded by a weedy, lotus-filled moat. The ornately embellished, Chinese-style Ngo Mon Gate leads to the Imperial City and Forbidden Purple City, now a hushed, abandoned area largely overgrown with vegetable patches and grass. It is a smaller, quieter Vietnamese version of Peking's Forbidden City, with the Halls of the Mandarins and the Tha Hoa Palace. But the library has been renovated, to house a gift shop.

The top of the gate looks out on the 37-meter "Kings Knight" flag pole across the road. The North Vietnamese flew the National-al Liberation Front flag here for weeks during the Tet Offensive, a scene I recall from news photos long ago.

But there is much more to Hue than wartime relics. Nguyen Dynasty kings (1802-1945) built their tombs in complexes spread over a large area along the Perfume River. It is a latter-day Ang-kor Wat (Cambodia's famous ruins), though not as grand or ar-tistic. Picking out the complex furthest from Hue, we direct our driver, who is obviously tiring of sightseeing, along the deserted back roads through the jungle.

With no road signs, we could quickly get lost, so we follow the foreigners cycling among the ruins. At the Tomb of Khai Dinh, a backpacker says it is easy to avoid the entry fee to all the tombs, and disappears around the side of the hill. We pay the US$3 and walk up the steps to meet a phalanx of stony honor guards as intimidating as a regiment of unpainted garden gnomes.

One of the more recent tombs (built from 1920 to 1931), Khai Dinh is a stunningly gaudy mishmash of colored bits of porce-lain and glass slapped onto a reinforced concrete structure. The guidebook says it is an amalgam of East and West, though nei-ther culture should accept the blame.

By now, the Danang duo is strongly agitating to head home, but we insist on seeing another tomb, Tu Duc. After 45 minutes of aimless driving around the jungle roads and countless stops to ask directions, we finally find it. The bicycling gatecrasher is already there, climbing over the fence.

Tuc Duc, spread over 225 hectares, is more extensive, older

and more tasteful than Khai Dinh. It is a pleasant atmosphere, like a busy urban park on a Sunday afternoon, as Vietnamese families stroll among the tombs and follow tiled paths past viewing pavilions, small lakes and temples.

Finally, with the late evening light slanting across the temple wall, we ask our dejected escorts to take us back to Danang, anticipating a sunset ride through the countryside. But it is not to be.

On the way out of Hue, our driver gets lost.

LAOS

LUANG PRABANG

Liquid Sunsets

February, 2000

LIKE a star performer exiting a stage, the vivid vermilion sun plops into the Mekong River, turning the water a liquid gold. Time for another Beerlao. Watching the dramatic sunsets from an outdoor cafe on stilts over the riverbank is as exciting as nightlife gets in Luang Prabang, former royal capital of the kingdom of Laos.

Which is just fine for visitors, who savor the leisurely pace of the scenic town, 367 kilometers northwest of Vientiane, now the Laotian capital. Crowing roosters greet the dawn in front yards lining unpaved streets, and goats rummage around the underbrush in this small riverine community. Groups of young boys with shaved skulls wearing robes the color of a Mekong sunset stroll the streets like their teenage counterparts wearing jeans and T-shirts in other Asian cities. Five years ago, traffic was mostly bicycles. Today it is mainly three-wheeled vehicles, with many Bangkok-style tuk-tuks (motorized trishaws) plying the streets. Soon, it will be four-wheeled vehicles, and some of the bucolic charm will be lost.

The town, with its lost-in-time aura, is perhaps the best-preserved in Southeast Asia. In recognition of this, UNESCO designated it a World Heritage Site in December 1995. An incredible 600 buildings are classified, with 33 temples and 111 historic Lao-French buildings listed for restoration.

For so small a town, Luang Prabang has numerous worthy sights, plus several pleasant excursions. Like many visitors, I get my bearings by climbing the "mountain," a 150-meter-high, pagoda-topped hill called Mt. Phousi. This is about as challenging as walking up to Hong Kong Park from Central District, and worth the effort. Stairways lead past rustic homes and small temples, with young monks hanging about, to a drowsy ticket taker collecting 8,000 kip (about US$1), the entry fee to the hilltop wat (temple compound).

A rusted old Russian anti-aircraft gun perched near the top provides momentary entertainment to visitors, who twirl the barrel around and sit in the gunner's seat posing for photographs. The peak, with the modest Wat Chom Si, provides a lofty view of the old town, set on a peninsula where the small Nam Khan River meets the Mekong.

From here, I glimpse some of the dozens of Buddhist temples scattered among the palms, including the five-tiered Wat Mai, and That Makmo, ostensibly shaped like a watermelon. Luang Prabang has so many temples, and relatively few tourists, that I often have one to myself -- or with the company of a young monk, eager to chat in English.

Restoring long-neglected religious structures is a major enterprise here. In a wat compound back down in the town, elderly monks oversee red bricks being laid for a new stupa and novices help unload ferroconcrete reinforcing bars from a three-wheel delivery bike while several of their robed brethren stroll by bearing paint rollers over their shoulders like sacred icons.

Only a few other visitors wander about Wat Xieng Thong, the town's grandest, most popular temple, the evening I arrive. The compound of elaborate, ornate chapels is set in a fragrant tropical garden of bougainvillea, frangipani and hibiscus, among banyan and palm trees. In one corner, the small royal chapel, shimmering like a jewel in the evening sun, houses an elaborate golden hearse, a huge, gilded and ornately-decorated funeral chariot, incongruously set on rubber tires.

One morning, not too early, I wander down to the riverbank to arrange a visit to the Pak Ou caves, a Buddhist shrine about 35 kilometers upstream from Luang Prabang. Locals hanging around the river ask for $15 for the boat trip, but readily agree on $13. This is easygoing Laos.

It is a pleasant, if buttocks-bruising, ride upriver in a long, narrow boat past empty, sandy beaches, a line of trees like huge ferns and rounded, forest-clad hills. Men load big burlap bags onto cargo boats; women wash themselves, their children and their clothes in the river; fishermen perch patiently on flimsy dugouts; and farmers tend their vegetable patches.

A school of noisy, Thai-style long-tailed boats roars by, spewing spray and exhaust fumes, disturbing the tranquillity; soon, it is peaceful again. Fortunately, these offensive craft have been banned from around the city.

Two peaceful hours from Luang Prabang, the boat approaches high, flat cliffs with a darkened cave mouth showing. A steep staircase leads to a little landing, where lazing locals collect the 8,000-kip entrance fee while their sisters sell sticks of incense. A pack of backpackers is leaving the lower cave as I arrive, so I have it to myself. This is so often the way in Asia; a place is swarming with tourists, or it is deserted. In pre-Buddhist days, a sign informs us, locals worshipped Phi, the spirit of nature, here. In more recent decades, the faithful have placed more than 4,000 gilded and wooden Buddha statues in the cave, a whole army of figurines, some old and artistic, others like cheap souvenir dolls.

After renting flashlights to explore the higher, deeper cave, then buying a token souvenir, a hand-stitched purse from the hill tribeswoman waiting below, I cross the river to a collection of makeshift restaurants. For a serene hour or so, I sit on a tiny stool set out on the sand, the reflection of the water shimmering on the thatched palm roof, drinking beer and eating boiled eggs and noodles.

I return to Luang Prabang in time for another excursion not usually on tourist itineraries: a visit to the grave of 19th-century French explorer Henri Mahout. The first European to see the fabulous temples of Angkor Wat while exploring the natural history of the Mekong River, the young Frenchman died here of jungle fever in 1861.

Setting off into the countryside on a rented minivan, I pass classic Southeast Asian rural scenery of jungle, thatched farm houses, water buffaloes, and half-naked children. A faded and chipped yellow sign, partly hidden by the foliage, says, simply, Henri Mahout.

The driver parks by the road and lights up a cigarette while I walk down to the sandy riverbank and follow a not-very-well-worn path. Soon, another faded sign points me back toward the jungle, and a few meters from the river, I find the famous French explorer's tomb. It is a simple, peaceful site, secluded and shrouded in the thick jungle. And there is not a souvenir or snack salesman in sight.

Back in Luang Prabang, there are so many historic buildings that, like most visitors, I sleep and eat in heritage houses. The Villa Santi, a French colonial mansion once home to a Laotian princess, is now a fine hotel with the pleasant Restaurant de la Princesse. Tables on the verandah overlooking the street are ideal for a long lunch or dinner.

The grand old L'Hotel Souvannaphoum's pleasant White Elephant bar is another atmospheric spot for a leisurely beer or Mekong whiskey. The quiet little room evokes colonial times, with crossed swords on the wall, old-style gas lamps as wall sconces, an ancient wooden gramophone, rattan tables and chairs, and a lone gecko clucking and skittering along the wall in search of wayward insects.

But when dusk approaches, I head back to the river, find an

open place on stilts over the Mekong, and end another peaceful day with fish curry, noodles and fried rice, and an iced Beerlao as the sun sinks into the Mekong.

BURMA

PAGAN

Temples on the Plain

June 2001

NEITHER mad dog nor Englishman, here I am, out in the scorching midday Burmese sun. Baked stones sear bare, tender city soles, sending me dancing down the path to the coolness of the shaded pagoda.

Aside from hot feet and the indignity of scurrying for cover, touring the ruins of Pagan (now Bagan) is a truly awesome experience, even for more jaded travelers. And I can now appreciate why both canine and man wander out in Noel Coward's nonsensical song.

Pagan, 315 miles (470 kilometers) northwest of Rangoon, Burma (Myanmar) is accessible from the capital by plane, train and bus. The Arrow Express bus takes about 12 hours, Air Mandalay about 80 minutes. The flight is worth it for the view, coming in over the flat, dry grassy plains, of the odd bumps that are the fantastic ruins, then, just as we are descending, of a gold stupa shimmering off in the distance.

The late 13th-century royal capital spread across Burma's central plains, one of the world's prime architectural wonders, equals Cambodia's Angkor Wat, Indonesia's Borobudur, Peru's Macchu Picchu or Guatemala's Tikal. Yet it is perhaps the least known, and appreciated of these.

At Pagan's small airport, we pay the compulsory US$10 for entrance to the monuments for two days, declining the extra fee for additional days. No one checks while we are there, so we don't pay anything when we decide to stay longer.

The ancient site, once known as "The city of four million pagodas," is actually a village of 5,000 pagodas, gathered around 2,230 monuments. Numbers aside, that is enough for the most insatiable sightseer.

On our way to the modest Thante Hotel in Old Pagan, one of the few still there, we pass some truly magnificent ruins, in many shapes and degrees of disrepair. But they are not even important ruins worthy of guidebook mention. Out hotel is a collection of wooden bungalows scattered around parklike grounds alongside the Irrawaddy (Ayeyarwady) River. Around us, they are building new bungalows, out of brick and terra-cotta tiles in what appears to be a kind of neo-Bagan Ruins style of architecture.

Flicking away a scorpion, or some other kind of deadly insect, from our bathroom with a towel, I inspect our room. It is plain and basic, but the setting superb, with a porch overlooking the river and hills on the other side, one topped by a monastery.

We can explore this superb 42-square-kilometer collection of ruins by car, horse cart or bicycle. Over three days, we try all three. It is impossible to see every ruin, so we abandon any plans and visit sites by whim, like attending a great sightseeing buffet, sampling a Mon-style temple here, a tiny stupa there. Vegetation, weather and vandalism have reduced many of the structures to mounds of rubble, but numerous intact temples tower over the dusty, scrub-covered plains like cathedrals in the wild.

There are some "musts," however: Bupaya Pagoda, the oldest in Pagan, for its riverside setting; Nathlaungkyaung, the only Hindu temple; Thatbyinnyu, the tallest in Pagan, a squarish structure with a dome in the middle; and Ananda temple, one of the largest and best preserved, with its elegant stupa and long shaded arcade of shops selling lacquer ware and gilded objects.

While strolling the arcade there one day, I hear the tinkling sound of a temple bell which attracts me to one shop. There, a cheerful lady, her face plastered with white powder, is selling the bells, as well as flowers, the wonderful scent of jasmine mixing with that of incense and burning candle wax from the temple.

At another stall, where I buy a copy of George Orwell's classic Burmese Days, the young salesman asks me for Canadian maple leaf pins. Apparently, such national symbol pins are popular here, the girls wearing them as earrings. He wants them for his sister, and I am able to give him a matched pair.

These sites are so spread out, that touring Pagan is a peaceful affair away from a few of the most popular pagodas. Often, the only sounds are temple bells, birdcalls and the clinking coming from the bamboo scaffolding as workers rebuild a crumbling temple.

Back at the hotel that evening, we sit on the porch watching the sun set, listening to the chugging of diesel engines coming from boats on the river packed high with bananas, and shouts from children playing in the river. Along the muddy shore, they run this way and that, changing directions like a flock of brown birds.

At dawn, we hire bikes from the Co-operative Hotel for 150 kyat (just over $1) a day. These aren't the stylish, sturdy knobby-tired mountain bikes preferred by hardcore modern cyclists, but girls' bikes, with basket carriers in front. They are adequate for this flat, paved terrain, however. Starting at about 7:30 am, we peddle down the dusty, betel-nut splattered road and onto the highway, heading south to New Bagan, a village created several years ago when the government forcibly moved the residents from the original Pagan.

Even on the main road, traffic is limited to a few buses, some horse carts piled high with rural folk, open-backed vans packed with passengers, and longyi-clad opportunists with Mickey

Mouse T-shirts scooting by on motorbikes shouting out "Good morning, my friend," "Hello," "Bye-bye," and "Buy rubies?" A woman follows us on a bike, wants to change money, and offers "flim" for my camera.

A well-preserved temple off the road to the left attracts our attention, so we bike over. It is Nagayon, now locked, but the drinks vendor smoking an acrid-smelling brown cheroot, like French Gitanes, sends for the key keeper to open it. We take off our shoes and scramble barefooted over the scorching ground to the cool inner temple. Dark corridors lead to a chamber with small terra-cotta Buddhas in the alcoves, staring out of the gloom. We have this magnificent historic relic all to ourselves.

Are there are snakes here? I ask a woman vendor outside the temple, making a waving motion with my hand. She understands immediately, and laughs. Not in the temple, her son says, because it is cool. They like to be in between rocks in the hot sun. That is good news.

Later on our random sightseeing, disaster strikes. Midday, miles from our hotel, at the main New Bagan intersection, one of the bikes gets a flat. It is the hottest part of the day, the temperature pushing three figures Fahrenheit, and there is not a garage in sight. What now?

The enormity of the situation has hardly set in when Mr. Ko Nine Win from the Khan Wa Restaurant comes out, his cheery smile displaying betel-nut-stained teeth. Sending his son to the village to get the flat fixed, he sits us in rattan planters' chairs on his restaurant's breezy porch and serves beer and excellent French fries with a sweet-and-zingy sauce. Twenty minutes later, his son is back with the bike. Drinks, food and bicycle repairs come to 210 kyat (less than $2). And he probably doesn't even know it is Visit Myanmar Year.

Down the dusty road, a sign catches our eye: "The only first class restaurant in Bagan serving traditional Myanmar cuisine. For reservations, telephone 01 60228." True to its word, the Riverview, though modest, proves to be the town's top restaurant, for setting as well as food. Sitting under a neem tree, which drops its minuscule blossoms on the table and on our hair, we study the extensive menu. The kitchen offers soups, quail's egg or duck's web salad, Myanmar-style chicken, pork or prawn curries or diced chicken with chili (large crispy dry-roasted chilies as red as the Burmese rubies). So we feast on chicken with cashew nuts, minced and fried pork, a whole river fish, noodles and rice. A good lunch for two, with Chinese beer, the cheapest kind in Burma and a tasty brew, comes to less than 1,500 kyat (about $13).

As we are leaving, I hear the Englishman at the next table comment, "I still have half my quacks left." He is not, apparently, talking about ducks on his plate, but the kyats.

Another day, we hire a car to go north, to Nyaung Oo, an interesting, but messy village with betel nut shops and women collecting water at the village well. At the market, hopeful hawkers peddle attractive marionettes, betel nut cutters, rubies, slippers, longyis (sarongs) and monk's bags (called Shan bags here) beloved by latter-day hippies, and necessary for locals because longyis don't have pockets. Like so much of Burma, the simple village seems to be lost in the 1960s.

Nearby, the glittering Shwezigon Temple is a dazzling, living place of worship compared to the somber stone temples of Old Pagan. In this age-old scene, mischievous young monks and worshipping grannies stroll the open, paved grounds under sun umbrellas, while gaunt temple dogs doze in the shade, not the midday sun.

Later, back in Old Pagan, men with horse and carts hustle their services around the main hotels, offering private tours for $10 a day. That evening, we take a sunset tour with EyEy and his horse, Madonna, a name favored for Pagan horses, for some reason. As we trot off, EyEy tells me his name was Koko, but there were too many of them around, so he changed it.

The little horse takes us on a circuit of some of the nearer temples and pagodas, those most popular with mini-bus tourists on a tight schedule. When we linger inside the small Ananda

Okkyaung temple, trying to escape a voluble French group, we get locked inside the dark, dank sanctuary. It is like being in jail until our shouts bring the key keeper, who tries to solicit a tip for letting us out. Later, we hesitate before entering the long, low Shinbinthalyaung temple, but there are no potential jailers here. Inside, the reclining Buddha, thought to date back to the 11th century, lies like a giant taking a perpetual nap.

At dusk, Koko and Madonna deposit us at the great, squarish, Shwesandaw, the current temple of choice for sunset viewing. Koko and Madonna got $10 -- a good day's income in that impoverished country - and they head off happily down the road, the sun flashing off the carriage's brass fixtures.

It was money they would never have earned if we had succumbed to the call to boycott travel to Burma. Some Western liberals urge tourists not to travel to Burma, and 1991 Nobel Peace Prize winner, opposition leader Aung San Suu Kyi, has called for a boycott of Visit Myanmar Year 1996. (Curiously, the spirited lady's weekly appearance to speak to her followers outside her house has become one of Rangoon's tourist attractions.)

These Westerners will let ordinary Burmese suffer for the Westerner's ideals, arguing that all funds from tourists go to the government. Nonsense. The sweet little girls selling lacquer ware in the temples, the taxi drivers, the charming, cheroot-puffing elderly ladies hawking delicious, ice cold Mandalay lager, all profited from my visit to Burma, as they will from others who sensibly ignore the boycott.

With that thought, I head up Shwesandaw's steep, narrow stairs leading like stone ladders up the five receding terraces on four sides. At the temple-top vantage point, dozens of visitors from around the world, all ignoring the boycott call, gather for the nightly show. The dying sun turns the dry land all around us the reddish hue of monk's robes, illuminating a fantastic panorama of temples stretching to the hazy horizon. As the great red ball drops down behind the hills across the powerful Irrawaddy River, an ox cart passes below, only the squeaking of the axles breaking the silence.

The complimentary solar show concluded, baggy European tourists scramble down the high steps sideways, like great pink crabs, and clamber onto mini-vans or bicycles. And we climb into the pony cart for the ride home, as a majestic silver disc floats in the sky behind the ancient pagodas, the moon over Myanmar.

MALAYSIA

MT. KINABALU

Struggling to the Top

July 1983

IN the crowded Sunday Market in Ranau, Borneo, the hot, damp air smells of fresh and dried fish, pungent local spices and grilling chicken wings. Ethnic Kadazan women chewing huge wads of tobacco gather round aggressive city hawkers peddling cheap manufactured goods spread out on blankets before them. Placid, passive country folk in towel turbans or cone straw hats squat under umbrellas before pyramids of produce from jungle gardens.

Ranau's golden-onion mosque glows in the haze. An itinerant sorcerer displays sections of tiger's penis (for virility) and charms offering protection from forest animals. The thumpthumpthump of Kadazan tapes overpowers the rock music, hoarse-voiced hawkers, and a blind beggar squatting in the dust playing Three Blind Mice over and over on a harmonica.

Over this hectic Asian scene, poking through the grey morning mists, broods sacred Mount Kinabalu, Southeast Asia's highest peak (4,101 meters) that I will try to climb tomorrow. Kinabalu will prove to be more than a walk in the rainforest.

* * * * *

Going downhill is a hell of a way to start a mountain climb. Some 30 hours from now, after climbing a mountain almost as high as Mont Blanc in the French Alps, I will have to struggle back up this steep gully in sadder shape than I am now. The skreeching, skrawking, whistles and rustles of the jungle around Mt. Kinabalu Park headquarters cabins give way to twittering bird songs greeting the pale dawn light. Half asleep, I haul my cameras, a few chocolate bars and a packet of cold, greasy rice to the warden's office to arrange for a guide. A smoke-belching pickup drops Benati, a frail. yet fit and silent Kadazan, and me at the power station at the foot of the mountain. From here, the trail dips down into a riverbed before steeply zigzagging up the mountainside.

Last year 10,378 climbers attempted the peak located some 90 kilometers east of Kota Kinabalu, Sabah's capital. Some 1,749 failed to make it to the top -- something to contemplate as I stumble up the rough, irregular trail. Ankle-turning rocks and twisted roots snaking through the thick, lush primary rain forest at the base of the mountain make the going hard. Already, I am puffing like an ancient steam engine while my guide follows effortlessly like a silent wraith, contemplating the Kadazan spirits that inhabit the top of the sacred mountain.

All morning, with many rest stops, I struggle up the forest path dappled with light filtering through the tall trees, over ground covered with tree roots like veins on an old, brown hand. I climb up rickety staircases with bamboo banisters and along a ridge of mossy forest with giant, trees dripping Tarzan-like vines, hanging orchids, lianas and ferns.

When my rasping breath quietens, the only sounds on the lonesome trail are the drowsy buzzing of flies and unseen little forest animals scuttling through the underbrush. We stop to suck water from a break in the plastic pipe running down the hill. Steam rises from the damp jungle in the burning mid-morning sun. My sticky-hot, sweat-soaked T-shirt turns chilly in a sudden

breeze. Old Benati waits patiently until the tuan, the white master, can resume the climb.

I wonder at the strange appeal of mountains that attract even
un-athletic, non-outdoors types. I have climbed Japan's sacred
Fuji-san, Tanzania's Mt. Kilimanjaro and Australia's Ayers Rock,
and hiked hills in the Andes, the Himalayas, Papua/New Guinea and northern Thailand's border with Burma, where hill tribes-
man in strange costumes still cultivate the poppy which ends up
in North America and Europe as heroin.

The thick jungle gives way to oaks (some 30 species), then a
cloud forest of smaller, moss-covered trees, ferns, bamboo, rho-
dodendron and evil, hungry insectivorous pitcher plants. Somewhere grow rarely seen Raffelesia, the world's largest blossoms.

The jagged peak we aspire to bears the name of one Hugh Low,
the first to ascend the mountain, in 1858. Today, a mixed collection of climbers stops for a break in a clearing at Carson's Camp
as cool, wet mists begin to blot out the sun: a group of laughing
Malaysian high school students that scampered up the mountain
with ease; stern German hikers ("You must not stop too long. You
must continue now."); and intense, well-equipped Japanese.

Japanese are well turned out in mountain gear even for the
six-hour hike up their own Mt. Fuji. Japanese tradition says a
wise man climbs Mt. Fuji, only a fool climbs it twice. The one time
I climbed it, I joined them on one of five ant-like trails leading
up the volcanic mountainside, the pilgrim/climbers stopping at
each station to get its mark seared into their walking sticks. Some
reach the peak in the evening, some stay overnight in mountain
huts and climb the last few hours in the dark, but they all gather
at the peak to greet the rising sun, (as all we Kinabalu climbers
hope to do tomorrow).

As I pause for a break, a small group comes up the trail behind me: a slightly paunchy lepidopterist from the University of
Rome (if he can make it, I certainly can) and several members of
the Brunei branch of the Hash House Harriers, those strange folk
who race through the jungles following trails that inevitably lead

to a beer truck.

The cold mist pushes me up the mountain, so at 2 p.m. I break through the gnarled trees of the alpine terrain to a slight rock face and the rest hut, Panar Laban, the place of sacrifice. I am so exhausted I can't even climb the short flight of stairs to the hut without stopping to rest -- but I have made it on day one, right on time according to the park climbing schedule. Decades of marathon-runner-like carbo-loading on spaghetti and beer have paid off in endurance.

Inside the bare, basic hut the Harriers and the Italian moth man, all there long before me, are stretched out on the plank bunks snoring. The Malaysian school kids romp around with odious vigor. I collapse on the bunk in a thin, rented sleeping bag. But the night is not near as cold as in the shack high on Kilimanjaro where I was perhaps the most ill-equipped climber ever: socks for gloves, a blanket over my shoulders and a towel draped on my head like on an Egyptian pharoah's. The Sierra Club American group I joined, with their expensive L.L. Bean and Eddie Bauer mountain gear, seemed to resent the outsider who made it to the top in street shoes.

At 3 a.m., climbers and guides stumbling around in the inadequate light of a soot-blackened kerosene lamp startle me to resentful wakefulness. After a breakfast of a packet of sugar from the Kota Kinabalu Hyatt and an icy tin cup of water, I set off in the blackness up the steep, twisted path behind the hut.

It is even worse than yesterday, the path so steep through the dense dwarf forest that in places we pull ourselves up by our hands along man-made ladders and natural staircases of Leptospermum roots. The full moon and occasional bright stabs from Benati's flashlight light the way. The only sounds now are the shallow, quick panting of climbers trying to suck in more oxygen-thin air.

At 4:30 a.m., Benati and I break out of the stunted forest. Pinpoints of light far ahead and above show the other climbers. We traverse a bare rock face, clutching thick ropes strung along and attached to metal rings in the rock for support, to reach Sayat Sayat, the last huts on the mountain where the others are resting.

The bare, pointed peaks loom ahead like a monstrous, multi-nippled breast. Walking is easy on the smooth rock, following cairns and piles of rocks, but progress is slow at this altitude. Even the guides stop frequently to gasp for breath. Altitude sickness begins to hit some of us, causing sharp headaches, nausea, shortness of breath. One of the Hashers stops to throw up, the hack-hacking carrying far in the cool, thin air. "I can't go any further," he groans, retches, then plods on. But eventually, this man who runs for recreation, has to give up, defeated more by altitude sickness than fatigue.

The light of the silvery moon bathes the stark, sheer peaks around us: the Ugly Sisters, Donkey Ears and, high ahead, Low's Peak.

An agonizing, chest-searing, throat-parching hour later I finally scramble up those giant boulders to plop down on the peak, panting, beside the signs and banners of previous climbers. The overweight Roman bug professor has been there for more than half an hour. We all sign the summit book. Then, right on cue, whoever arranges such things has the giant red sun rise like a bloodshot eyeball over the granite cliff to the east to glare at our shivering, jubilant group. Slowly, the rays light the jagged peaks and the valleys far, far below. Absolute silence. An awesome, otherworldly beauty and peace.

Resting atop the peak for the descent, I recall other times, other peaks; Japan's Fuji-san, 12,388 feet, where dawn-greeting Champagne -- even cheap Japanese Champagne -- blows its cork even more at that altitude; celebrating atop Gilman's Peak, three hard days up 19,340-foot Mt. Kilimanjaro, with mini-bottles of airline brandy. Today, the total serenity is disturbed only by the thought of the painful five-mile, six-hour hike down to a hot shower and cold beer.

Sir Edmund Hillary and Sherpa Tenzing Norgay, alone 29,028

feet atop Mt. Everest in 1953, could not have felt more fulfilled.

Postscript

While the climb is possible for anyone moderately fit, it is still not a walk in the park. Kinabalu has claimed nine lives since the park opened. Each year, a team of some 20 rangers deal with a number of minor injuries and accidents, usually of climbers with scrapes, broken bones or overcome with exhaustion and altitude sickness, although there are more serious cases.

A few years after I climbed, in 1987, when five climbers were scaling the mountain, three went ahead, while the leader stayed back with the slowest member. Very soon, the weather changed, as it often does on the mountain, and visibility was reduced to almost zero for three days. The two lagging behind disappeared and although rangers looked for them for a month, they never found the men.

Another case, the most famous rescue ever on the mountain, made international news headlines. Ten British and Hong Kong soldiers attempted in February, 1994, to become the first to descend Low's Gully. Five became trapped on the towering cliffs. More than two weeks after the expedition began, the other five climbers stumbled out of the gully and raised the alarm. Park rangers, the Malaysian army and a British mountain rescue team all joined the hunt.

Nine days later, the stranded climbers were spotted and winched to safety aboard a helicopter. They had attempted to abseil down the notorious Low's Gully, a mile-deep cleft down one side of the mountain. A month later they had to be rescued, having apparently survived the last week with no food other than mints. Their story was made into a movie, In the Place of the Dead.

In August, 2001, Ellie James, a 16-year-old girl from Cornwall, England, got separated from her group on a descent during bad weather. A search and rescue team found her body a week later. Local guides feared "spirits" had lured her astray.

SARAWAK

Hornbills, Headhunters and Tattooed Ladies

January 2001

I'M afraid Jalan, my Iban guide, is going to have a heart attack when he almost steps on a slithery, prehistoric monster. And he is a descendant of headhunters. I'm just a city dweller, and I'm sure I'll have a cardiac arrest when the huge, startled monitor lizard crashes through the underbrush just feet in front of us. Jalan has never encountered one of these saurian eyesores so close up, even though he is from the area.

This is Sarawak, wild land of hornbills, headhunters and tattooed ladies. The unusual, the outlandish and the just plain bizarre are commonplace in this Malaysian state on the north coast of the island of Borneo. Oddities include comical orangutans, flabby-nosed proboscis monkeys, flying lizards, bearded pigs, squirrels with wings, insectivorous pitcher plants, the world's largest flower, the Rafflesia, with blossoms a yard wide, and rhinoceros hornbills (birds) with huge beaks and colorful "helmets."

With its more than 26 indigenous ethnic groups plus a variety of newcomers, Sarawak has its human oddities as well. Once, it was a land of marauding pirates and tattooed headhunters whose most distinctive interior decorating item was a string of human skulls hanging from the rafters of their longhouses. Instead of merely applying lipstick and eye makeup, the women of some interior tribes tattoo themselves from neck to knee.

Three-quarters of Sarawak, Malaysia's largest state, is mountains covered by the world's oldest rainforest, much of it protected in national parks and reserves. Rivers penetrating the interior, where most inhabitants still live in distinctive communal longhouses, serve as highways.

Borneo makes its first impression on me right at Kuching airport, with its warm, tropical vegetation smell, like overripe fruit, and the rich, sweet perfume of the local clove cigarettes. Kuching, the state capital of low-rise shophouses, austere mosques and elaborate, colorful Hindu and Chinese temples, remains one of Southeast Asia's most charming cities.

But even the city still borders on the wild. The day I arrive, I witness a big orange bundle of fur swinging through the trees high above, like a hairy Tarzan on steroids. With tremendous agility, speed and power, the long-armed orangutan ("man of the jungle" in Malay) scrambles from branch to branch, vine to vine, in the jungle canopy at the Semengoh Wildlife Rehabilitation Center, just 30 kilometers from the city center.

This is an early taste of wild Borneo, and the next day, I head north along the new Pan-Borneo highway, bound for the Hilton Batang Ai Longhouse Resort 270 kilometers north of Kuching, in a center of Iban culture. Along the way, I learn more about Iban customs -- notably headhunting -- from my driver/guide Mas.

Sarawak's original inhabitants include Land Dayaks (Bidayuh), Sea Dayaks (Ibans) and Upriver Dayaks (Orang Ulu). "In the old days, an Iban man had to take the head of an adult male from another tribe before he could get married," Mas informs me. "No head, no honey," he adds. "Today, it is no money, no honey."

Iban men had their bodies, arms and legs tattooed, but could only tattoo their fingers if they killed a male older than 18 from another tribe. "Headhunting stopped about 50 years ago. It's not popular anymore," Mas shrugs.

The highway through the rainforest follows a mountain range on our right, separating us from Kalimantan, Indonesia. On the way, we pass palm oil estates with tree branches like gargantuan feather dusters and pepper plantations with orderly rows of tall cylindrical pepper trees.

Mid-morning we reach the 90-square-kilometer artificial lake that the Batang Ai hydro-electric created with a dam it built 18 years ago. In just 15 minutes, a modern speedboat speeds us to our home for the next few days. Opened in 1995, the unique Hilton Batang Ai Resort, the most luxurious in Borneo, combines Iban longhouse architecture with modern amenities.

Traditional longhouses are villages of up to 200 people living under one roof -- long buildings with private "apartments" off a communal verandah, where public life goes on. The Hilton resort's 100 rooms are in 11 large, authentic-looking, but modern Iban-style longhouses made with smooth, dark local hardwood and mostly natural materials. Traditional Iban carvings, textiles and handicrafts decorate the wooden structures. Landscaped gardens with local flowering plants to attract wild birds surround the resort, and a nature walk winds through the nearby jungle.

Some 90 percent of the staff are locals, friendly Ibans with a natural charm. Headhunters make good head waiters, I find. My first stop is the Nanga Mepi restaurant to sample some Iban food. The chicken and coconut soup with slices of young coconut, and the baked red tilapia, a local freshwater fish served with garlic rice and wild jungle ferns is delicious, as is the bamboo chicken I try another night.

From this base, guests explore traditional Iban communal longhouses and the 240-square-kilometer Batang Ai National Park. My Borneo Adventure tour company day trip starts next morning at 9am when I board one of a dozen longboats at the resort dock. With James driving the long, narrow boat and jungle guide Jalan navigating from the front, we cross the lake, pass some freshwater fish farms, and leave the modern world behind. It is soothing this brilliant Borneo morning sitting low in the boat, savoring the blue sky, white clouds, green jungle and brown river, while lulled by the hypnotic hum of the 15-horsepower outboard and the water slapping at the bow.

At the end of the lake, Jalan, giving hand signals, guides

us through a maze of upright dead tree trunks, stumps, sticks, branches and floating driftwood. Entering a river, we pass a few dilapidated longhouses looking like long-abandoned summer homes up on the bank, then patches of cultivated land and orderly rows of pepper trees up on the hills.

Suddenly, the river narrows, and a powerful current rocks the narrow boat. With James driving and Jalan fending off rocks with a pole or paddle, we fight our way past the rapids. I search the trees above, looking for hornbills and proboscis monkeys, nature's little joke, with their weird, pendulous elongated noses. Ahead, I spot a vine -- or a thick, grey snake -- stretched across the river. But it is only a power cable bringing electricity to the ranger station.

An hour-and-a-half after leaving the resort, we reach the Batang Ai National Park ranger station. In the office perched up on the bank, I see by the guest book that I am the first visitor in three days, and the last person here was a forestry officer.

Back across the river, Jalan and I slather on insect repellent - especially on our ankles to ward off leeches, which are common here - and head up some wooden steps on a jungle trek. Along the way, he points out several ancient Iban graves with large clay pots on them to hold sacrifices (or funeral items), and one more modern one with a small tin trunk. Only warriors are buried up here, he explains.

Puffing and sweating in this jungle heat and humidity, I climb to a ridge and walk along, catching occasional glimpses of the valley on both sides. Jalan tells me about the different types of foliage: the pandanus used for thatching roofs and weaving baskets and mats; ferns for making bracelets and armlets; and the large hardwood trees used to build longhouses and longboats.

It is here we encounter the lounging lizard sunning itself at the side of the path. It is a startling sight, the size of a Great Dane, on Pekingese legs, with a long tail and a Jurassic Park monster's head.

When we get back to the river, James is cleaning five silvery fish he caught while waiting for us. On a small pebble beach nearby, he salts them, impales them on sharpened sticks, and roasts them over a campfire. They make a tasty supplement to our packed lunch. Jalan promises me that "Next time I'll catch the monitor lizard, and we can eat that as well." I think I will pass on that.

After lunch, we make a short visit to a functioning longhouse. Rough cement steps lead up to the communal home, but inside it is still basic. The only modern objects are some kerosene lamps, a few plastic containers, nylon fishnets hanging to dry and a John Player cigarettes poster. Hand-woven baskets, mats and fish traps hang on plain, unpainted wooden plank walls and a handful of pig-sticking spears leans against the corner next to a stack of firewood. Deer, not human, skulls decorate the support posts in this longhouse. The smell of wood smoke lingers in the air. Roosters crow, flies buzz, dogs snuffle around.

Jalan urges me to be careful walking over the springy bamboo floor so I don't plunge through. "You have a strong body," he says - meaning heavy, and I do weigh far more than these small, wiry warriors who are built more like junior gymnasts than boxers or wrestlers.

Only a half-dozen members of the 22 resident families are around this afternoon, the men in shorts, the women in batik sarongs. In Iban fashion, they gather around to greet me. The oldest man's back, arms and legs are completely covered with dark tattoos. Among the traditional patterns, he proudly shows me one of a naked lady on his arm, done in Kuala Lumpur with a modern tattooing needle. I note that his fingers are not tattooed, so he is no headhunter. The old women also have dark blue tattoos around their arms.

Feeling like Santa, I hand over the large plastic bag of candy and chocolates that I'd been told to bring as a traditional present. With all this concentrated sugar, I feel like I'm contributing to future dentists of Sarawak, but the oldest woman gives me a thumbs up, so the gift is a hit.

"How big is your longhouse?" asks the older man, who I take to be the chief. I wonder how to explain Hong Kong apartment blocks, before simply replying, "Quite big."

As I squat on the floor, I am introduced to the most amicable of Iban customs. Whenever welcoming visitors, these hospitable people break open a bottle (or more) of tuak, the local rice wine. It is surprisingly tasty, and the chief keeps refilling my glass. I'm too well-mannered to refuse.

Iban welcomes can go on for days, with extensive drinking, singing and dancing. But tuak apparently packs a powerful punch, and Jalan says our good-byes after we finish the first bottle. With a mixture of relief and reluctance, I board the boat and we head back to our own longhouse. In this wild and wonderful corner of the world, there are more adventures to come.

PHILIPPINES

ATI ATIHAN

Days of Madness

January, 1983

WHEN the doors of the Philippine Airlines' plane swing open a
band of sooty-faced natives in pseudo-Zulu outfits bearing a sign
"Black Beauty Boys" advance on us waving spears and bashing
bass drums.

Screaming, "I gotta get this sound; we may not hear it again,"
Matt, a CBC correspondent, shoves past me down the stairs.

Blunt fingers jabbing at the black piano-key controls of his
Sony portable tape recorder, he marches towards the wild, shuffling band, his mike held forward like a bayonet. But the natives
are friendly, here to greet junketing politicians from Manila, a jet
hour to the northwest.

The occasion is the annual January Ati-Atihan Festival in Kalibo, Atlan district, the biggest and best in a land of festivals. But
Matt need not fear missing the sound. For the next two days we
can't escape it.

It drives him over the edge, until he buries his head under a
pillow at night screaming, "The drums, the drums," like a melo-
dramatic colonial officer in a 1930s adventure movie.

We learned of the festival a few days earlier while lounging pool side at the Manila Hilton, sampling exotic fruit juices and baking ourselves to the toasty brown of the Filipinos. We were resting from an exhausting tour of the country, reporting on faith healers, dog eaters and cockfights, seeking out the perfect secluded beach and sampling local delicacies like balut (fertilized duck eggs eaten from the shell, tiny bodies with feathers already formed, reputedly a potent aphrodisiac).

My companion was a London-based radio reporter. His area, the world; his beat, the bizarre. And with his trained eye for the offbeat, he spotted the item in What's On in Manila.

"Here, look at his," he said one afternoon, pushing aside the crumbs from an adobo sandwich (chicken and pork steamed in soy sauce, vinegar, garlic, peppercorn and spices). It was a photo story on a little festival on a secluded island, a quiet celebration in the boondocks, far from the blaring jeepneys, the brash, non-stop disco in Manila's notorious del Pilar bars.

"We can relax for a few days, get some peace and quiet, maybe even get a story," Matt declared, slurping on his calamansi (lime) juice. "We'll go tomorrow. Carlos, can I see that menu again?"

By Sunday morning, last day of the festival, Kalibo looks like host city to a giant, noisy chimney sweeps convention. People from barrios (villages and districts) from miles around parade through the sun-blanched streets and open square with faces and bodies soot-blackened in imitation of the Atis, the original short, kinky-haired negrito inhabitants of the area. (Ati-Atihan literally means "make like the Atis.")

They march alone, in family groups of 10 to 20, or in ragged "tribes" of hundreds from the barrios, with names like D'Black Maharlikan Guards, Tribu Amazona or Sound Tripping. Some wear homemade costumes of woven palm leaves, straw, seashells or coconuts, others dress in camouflage ponchos, T-shirts or hats, mechanics' overalls and Arab headdress, or military uniform with wooden guns.

A few parade more elaborate costumes: a prisoner with ball

and chain made from silver-painted basketball, a giant baby sucking on a quart of local rum with rubber nipple, a 120-pound, green-faced Incredible Hulk, a Jesus Christ with fake blood dripping down his face from a crown of thorns (expensive cowboy boots showing beneath his crimson gown). And each group carries a white-skinned, blue-eyed doll dressed in red cloak -- Santo Nino, the Christchild -- in a happy, if confusing blend of Christian and pagan celebrations.

Blackavised Atis shuffle to the pounding beat of military drums or bamboo tubes or beer bottles banged with sticks and stones. The incessant boomtataboomtataboom is broken only occasionally by a marching brass band, a tinkling xylophone or piercing tin whistle.

It is a smaller, less-organized version of the great, pre-Lenten Trinidad and Rio de Janeiro carnivals -- but also different. Trinidadian and Brazilian festival groups write their own music, songs that will be sung in bars and streets as the popular music for the rest of the year. Filipinos are the most musical people of Asia, providing nightclub and cabaret bands and singers to all of Asia and the Pacific. But I hear little singing at the festival, just the constant drumbeat and the slow shuffling dance.

A bus pushing through the human traffic jam blares Yankee Doodle Dandy on its horn. All morning, the dancing, shouting, eating, drinking groups wind through the streets, meet and mill around the jammed square.

A sooty fire-eater spews black smoke and flames into the sky in front of the cathedral: a motorcyclist splutters by with Santo Nino riding high on his side car; a chubby, straggly haired American girl waves a huge Confederate flag as she circles the square. Young girls from the local hospital bounce by in T-shirts promising, "Marry me and you will get free nursing forever."

As the sound level increases, so do the beer prices. Yesterday, a small San Miguel was three pesos. Today it is three-fifty. Street kids follow us around as if we were Pied Pipers of Hamelin, waiting for our empties. In the heat, we drain the beer quickly to be rid of the urchins, who squabble in the dust for our castoff bottles.

A radio announcer plucks us from the chaos to do a live interview on the local station. The soundproofing of the ground floor studio off the square almost muffles the hypnotic drumbeats outside.

Before we start, our interviewer sends out for quarts of icy San Miguel beer and a plate of dinuguan (pork innards stewed in fresh pig's blood and chili). Matt grabs a squiggly, lumpy bit and drops it down his throat. The Vu dials on his Sony quiver at his appreciative lip smacking.

After a short introduction in Tagalog, the announcer switches to English. "We are honored today to have with us two journalists who have come all the way from Canada to cover the Ati-Atihan Festival."

He turns suddenly somber. "Now gentlemen, what do you think of these foreign peoples, not Canadians of course, but these foreign peoples who come from Europe and America and Australia, who come here wearing just shorts and shabby clothing and taking part in Ati-Atihan?"

"I'll take this one," Matt says, dipping his pan de sal (bun) into the sticky, reddish-black sauce. "Yes, well, I think this is a wonderful example of international harmony and brotherhood, people of all nations getting together to enjoy this fine festival."

"No, no, that's not what I mean," the Filipino says, his eyes flicking over the microphones. "But these people who come here to live on the beaches and don't work or anything."

"Ah, yes, great show of Filipino hospitality, that," Matt says, reaching for a fresh quart of San Mig. "Very friendly people here."

The little interviewer turns desperate, almost pleading. "But these hippies ..."

"Oh them," Matt says, finally catching on and, licking the last red drops from his fingers, launches into his anti-hippie tirade.

Outside, the square has quietened down for the lunch time,

the bands have disappeared to restaurants or parks. One barrio group sprawls out under the blazing sun in the cathedral yard, surrounded by red and yellow bits of costume. We can still hear drumbeats from nearby streets.

Our search for a motorcycle taxi to take us back to the hotel for a siesta is interrupted by a high-pitched voice. "Yoo-hoo, boys, come over here." It is the young civil servant we met in Manila airport, now changed from his crisp, formal barong shirt and pressed trousers.

Batting mascara-caked eyes and pursing rosebud red lips he coos, "Come and join me for lunch at my friend's house. He is a newspaper publisher who would like to meet you." And fluttering a long silk scarf behind him, he leads us down the street.

The house is a cool, high-ceilinged sanctuary from the burning street, a typical Filipino household with women cooking in the kitchen, men drinking rum and beer in the living room, and children underfoot everywhere. One of the daughters, a typical long-haired Filipino beauty in her 20s, sits with the men, privileged because with her American university degree she has a good government job.

She explains to Matt's ever-ready Sony the origins of the festival. One complex legend involves the arrival of Bornean chieftans here hundreds of years ago. They bought land from the Atis and during a feast to celebrate the transaction, smeared themselves with soot to look like the natives.

A beaming matriarch comes to the door to announce that lunch is served, then swats children away from the groaning table so the guests can have first go at the fried chicken, salad, huge chili prawns, lumpia (spring rolls stuffed with shrimp, pork, chicken and tender heart of young coconut), tropical fruit and lechon, fat, suckling pig roasted deep honey-brown with a crispy skin.

Dipping a slab of pork into the liver sauce, Matt juggles with his microphone and pursues his investigation into the festival's origins. Where do the Christian elements, the Santo Ninos, come from?

"Spanish missionaries introduced the Holy Child Jesus and his feast day to the negritos many years ago," the young woman explains, delicately nibbling at a peppery prawn. Each year the Atis came down from hills to celebrate the Christian festival in their own pagan way, sacrificing pigs and singing and dancing in the streets.

The idea became popular with the Filipinos, who started covering their faces with soot to resemble the Atis. While once Ati-Atihan was celebrated during harvest, now the week's festivities culminate on the second Sunday after Three Kings, the Spanish day of the Feast of the Holy Child Jesus.

While Matt is interviewing, and eating, I strike up a conversation with one of the matrons. She promotes one of her nieces as a good prospect for marriage.

"She is almost a virgin," she boasts.

After seconds on the buko pie, made from young coconut, we plunge once more into the maelstrom of color and noise in the streets. The festival has reached a fever pitch, the streets choked with jiggling, bouncing, writhing bodies, like ants in an overturned hill.

Matt, in his CBC correspondents' uniform of brief white shorts, belly bulging through blue tank top, cowboy-style neck scarf, European tinted glasses, monitoring earphones, large microphone and tape recorder dangling from his shoulder, plunges into the milling mass.

Always working, he attempts to interview a craggy old man in net stockings, brief dress and sun umbrella. "Now my dear, how are you enjoying the festival so far?" But the background noise is too much, the needles on his Vu meter bounce madly to the drum beats.

Matt screams in my ear, "This is even louder than the flight deck of the aircraft carrier USS Enterprise where I ... " but the rest is lost in the noise from the White Castle Whiskey float.

By dusk on this, the last day of the festival, revelers are marshaled into some chaotic order for the final parade. For hours frenzied devotees shuffle past, Santo Ninos carried on floats lit with portable generators or gently cradled in the thin arms of poor farmers. A noisy group marches by sponsored by Hilda's Shoes, another with a hand lettered cardboard sign "Hey, Joe." We've heard the WWll comic book cry for the past days as marchers called us to join their groups.

Three hours later, the last float passes, the revelers slowly head out of town, the din gradually dies. We squeeze into a tricycle taxi to return to the hotel. A few rowdy Atis drinking rum under a street light give a last few beats on their bass drums.

And blessed silence falls on Kalibo, Atlan, Philippines.

THE VISAYAS

Winging It

March 1991

"HEY JOE" yell the schoolboys, squealing with delight at the unexpected sight of foreigners riding a modified jeep through their Philippine village. I feel like an extra in a WWII movie.

We are touring Legaspi in southern Luzon Island, an area seldom visited by mainstream tourists despite its scenic and historic attractions. The Philippines, a tropical archipelago of more than 7,000 islands, lacks adequate roads or ferry services. Bus and rail travel are slow, sea travel infrequent and inconvenient, and most flights originate from the Manila hub, forcing travelers between rural cities to return to the capital.

So moving around the country has always been arduous. Then the Blue Horizons tour company flew into the picture with its air safari, a week-long jaunt by private aircraft that opens the southern Philippines to adventurous travelers willing to tolerate some provincial discomforts. So I am island-hopping Luzon and the Visayas islands in an airborne limousine with a congenial band of traveling companions, including a Swiss anthropologist/journalist, roving British lady diplomat, Filipino tour operator and a Canadian expatriate woman on holidays from Hong Kong.

This is traveling, not tourism. From the time the green and white Cessna takes off from Manila until it touches down there again a week later, the only tourists we see are a few rugged backpackers and a hardy coterie of brightly garbed Japanese scuba divers. Besides our private aircraft, we travel aboard jeepneys (the colorful Filipino jeep-turned-bus), bancas (outrigger canoes), speedboats and bicycle rickshaws.

Leaving Manila on a cloudless morning, we fly low over lakes, rivers and a patchwork of farmland, then skirt flat-topped, Fuji-like Mt. Iriga and pointed Mayon Volcano, rising out of the green fields. After just over an hours scenic flight, the twin-engine, six-passenger turboprop aircraft deposits us here in southern Luzon. This is normally an all-day, bone-bashing bus ride from Manila that discourages most visitors.

Real adventurers can climb Mayon, a several day expedition involving camping overnight. We merely board a brightly deco-rated jeepney called "Heart Breaker" to ride through Legaspi, a typical Filipino provincial town, to the tragic Cagsawa historical site. Only the Daraga Church tower jutting above the volcanic ash deposit marks the site of the town buried by Mayon's erup-tion in 1814. Nothing else in this peaceful setting - a Coca-Cola shack, a few chickens scratching in the grass and a village wom-an spreading grain to dry on the seldom used road - recalls the town's violent past.

Meals in the rural Philippines prove an unexpected treat. Today's lunch at La Trinidad Hotel is a felicitous Filipino-Chi-nese hybrid with cool, delicious juice from the lemon-like cala-mansi fruit, slightly sour but luscious sinigang soup cooked with tamarinds and prawn, chicken with coconut, grilled fish and rice as fluffy as the clouds surrounding Mayon Volcano. And prices in the provinces are right, with San Miguel beers starting from about eight pesos.

"Forty cent beer and 90-degree temperatures. That's para-dise," notes the journalist.

After lunch, we strap ourselves into the Cessna once more and our airborne limo conveys us south of Luzon to the Visayas islands of Samar and Leyte. Circling Southeast Asia's largest bridge, the San Juanico, we set down at Tacloban. The Leyte Park Hotel, Imelda's Folly, was built as a resort in this area of few tourists that was also the former first lady's hometown. Rural Filipino accommodation generally runs the complete range from basic to even more basic. This is one of the better hotels, clean, with private showers and hot water. Usually.

The Leyte's bar special, MacArthur's Landing, a tasty fruit juice and rum combination, recalls an important historic local event. American General Douglas MacArthur did return to the Philippines, as promised, landing at Red Beach near Tacloban in 1944. A giant, larger-than-lifesize monument of him purposefully striding ashore now marks the spot.

At dawn, a motorized banca transports us across the peaceful bay and up the Basey River, past jungle and mangrove with its distinctive, decaying sweet smell. The riverside life and the villages of faded bamboo houses on stilts, all weathered and sagging with age, is reminiscent of the middle reaches of the Amazon. Riverine folk gather nipa palm in the jungle to weave rooftops, paddle simple dugouts piled high with plastic containers of cooking oil and bags of rice back to their small farms or wait for banca buses at shelters on stilts -- one with a faded and unlikely "Welcome Visitors" sign. A young river urchin sends a different message, gleefully mooning us from shore, encouraged by his waving and shouting cronies.

The Basey River gradually narrows until it squeezes through a canyon of high limestone cliffs worn into eerie shapes -- the Sohoton National Park. Beaching the banca, we hike a path up the bank to a jungle picnic site with concrete tables and chairs. We are the only visitors in the park. The crew lights a charcoal fire, grills pork chops and chicken, and sets out a tasty lunch on a large banana leaf tablecloth.

While the boatmen set to work on a gallon jug of brown tuba, a potent liquor made from the sap of coconut trees, a guide takes us to the nearby caves. Leading the way by lamplight and flashlight, he shepherds us through a maze of stalactites and stalagmites. Where the cavern narrows, we squeeze around tight corners and crawl on our hands and knees. When we stop to rest, we hear only our panting, the hissing lamp and bat squeaks.

Back in a larger cavern, the guide points out oddities such as "the igloo," a small, sparkling white mini-cave; "ice cream," a cone with a white flat top; the stairway to heaven; and a "Madonna," who resembles the sacred, rather than the current profane rock version. After hours of spectacular spelunking, we emerge from the dank caverns, squinting like moles at the sun. Compared to the netherworldy silence of the eerie caves, the jungle seems clamorous with insects screaming, birds calling and wind rustling through the trees. The boatmen polish off the tuba and, with cicadas screeching at us, we drift back downstream, back to the plane.

A geographical oddity awaits at the next island, Bohol, where we park the plane and embark on a rough 55-kilometer ride along a bumpy potholed road into the interior. This is rural Philippines, with sleek, belligerent fighting cocks tethered in yards, carabao (water buffaloes) and stooped women in straw hats working the shimmering green rice paddies. Aged carabao cowboys, bush knife swinging from hips, ride along the roadside. Bright bougainvillea and hibiscus hedges line village yards and copra dries on the ground.

The road gradually leaves the agricultural land behind to climb into the mountains and through mahogany and rattan forests. Our destination is the so-called Chocolate Hills, which turn brown when their thin grass covering dries in the summer. Today they are minty-green. Climbing steps up the highest hill, we survey the mounds stretching to the horizon.

"They look like drums," says the lady diplomat.

"Like upturned cooking pots," remarks the Canadian woman.

"Like a field of perfect breasts," murmurs the journalist.

At the end of the week, we bounce through the air over the mountainous Cuyo Islands in Northern Palawan Island, set down along a palm-fringed rough dirt runway, and taxi to the "terminal" -- a thatched hut on stilts. This is the most remote place yet. After gulping delicious coconut water from big green nuts, we walk across the sugary sand and knee-deep through warm sea water to a seagoing banca (outrigger canoe).

Isolated El Nido Resort, nestled in a little cove on a black marble island of its own, is not a typical slick getaway. Built like a native village with communal toilets and showers, its basic cottages are set in a row on stilts over the water, along the beach and clinging to the cliff.

Although it has snorkeling, water skiing, wind surfing, this is essentially a diving resort. Schools of athletic Japanese clad in brightly colored dive suits and outfitted with the most expensive equipment and underwater cameras set out twice a day on the great outriggers to nearby dive spots. We non-divers explore El Nido island aboard a small motorboat, passing sheer, black marble cliffs and tiny, perfect white beaches like settings from a travel agency brochure. Turning in to a crevice in the cliffs, we squeeze under a tiny gap in the wall, ducking our heads, with just inches to spare. Inside is a fantastic lagoon of deep, jade green water surrounded by sheer cliffs jagged and black as sticks of charcoal. It was, I thought, the perfect lagoon, lacking nothing. Until back at the resort, when a Filipino waiter asks if I saw Brook Shields in the lagoon.

That evening, we set off fishing for our dinner from a banca, trolling, then bottom fishing in the gathering dusk. Sunset this night is as dramatic as any I have ever seen, the sky awash in reds and purples, bright as bougainvillea, the clouds tinged a soft, flamingo pink. It is a moment of perfect peace, the water slapping against the boat, swallows chirping from nests high on the darkening, brooding cliffs.

Peace, but no fish. We return in the cool late evening to the resort to eat chicken and pork.

Next morning, a 5 a.m. wake-up call of jungle noises drives us out of bed, and we return by banca to the dirt strip for our last departure. There, two village boys on a primitive sled without wheels, hauled by a forlorn carabao, come to see the strange apparition of a flying machine. Our pilots crisply run through the pre-takeoff checks, rev up the twin turboprops and release the brakes. We surge down the rough runway, engines roaring, kicking up a trail of dust, lift off just before the land gives way to sea, and make a banking turn into the sky, back to Manila. Three pairs of wondrous brown eyes watch our departure to a mysterious, far-off world.

INDIA

DELHI to AGRA
Take Me to the Taj

February, 1984

THE ancient Indian sun hangs like a saffron disc in the sky to our left as we leave New Delhi. Squatting figures with brass jars of water line the horizon, beggars rise along the sidewalks like rag dolls come to life. Sacred cows graze in the streets, ancient women in thin saris hunker in the shade making dung patties for fuel, babus in loose dhotis (loin cloths) and suit jackets carry brief cases and umbrellas to another day of bureaucrating. Mother India rises to another chaotic day.

The 15,652 kilometers from Vancouver to Tokyo, Bangkok and New Delhi on Japan Airlines was easy. The 203 kilometers to the ancient holy city, Agra, prove more complicated.

"Take me to the Taj," I instruct Mr. Murkejee, my driver. "Yes, sahib," he says, sliding behind the wheel of his grey Ambassador, a copy of the classic 1959 Morris. My driver speaks commendable Subcontinent English.

Two-wheeled tonga horse carts, three-wheeled scooter taxis, fearsome Sikhs in magenta turbans astride khaki Enfield motorcycles, brapping Tata buses spewing black smoke and noise into the morning air and trucks garishly decorated with Hindu gods race down Delhi's broad streets. As we jolt along the unfinished road, I envisage approaching the legendary Taj Mahal through the red sandstone arched gate, its perfect white dome reflected in the long pool, as it is traditionally photographed and described by romantic travelers.

"You no smoking?" Mr. Murkejee asks, lighting up a beedi, a cone-shaped cigarette wrapped in a leaf. Soon the car smells of cloves, like an old dental surgery.

Elegant script on the back of every decorated truck exhorts, unnecessarily, "Horn Please." Mr. Murkejee honks happily, his brown sandaled foot stabbing at the brake pedal. "To drive in India, sor, you must have good horn, good brakes, good luck." A good Hindu reincarnationist, he swerves to avoid birds feeding on grains of rice on the road.

Past the Siddhartha Ferro Alloy Ltd., road signs warning "Liquor Licks The Driver," and billboards touting Compa Cola, Thums Up and Disco Duble Seven soft drinks, we escape the crowded capital -- for the crowded countryside. Bullocks and bicycles with up to seven passengers, flocks of goats and white oxen with painted horns pulling carts now block the narrow road. Ominous, scrawny-necked vultures with wings like broken umbrellas hop clumsily as they land on the road to squabble over some flattened carrion.

Country maidens with big clay jugs clustering at village wells coyly let slip their veils to peek at passing cars. Camel drivers park their humped mounts at mud huts to squat on charpoys (string beds) sipping tea. Can we stop at one of these for a break. "Of course, sir, is coming," Mr. Murkejee nods, pulling into a government rest house with souvenir shops, trimmed lawns, a camel to and a mahout posing with his elephant for photographs.

"Ship me somewheres east of Suez, where the best is like the worst,

Where there aren't no Ten Commandments an' a man can raise a thirst;" (Kipling)

India's heat and dust has indeed raised a thirst. Time for a

Rosy Pelican beer.

Down the road again, Mr. Murkejee points out the Hare Krishna world headquarters and Mathura, Lord Vishnu's birthplace. Hindu India has plenty of gods to go around.

Outside Agra, my self-appointed guide escorts me through Sikandra, the emperor Akbar's multi-storied, minareted mausoleum, a "little Taj" where monkeys impudent as street urchins cavort among the fusion of Hindu and Muslim art and architecture. But the Taj, the marble monument to love Emperor Sha Jahan built for his favorite wife, Queen Mumtaz Mahal? "Coming next, sir."

At the Dayal Bagh, headquarters of the Radha Soami sect, an offshoot of Hinduism, we join pilgrims in khaki sackcloth to gawk at the white marble temple still a-building, clothed in scaffolding. The Taj?

"Yes, Sahib," Mr. Murkejee says with that little subcontinent, broken-necked head wiggle. Passing Agra, my driver-cum-guide parks the Ambassador before the elaborate tomb Empress Nurjahan built for her father in the 17th century, a forerunner of the Taj. But not the Taj. An English speaking Indian guide explains my demands to Mr. Murkejee. Amidst much shaking of heads, I hear the words "Taj" and "fort" repeated. "He will take you now," the man promises.

Crossing the Jamuna River on a narrow railway bridge, we plunge into the midday melee of Agra, a confusion of animals, people and machines. Half-naked men in towel turbans unload rice bags from trucks amid sadhus, yogis, Gandhi-ji clones, gurus, young Americans and Europeans in white muslin dhotis (the Kharma Kola kids), black water buffaloes and white sacred cows. The hot air in the narrow alleys is pungent with coriander, cumin and camel dung.

"In the epic 3rd century BC Mahabharata, this town was called Agrabana or Paradise in Sanskrit," Mr. Murkejee recites. "In the 2nd century, Alexander the Great's geographer Ptolemy showed it on his map as Agara. Moghul emperor Akbar made Agra his capital and built the massive red sandstone Agra Fort."

"Very good. But go straight to the Taj now," I demand.

"Of course, sir."

We next stop at the Red Fort where, like a mad dog or Englishman, I go in the hot midday sun to explore the serrated battlements, flanking bastions, turrets and machicolations. Through the latticework, the elusive, far-off Taj Mahal floats like a burnished opal along the sandy riverbank.

Outside the fort, a horde of mendicants, snake charmers, fakirs, touts, peddlers with wiggly sandalwood snakes and "Kama Sutra postcards" of the Khajuraho temple rock carvings swarm around with more grasping hands than the multi-armed goddess Kali.

Resigned that only the fool of Kipling's "epitaph drear" would hustle, or hurry, the East I crawl back into the car to await Mr. Murkejee's next move. We drive to the bazaar of souvenir shops and carpet emporiums, the Koh i Noor Jewelers, Krishna Footwear and the Agra Marble Works where craftsmen labor over spinning emery wheels.

"Sahib would like model of the Taj?"

"Sahib would not like model of the Taj."

"Only looking, sir, not buying."

Inlaid marble tabletops, lamps, chessboards, stone elephants and 100-pound scale-model Taj Mahals line the shelves of the cool, damp, tombstone-like basement storeroom. After a cursory only-looking-not-buying, I exit, as popular as purdah among feminists.

By late afternoon, we finally approach the Taj -- and drive by, to the river. "Very nice here, sir. You take boat ride."

Baba Shree Kant, a young entrepreneurial holy man with red-powder third-eye-tikka marking his forehead and long matted hair, offers us his wooden boat. The holy man, his ancient boatman and I pole out onto the sluggish river for an unusual rear view of the magnificent Taj Mahal. We watch silently a moment as the river ripples against the boat and the plop, ploplop, plop of women washing clothes echoes from the far riverbank.

The young holy man elbows me and winks, pointing out two Muslim girls calling from the far side. The only flesh they display are hands, feet and face. "We can giving them a ride?" he asks, as excited as a teenager cruising the suburbs in his dad's car.

"What will they say at the temple, a good Hindu holy man with Muslim girls?" I chide.

"Oh, no, sor, it is not like that," he chortles as he helps the draped sisters aboard.

Back ashore, the mercenary holy man and I banter over the few rupees charge, and once more I am in the charge of the single-minded Murkejee. And at last, with late afternoon shadows falling, I pass through the red sandstone gate to see the perfect marble mausoleum reflected in the long shallow pool.

Women with bangled ankles and brilliant saris, clamoring children, holidaying Hindus in Nehru hats and black-veiled Muslims swarm across the marble monument in a crowd scene from Gandhi. Bare feet slap against the cool, smooth as plastic marble floor. Elaborate Arabesque and Arabic inscriptions and inlaid semiprecious stones decorate the great white exterior walls. Inside, the tombs of Shah Jahan and his favorite, Mumtaz, lie side by side in soft light diffused by the translucent dome and pierced marble window screens.

Sha Jahan imported craftsmen from Italy, Turkey and Persia for the fine, delicately-latticed and inlaid stonework. The Moghuls, they said, "designed like giants and built like jewelers." This marble mausoleum has excited more awe than any other of India's many wonders; "The Ivory Gate through which all dreams come," a dream in marble, a sigh made stone, a fragile, delicate soap bubble.

A perfect Gibson cocktail onion.

And Mr. Murkejee was right. The Taj is best seen not when the harsh glare of the midday sun burns it bone white, but in the softer flush of the dying day. Outside Agra, we pause at an English Wine and Beer Shop to toast the Taj with a Guru beer before turning the Ambassador north to the capital. The ancient Indian sun hangs like a saffron disc in the sky to our left as we enter New Delhi.

BOMBAY

India's Bombastic Manhattan

June 1986

ON a sweltering weekday rush hour morning, bulging-eyed stone gargoyles high atop the ornate, Indo-Gothic Victoria Terminus Station stare as if in permanent disbelief at the chaotic scene below. Tiffin-wallahs sort out metal lunch buckets for delivery, paan-wallahs roll betel nut and lime mixtures onto leaves. Colorfully garbed migrant women laborers from Andhar Pradesh and Mysore provinces jostle aside scrawny, hairy holy men.

Red London-style double-decker buses, yellow-topped Ambassador taxis and upcountry trucks emblazoned with the most popular Gods of the Hindu pantheon clamor along the crowded road. Bombay's Victoria Terminus, VT to the acronym-loving Indians, is an imposing European structure with a tumultuous crush of Eastern humanity milling before it.

The busy, booming Maharashtra state capital of 8 million people is a rich, cosmopolitan human stew. Urban Bombayers include Parsees, descendants of refugees from Muslim religious persecution in eighth century Persia, dark Tamils, tall, turbaned Sikhs, Gujeratis, Rajasthanis, Sindhis, Goans and all the races of the sub continent bubble along in this pot that does not melt.

The Portuguese, who built a fort in these low-lying, malarial mud flats, bequeathed it to England's King Charles II as a part of a dowry in 1661. After the British government leased Bombay to the British East India Company for £10 gold annually in 1668, its long and prosperous years in the British Empire began. Bombay reached its "Golden Years" in the Victorian reign. Today, India's most modern, prosperous city aspires to be the most Western.

"This is India's Manhattan," boasts a Bombayite, pointing out the solid row of skyscrapers overlooking the Arabian Sea. This curve of Marine Drive, now Netaji Subash Road, is called the "Queen's Necklace" for the way it twinkles with lights at night. If a map of Bombay resembles satan's profile, Malabar Hill, at one end of Marine Drive, is the hook nose. The hill is India's most expensive residential area, with spacious, Western-style homes.

Behind the skyscrapers and tree-shaded homes, the Banganga area is village India. Tin smiths in ice cream-vendor hats squat before open forges under the eyes of god calendars, insolent children prance noisily around offerings before a gaudy, incense-scented shrine, and in a temple compound, ancient priests prepare vats of spicy food for the poor.

Local fisherwomen in dazzling, day-glo saris and heavy silver jewelry dripping from wrists, ankles, ears and nose, wash clothes in sacred bathing ghats. Bathers claim that the pond, and the surrounding shambles, is as holy as Benares. Looking down on rotting flower blossoms floating on slime-green water, a passing policeman remarks on their beauty. Jabbing his steel-tipped lathi stick at logs as thick as corpse's legs piled in a nearby compound, he adds, with civic pride, "Very nice cremation grounds." Bright paintings of the Virgin Mother and Child, Ganesh the elephant god, and Saint Sai Bapu discourage men from urinating on the compound wall.

A holy man with trident and begging bowl walks barefoot past the nuclear research center in the heart of chaotic Bombay. Beneath elegant Malabar Hill, one of the world's most expensive residential areas, Hindus wash in the Banganga bathing ghats that are as holy as those at Benares. Goats and ravens pick through the refuse and festering vegetation around the holy pond. Logs like twisted corpses are piled nearby, fuel for the cremation grounds. At the washing ghats, dhobi-wallahs (washermen), part of the fourth, laboring, caste, steam, boil, wash and spread clothes out to dry in spaces they rent by the hour.

Religion intrudes everywhere in India. Paintings of gods --

Virgin Mother and Child, Ganesh, the elephant god, and great scholar-worker Sai Bapu -- stop men from urinating on walls. Hindu and Jain temples, Muslim mosques and Fire Temples of the fair-skinned Parsees, or Zarathustrans, are scattered throughout the city. Religious pictures decorate walls of the smallest curry stall or dry goods shop.

Chaotic Bombay is home to a nuclear research center, and Zoroastrian Towers of Silence, where Parsis dispose of their dead. Evenings, well-fed vultures circle the sky over the towers, near the city reservoir. Local legend has it that vultures dropped human tid-bits into the reservoir before it was covered.

One evening, scores of religious processions block traffic for hours as devotees bear statues of the pink, pot-bellied elephant god to Chowpatty Beach for his annual bath. Celebrating this Chaturthi festival, worshippers smeared with red paint play flutes, bang drums and dance through the streets. All of Bombay stops when Ganesh takes a bath.

In Falklands Road, the infamous Bombay Cages red light district, harsh fluorescent lights pierce the darkness. From behind iron bars, dwarfish girls of many different Asian races -- dark Tamils, Chinese-looking Nepalis -- clutch beseechingly at passersby. A block away, Ganesh followers prance and chant around their dancing god.

Things are never as they seem in India. Even Bombay Duck is a dried, fried, salted jelly fish (also known as stinkfish). India has as great a variety of cuisines as all of Europe, and Bombay is India's gastronomic capital. There is Kutchi food from the frontier with Pakistan, pungent Maharasthra fish, Goan prawn curries, spicy northern Mogul cuisine, more subtle Persian, or Parsee dishes, tandooris, vindaloos and even chow mein. (Bombay has India's best Chinese food). The curious, but cautious, diner may dip a tentative taste bud into the mulligatawny at any of the good hotel restaurants, especially at the Sunday tiffin buffets, or in regional restaurants such as the Khyber, Delhi Durbar or Copper Chimney.

Foreigners unfamiliar with India find doing business difficult. "We suffer diarrhea of words and constipation of action,"
goes an ancient Indian saw.

Dominating Bombay's vast harbor is Elephanta Island, with
its a monolithic Hindu temple devoted to Lord Shiva. Launches
for the island and the holy Sixth century Elephanta Caves leave
from the downtown Gateway of India, a Gujarat-style Triumph
Arch. Here, a chaotic collection of snake charmers with baskets
of cobras, monkey men with playful simians and "filthy-post-
card" wallahs selling bad reproductions of the erotic carvings of
Khajuraho attempt to squeeze a few rupees from the mainly-In-
dian tourists.

At the island, fat ladies, chapati-swelled bellies bursting from
saris, ride crude palanquins, wooden chairs roped onto poles,
up the steep steps. Monkey beggars demand banana baksheesh
(tips), from photographers.

Grandmotherly guides squabble over long pointing sticks, a
mark of office, then go on to give their own interpretations of
Hindu sacred art. All art in India is basically religious in nature,
a guide explains, as her flock studies Vishnu's consort, Parvati.
This hourglass female body, with perfect full breasts, narrow
waist and swinging hip, suggest that the ancient Hindu and
modern Playboy magazine physical ideals of womanhood are
identical.

Yoga, too, is religious, a guide says. "Not just head down,
legs up." Statues depicting normal solitary figures doing yoga
have only two arms. The windmill effect of multi-limbed gods is
meant to illustrate motion. "Like you make Mickey Mouse film,"
the guide explains.

Film? Bombay is South Asia's Hollywood, the world's largest film-making center, its dozen studios churning out half of
India's 800 pictures a year. Every film, in Hindi and regional languages, is a mixture of romance, adventure, music, action, drama
and dancing. The genre is known locally as marsala, a mixture
of spices for curry. Most action consists of chubby girls running

around trees singing and batting kohl-darkened eyes at porky heroes.

Plump is sexy, and successful, on the subcontinent. Western stars balloon up on Indian billboards; poster artists make even Jane Fonda pleasantly plump.

A tattered hoarding breathlessly promises "RAPE-MURDAR AND ROMANCE FILM" with "Sex Bomb Silk Smita." This in a country that barely tolerates on-screen kisses.

Glossy Indian film magazines, the Bombay weekly city magazine, Business India, and Debonair, a down-scale, modest Playboy, keep the Bombay sophisticate posted as to what is happening in his swinging city.

The bar guide in a local weekly says, "the Hi-Time has a balcony reminding you of bars in the Wild West." Not that western, though. A wine-glass-shaped menu card on the bar proclaims: "Dear Guest. The State Prohibition & Excise Notification No. FLR 1079/105-A PRO dated 20-9-79, prohibits the sale of alcoholic beverages to Indian Nationals on 'dry days'."

In the evenings, much of Bombay gathers at Chowpatty Beach for a sunset circus. Couples who have escaped from the watchful eye of parents, snuggle on the rocks. Pan salesmen roll betel nut and spice mixtures on betel leaves to sell. Children line up before crude, hand-powered miniature merry-go-rounds. Yogis bury themselves in the sand like human crabs, waving their arms for alms.

Bombay is like a Maharashtra curry, mysterious and overpowering at first, rich and wondrous to those with the taste.

RAJASTHAN

Castles in the Sand

September 1997

"Your conveyance is approaching sir," the giant Punjabi door-man in the tightly wound turban announces, a smile as bright as the desert sky creasing his fierce, bearded face.

A white Ambassador Nova, a replica of a 1950s British Morris Oxford with rounded fenders and roof, pulls up under the Oberoi hotel's porte cochere. The uniformed attendant opens the door, stiffens to attention, and throws a snappy salute worthy of a Rajput warrior.

I am off on a tour of maharajahs' palace hotels in Rajasthan, the desert state south of New Delhi, India's capital. Until Indian independence 50 years ago Rajasthan, Rajputana of old, was a turbulent land of fierce people, of 22 warring princely states. But the maharajas and maharanis lived in regal splendor rarely seen elsewhere in the world, creating an imposing architecture of magnificent forts, palaces, castles and sandstone cities scattered across the desert.

I settle into the back seat on the carpet-like tiger print seat cover as Suress, the driver, points the blunt-nosed car into Delhi's morning traffic of soot-belching buses, three-wheel scooter taxis, ancient khaki colored motorcycles, numerous other lumpy shaped Ambassadors and grazing sacred cows. Road travel in rural Rajasthan is for the adventurous who can tolerate some discomfort and intimidating traffic, I quickly discover.

On The Road

The main Delhi-Jaipur highway is like the world's longest dod-gem-cars track, the chaotic animal and mechanical traffic reflecting the anarchy of India. Jeeps, cars and huge TATA brand buses with passengers overflowing out the doors weave past Sikhs on cycles, bicycles piled high with carpets and baskets, tricycle taxis bearing a half-dozen passengers, bullock carts, white oxen with brightly painted horns, camels and donkeys.

Caravans of boxy, brightly decorated trucks embellished with illustrations of Indian gods crowd the road, every one with the elegant script on the back urging "Horn Please." It is an unnecessary exhortation on this highway, as Indian drivers use the horn as much as the accelerator or brakes. With the chaos, color and craziness, India is not for the faint-hearted, but it provides endless entertainment.

In roadside villages, men in loose-fitting white cotton dhotis sit or lie around on their charpoys (rope beds on simple wood frames). Barefoot women with ankle bangles and flowing. brilliantly colored saris balance huge tin or clay pots on their heads as they stride along the dusty road, as graceful as models. India is a land of incredible color, from the iridescent tails of the peacocks, India's national bird, to the fantastically decorated temples and the fluorescent flash of women's saris.

And it is a land of constant surprises and anomalies, such as village merchants naming their businesses for deities -- the Ganesh Cleaning Service, the Siddhartha Restaurant, the Shiva Metal Works.

Loo With a View

After two hours (and just 76 miles) of frenetic driving, we spot the Neemrana Fort-Palace, like Disney's castle clinging like a limpet high on a cliff in a fold of the Aravalli mountain range. The incredible structure, India's oldest heritage resort and the closest palace hotel to Delhi, was built over five centuries, starting from 1464 A.D..

Halfway up the hillside, we park at the foot of the stepped palace, spreading across three acres. Beyond the imposing gates, a steep, winding stone ramp leads into the fantastic, multilayered structure, with four wings rising nine levels up the cliffside. It is a maze of hallways, stairwells, overpasses, turrets and dead ends. Meals are sometimes served on balconies or terraces atop small towers, with views over the plains far below.

The 35 suites and rooms with such romantic names as the Palace of Breezes, Cloud Palace, Sky Palace, Palace of the Goddess and Abode of Peace all have private balconies or courtyards facing panoramic vistas, perfect for the old Indian custom of sundowners. One suite even has a "loo (bathroom) with a view."

Time for a Tiger

Further south, a road off the main highway leads through ancient, rural India, with horse and donkey carts, women in vibrant dress working the fields, and farmers in huge, bright turbans herding long-horned cattle, water buffalo, camels and goats. The temperature rises into three figures Fahrenheit as the surroundings become more desert-like, and bridges cross over rivers of fine sand.

At the entrance to the Sariska Tiger Reserve, once a maharajah's private hunting grounds, we reach our second palace. Huge gates lead to palatial grounds, and the grand, if not particularly maharajah-like, Sariska Palace Hotel. Maharaja Jai Singh of Alwar built the place at the turn of the century as a royal hunting lodge.

With the main structure curved like a ship's hull and towers at each corner, the architecture seems Indo-art deco with Saracenic touches, such as arched doorways. It is grand enough, but needs a touch up. Fortunately, renovations are proceeding and painters are at work in the dining room as I check in.

Several stuffed tigers prowl the lounge, and the hall walls are hung with ancient black-and-white photographs of hunters posing before supine felines. The great hunting parties of the past included hundreds of men: maharajah's cradling their rifles, fierce retainers in tight turbans, dozens of beaters, gun bearers, professional hunters and elephants with costumed mahouts posing sternly on the howdahs. And standing among them is an occasional colonial Brit, out hunting in pith helmet, three-piece suit and tie. No wonder they sang of mad dogs and Englishmen out in the noonday sun.

Like many of the remote palace hotels, Sariska is not deluxe. Accommodation is clean, but basic -- heavy on character, light on maintenance. "In India, we are big on ambiance, light on amenities," shrugs one mustachioed retainer.

Jackals and Hide

At dawn, an open Maruti Gypsy jeep appears in front of the palace. As in the African game parks, the lodge provides game viewing safaris into the park, daily at 6 a.m. and 4 p.m.. It is off-season, so I am the only guest going out.

Past the entrance, we follow the paved road into the park a short distance before turning off on a dirt track through the dry brush, thorns, bamboo, prickly cacti and flame of the forest trees. The Sariska Sanctuary, spread over 335 square miles of dense, dry forest, streams, steep ridges, valleys and hills, is considered one of India's finest. The number of tigers here has increased from 15 when it started in 1979 to 24 now. While April to June is sizzling hot and dry, it is the best time for game spotting, as the animals come down to the waterholes.

In a sudden flash of color ahead, a peacock flutters across the road trailing its iridescent tail behind it, like a flamboyant opera star flaunting a flashy cape. These grand creatures are everywhere, perched in the trees, flying through the air, scurrying along the ground.

Deep in the bush, the driver points out some high stone watchtowers. Not so long ago, hunters would dismount from elephant back onto these hides, and shoot tigers from the vantage point.

Small herds of ungulates graze these dry, scrubby trees -- spotted deer, four-horned antelopes and large blue bull antelopes, who give warning honks like a TATA bus horn before leaping into the bush. In the open jeep, we approach within yards of porcupine, mongoose, civet cat and wild boar crusty with mud. And we see large groups of two kinds of monkeys: rhesus, with no tails and dangerous dispositions; and gentle brown langurs, with long tails and black faces.

At one waterhole, adolescent langurs playing like errant schoolboys drop out of tree branches, furry cannonballs hitting the water with a splash. A brilliant peacock, tail spread out in a great fan, does a strutting mating dance, trying to impress a pea hen with its avian antics.

When the driver stops and turns off the engine, it is remarkably peaceful, with only the wild sounds of the high, two-toned screams of peacocks, bird calls, the shrill clicking of cicadas, animals rustling in the underbrush. It is remarkable that tiger, leopard and panther prowl these forests just a few hours from Delhi.

Later, on a jungle walk, we follow an ancient aqueduct along the river and into the forest. The guide, armed only with a makeshift swagger stick, points out a spot nearby, where tigers come down to drink. Farther on, we find a pile of peacock tail feathers. "A leopard had his lunch," he explains.

A half-hour later, we reach the Royal Watchtower, from where the maharajah and his fellow hunters once shot tiger. Guests can stay overnight here, sitting up by candlelight, and in the morning watch game coming down to the river to drink. From the hide, they might spot jackals, deer, boar or even, if they are lucky, tiger.

Although it is the dry season, it rained a few days ago, and there is water in the forest. There will be no tiger for me today.

Pink Gin in a Pink City

Several hours later, driving into Jaipur, Rajasthan's capital, we turn off towards the hilltop Amber Palace and Fort. The city's major attraction is noted for its pink stone architecture, and its shops. Approaching the palace, the driver speaks his first English words today.

"Factory looking?"

"Factory no looking."

Rajasthan is known for its great variety of arts and crafts. Shops and factories sell hand-woven silk and wool carpets, tie-dyed fabrics in shimmering colors, hand-blocked printed muslin and silk clothes, wood and ivory carvings, and lacquer and filigree work.

Across the river, decorated and adorned elephants, their ears and trunks painted with vivid floral patterns, carry tourists up a rampart to the imposing hilltop fort. But the vast complex of ancient palaces, pavilions and fortifications is a fort for looking at, not staying in, so we continue on to Jaipur, the Pink City.

This 18-century planned capital, modern by Indian standards, was built of pink sandstone in the Mughal style, which makes it appear much older. Driving though the city, slowed to a camel pace by the frenzied traffic of vehicles, people and animals, we pass the elaborate Palace of Winds. The peculiar five-story facade of pink stone fronting the street was a kind of elaborate modesty curtain. Palace ladies could look out onto street activities through some 953 latticed windows without being seen.

On the outskirts of the city, the deluxe Rambagh Palace is one of the few palace hotels of international standards. As in most Rajasthan hotels, doormen are dressed like Rajput dandies, cultivating immense, curved mustaches, and wearing brilliant turbans, some with flowing tails flapping down the back.

The sprawling palace is a peaceful retreat of long, shady corridors, arched passageways, latticed screens, delicate cupolas and fountains. In the courtyard outside, snake charmers lure cobras out of their baskets and mahouts pose with their painted elephants for photographs.

Lunch is a delicious biriani -- sweet basmati rice with pieces of lamb and cashew nuts flavored with saffron and mint and served with raita (yogurt with grated cucumbers and spices). Musicians in turbans and dhotis sitting cross-legged at the end of the room playing the taula (drum) and the tanpura (a long-handled kind of sitar) provide the appropriate subcontinent background music.

Samode - The Far Pavilions

Some 25 miles (40 kilometers) north of Jaipur, Samode Palace sits majestically above a seedy village. Massive doors, high as a house and bristling with great metal studs to deter fighting elephants, swing open to let the Ambassador pass. Four-hundred-year-old Samode, a blend of Rajput and Mughal styles of architecture, is one of the most ornate, and best known, of Rajasthan's palace hotels.

From the parking lot (a few shade trees), a series of steps lead up to ascending courtyards of the multilevel palace. Bare stone stairwells and hallways lead to frescoed walls and audience halls, such as the twinkling Hall of Mirrors.

The ornate Durbar Hall (maharaja's court), patterned like an Oriental carpet from wall to ceiling, was the main setting for the British television production of author M. M. Kaye's The Far Pavilions. The maharajahs and maharanis must have abhorred the unadorned; every square inch of my room seems covered with some pattern or picture, from flowers and geometric shapes to battle or hunting scenes with warriors, fighting elephants and tigers in the forest.

During the day, guests can ride a camel three miles through villages and dusty desert roads to the hotel's Samode Bagh Mughal garden, to use the swimming pool and lawn tennis court. Or they can walk through the adjoining village, viewing the ancient wall paintings on merchants' homes and experiencing Indian peasant life in the raw. Outside the palace gate, two village boys, claiming to come from a long line of artists, display distinctive Rajasthan-style miniatures -- traditional paintings including slightly risque works featuring generously proportioned village girls in see-through blouses.

Next to the palace, a steep staircase of 376 steps leads up the slope to the 400-year-old ruins of one of three hilltop forts protecting Samode. At the top, a watchman unlocks a heavy door and I have the huge, well-constructed fort to myself.

Although in ruins, the basic structure is in good shape. It is a classic stone fort with parapets, loopholes, turrets, bastions and battlements. The watchman points out machicolations, holes in the floor over the outside walls, that were the soldiers' toilets.

It is peaceful up here, alone. The braying of a camel far below and the distant chattering of pilgrims walking along a path disappearing over the dry hills.

Castle Mandawa

Beyond Jaipur, the countryside, and the castles, become harsher, less genteel, but even more colorful. Sword-bearing guards with fearsome beards welcome travelers to Castle Mandawa, where two venerable cannons on large spoked wheels stand guard at the massive, spiked gate.

Much of the rambling, 240-year-old castle is still unrestored, with peeling walls, unpainted hallways and building materials piled in the corners. The rooms, though, are large and lavish. Mine is like a harem, lacking only the female companionship, with ornate white marble arches, delicately carved woodwork, little alcoves and a maharajah-sized bed.

The Rajputs have a great sense of showmanship and pageantry. Caparisoned camels and horses carry tour groups into the main courtyard as the musicians blow horns and drums roll the "Royal Welcome." In season, traditional Rajasthani artists give lively song and dance performances by candlelight, dazzling displays harking back to ancient days.

Another Roadside Detraction

Peacock cries are the wake-up call at Mandawa, summoning me to a fried eggs-toast-and-coffee breakfast. Heading back to Delhi, Suress takes a shortcut down side roads. These quickly degenerate to mere sand trails through the scrub and desert, where the only other traffic consists of camels pulling two-wheeled carts with huge rubber tires, piled high with firewood.

In this heat, Suress stops frequently at mud huts with wells outside to top up the hissing radiator. Finally, the diesel engine overheats and stops. I sit on a kilometer stone by the side of the road reading The Times of India while the driver walks back a village for a bucket of water. It is just another roadside detraction.

Driving through rural Rajasthan is like being thrust into Satyajit Ray's classic Pather Panchali movie of village India. Then, suddenly, we are back on the main highway to Delhi, and 20th-century traffic. Back at my hotel, as I arrive hot and dusty, the towering doorman snaps to attention and salutes.

"I trust you have had a commendable journey, sir."

BANGLADESH

DHAKA

Dhaka Days, Dhaka Nights

November 1994

THE sign "Flesh Pots" outside downtown Dhaka's Metropolitan Hotel was intriguing, especially in conservative Bangladesh. Curious, I walked up the dingy stairs to the second floor. Inside the door, the receptionist at the cash register whispered "Vegetable soup?" Despite the suggestive name, Flesh Pots is merely a restaurant serving such fare as "Chinese and American chop suey." The vegetable soup was on special.

Like the restaurant, the Bangladesh capital is an anomaly, an ancient city where some 200,000 bicycle rickshaws still ply the streets, but hotels have satellite communications and broadcast international TV news. Bangladesh evokes images of a hapless land of overwhelming masses, typhoon ravaged coasts, endless expanses of flooded fields and inundated villages, droughts and disasters.

The capital, set on the flat, fertile delta of the Ganges and Brahmaputra rivers, is not the most beloved of Asian capitals, for tourists, business travelers or, apparently, flight crews.

The crew on my flight from Hong Kong was gathered in the

galley at the back of the darkened Airbus when I went back to recharge my Champagne flute. Did they have to stay on and work the return flight to Hong Kong? I asked.

Yes, they did.

"That must be tough?" I sympathized.

"Well, its better than staying in Dhaka," replied a stylish miss applying crimson polish to delicate fingernails. Her companions nodded earnest assent.

My first impression is hardly favorable. The sly usurers at the airport banks are widely known to cheat unwary visitors, giving as much as 25 percent less than the official exchange rate. Stung visitors question whether it is the official bank policy, or if the employees simply pocket the difference.

The hustling extends to Dhaka taxis, which have no meters, so bargaining is essential. Drivers ask up to five times the price from foreigners for the ride from the airport to the city, but will usually settle for much less. Three-wheel motorcycle-rickshaws, like Thai tuk-tuks, here called scooters or baby taxis, are more commonplace. With these, too, visitors pay up to 50 percent more than locals. Bicycle rickshaws are practical only for short distances, or a nostalgic ride, evoking an experience of old Asia, not so long ago.

The country, and its capital, has definite, although sometimes elusive, attractions. Founded in the 10th century, this was the Mogul capital of Bengal (1608-1704) and a trading center for the British, French and Dutch before coming under British rule in 1765. Even the name is not what it was. Dacca, the Romanized spelling of the Bengali name, became Dhaka in 1982.

In its dated urban appearance, and its preponderance of non-motorized traffic, Dhaka is reminiscent of a more leisurely era, like Bangkok or Kuala Lumpur of a few decades ago. Two-, three- and four-wheel traffic -- bicycles, pedicabs and motor rickshaws, farm trucks and battered taxis -- clog the main streets such as North-South Road (formerly a canal). Even in the city center, crude, hand-drawn carts piled high with coconuts and produce, as well as rustics returning to the farm carrying huge woven vegetable baskets, slow the traffic flow.

Bangladesh's colonial past prevails in the sing-song English, and a few architectural remnants such as the High Court and Curzon Hall, a rose-hued Victorian-Mogul building that now houses the Dhaka University science faculty. Six local English-language newspapers (Observer, Times, Morning News, Daily Star, Telegraph, New Nation) as well as international publications bring the news to this poor country.

The capital of the world's most crowded nation does have peaceful, attractive areas, such as broad Crescent Boulevard lined with brilliant flame trees. A symbol of modern Bangladesh, the modernistic, angular concrete Jatiya Sangsas Bhaban (parliament building) looks as though it is floating on a lake. Its American architect, Louis I. Kahn, who thought it a modern version of the Taj Mahal, designed it so that every room is exposed to light and cool breezes. When the electricity goes (as it does here), the building functions without lights or air-conditioning.

This low-rise city's soft, muddy base, and a lack of investment funds have restricted the construction of skyscrapers. Most banks, airlines and commercial offices are in Motijheel (both the street and the district), the heart of Dhaka's business life. But this is no Manhattan of Bengal; the 34-story State Bank Building is the country's tallest.

Numerous mosques and historic buildings set against the city's more contemporary structures reflect the country's ancient Muslim heritage. But the Bangladeshis fuse faith and commerce in their own, distinct way. Yet another symbol of modern Dhaka -- and another paradox -- is the giant Baitul Mukarram National Mosque, resembling a mammoth sugar cube just like the Kaaba in Mecca. While the faithful pray in the main hall, shopkeepers in the thriving basement electronic bazaar hawk TVs, VCRS, satellite dishes, batteries and coaxial cables.

East meets West most curiously in the 18th-century Ahsan Manzil, formerly home of the nawabs (rulers) of Dhaka. The imposing pink riverside palace is now a museum. Inside, a row of portraits of ancient patriarchs in various configurations of beard gaze sternly down from the walls. Despite their archaic appearance, these men embraced modernism and endeavored to live like Victorian gentlemen.

Twenty-three galleries in 31 rooms display their life in the British colony, where they introduced such foreign innovations as plumbing and electricity to Bangladesh. In one room, a long dining table is set with crystal glasses and silverware. Other displays include a billiard room, the nawab's library, a bedroom with a four-poster bed and a drawing room with brothel-red velveteen walls.

When the national tourist organization, Bangladesh Parjatan Corporation, refers to this as "A land of hidden charm," it is being modest. There is more to East Bengal than the Lancers and tigers, although the big striped cats still prowl the vast Sundarbans (beautiful forest) west of Dhaka. Deer, monkey, wild bear and hyena are more common, however. Terraced tea plantations spread over the scenic hills at Sylhet north of Dhaka, while to the south at Cox's Bazar the world's longest beach stretches for 120 kilometers along the Bay of Bengal.

Social customs are similar to those throughout Asia. Businessmen may bring their wives for dinner "If they think they are presentable enough, in looks and education," explains one sari-clad executive. "Otherwise they might bring a secretary. People do want to be seen with a pretty girl," she adds.

In this predominantly Muslim country, alcohol is legal, and readily available to visitors, although some conservative (orthodox) locals may object to it. Pork is also proscribed, and although the ubiquitous Chinese restaurants serve it, getting a standard bacon-and-eggs breakfast is a problem.

"Bangladesh is Muslim, but not fundamentalist," a local businessman explains over morning tea. "You see Europeans in miniskirts, and local women do not wear veils. At least, very few of them."

As a Muslim country, Bangladesh has different days off. "On Thursday, we get Saturday Night Fever," the lady explains as she prepares to leave the office early. Many companies have a half day off Thursday, while banks, offices and government departments are closed Friday, the Muslim day of rest, when no alcoholic drinks are served. Multinationals and embassies are closed Saturdays as well, and everything is open on Sunday.

Thursday Night Fever is tamer than its Western counterpart. It is hard to boogie in Dhaka, a city of 1,000 mosques and about 20 bars, but no nightclubs. Locals socialize at private clubs, a legacy of the Raj, expatriates at diplomatic clubs. Entertaining is usually done in restaurants or in private homes, with cocktail parties and dinners.

Postprandial prancing and dancing is restricted in this conservative country. At the large, dark Sonargaon Hotel Khayyam Club, the city's only disco, a DJ plays neo-reggae while a few customers sit at the tables, eyeing the empty little dance floor.

The Bar off the Sheraton Hotel's lobby is pleasant, subdued, like a dimly lit private club, with high teak ceilings, large mirrors behind the bar and potted ferns. An innocuous house drink, the Dhaka Duck (orange, pineapple and lemon juice, Grenadine syrup and angostura bitters mixed with fresh cream), exemplifies Bengali nightlife.

But the bartender tells me Dhaka has more than 20 bars. Of all his suggestions, the Red Bottom Bar sounds most promising. Address in hand, I hail a "baby taxi" in pursuit of nocturnal adventures. But 10 minutes later, buzzing down a busy main street, I spot it: The Red Button Restaurant.

Dhaka has fooled me again.

COX'S BAZAR

Dunes to dusk

Fall 2001

THE exotic name Cox's Bazar has enticed me since I first heard it as a schoolboy long ago. Besotted by faraway places with strange-sounding names, studying maps of exotic climes, I made a mental note that I must visit it someday.

The name, and the brochure photograph of an elephant standing on the beach with head held high, a great orange setting sun perfectly framed in the curve of its trunk, attracted me to the town on the Bay of Bengal. Promoted as the "Tourist Capital of Bangladesh" with its miles of golden sands, Buddhist temples and excellent seafood, it sounds intriguing.

So I travel south from Dhaka, to see the sun set on the world's longest unbroken sandy beach, which stretches 120 kilometers, all the way from Cox's Bazar south to Burma.

To see something of rural Bangladesh, I travel overland by train and bus instead of flying. The arduous day-long journey is not for the faint of heart, with beggars pouncing on every passing foreigner, and villages with garbage and vegetation strewn in festering piles on the street - interspersed with bucolic rural scenes. Travelers concerned with comfort for body and spirit should fly.

Arriving in Cox's, tired and dusty after the long journey, I ride a pedicab to my seaside hotel, the Shaibal. Eager to sample the area's vaunted seafood, I immediately set off into town in search of a restaurant, and soon find a small place rich with local color. I am about to order a fish dopiaza (onions twice curry) when I spot the waiter combing his hair with a fork, then putting it back on the table.

The hotel restaurant will have to do, I decide, and scuttle back to the big, empty place I had originally spurned. In fact, it is a delightful surprise. The pomfret masala is delicious, as tasty as anything I have had in five-star restaurants. The whole fish, large enough to cover the plate, along with rice, vegetables and tea, comes to just a few dollars. So the brochures are right about the superb seafood.

The next morning at dawn, Inani Beach is already active. Children swim in the clear Bay of Bengal water; women in saris stroll the beach; and fishermen are out with nets at the end of long poles, pushing them like wheelbarrows, collecting tiny fish in big aluminum pots. A sign on the beach lists charges for showers, inflatable inner tubes and "kit kots," which I take to mean inflatable mattresses.

Over breakfast, I overhear a local refer to the many "anjos" (NGOs) in Cox's Bazar, and aside from tourism, foreign aid seems to be the main industry. Strolling the streets of the dusty, ramshackle but pleasant town, I spot numerous international relief organization offices. In a few short blocks, there is the Control of Communicable Diseases, Bangladesh. the Community Based Calamity Preparedness and Rehabilitation Program, the Cyclone Preparedness Program and others.

Sightseeing proves a challenge, even in such a small town. I commission a pedicab to take me to the largest bronze statue of the Buddha in Bangladesh, and climb aboard for the bumpy ride through the baking streets. Although it is the town's most famous sight, the driver drops me off far past it and wheels away before I know what has happened. But at least I am in Ramu, a Buddhist village about 10 kilometers from Cox's Bazar. After asking directions from several shopkeepers, I walk back down the road and along a deserted side street.

Finally, I come upon a collection of strange, rundown buildings, with worn teak floors and multitiered corrugated iron roofs housing Buddha statues from Burma. An old priest and I are the only ones there, and it is peaceful in the jungle setting. But it isn't the big Buddha.

Back on the main road, I find a more informed pedicab driver, who takes me further out of town and down a jungle path with paved strips for the pedicab wheels and brick in between. This leads to a complex of 19th-century khyangs, or monasteries, timber-framed, with multilevel pitched roofs and decorative fretted carvings in a sort of Indo-Chinese Carpenters' Gothic style.

The temple guardian, a stooped and frail woman who the driver swears is 110-years-old, silently appears, hand outstretched. Despite her three-figure age, her eyes are sharp enough to assess the bill I give her before she opens the temples for me. Inside, she indicates the big Buddha, and disappears like a wraith.

Left alone, I read a school scribbler I find at the entrance. In childlike writing, it informs me that this, the most famous Buddhist temple in Bangladesh, was built in 1877. The temple holds the large bronze Buddha, cast at the end of the last century, seven smaller Buddha images - six bronze, one white stone - and a row of plaster Buddhas. Another wood temple nearby is stocked with Burmese handicrafts and 23 Buddhas.

Anywhere else, a place like this would be overrun with tourists and lined with snack and souvenir shops. Instead, I spend an hour here in blissful solitude, savoring a kind of serenity I haven't experienced since traveling around Southeast Asia in the 1970s.

Back at Coxybar, as some call it, a band of locals resembling the 17th-century Mogh pirates who ravaged the Bay of Bengal loiter around an old blue Toyota. After hard bargaining, I rent the wreck for a short drive up the long beach. Although I am the only paying customer, a half-dozen of the driver's friends pile in the back, and we take off for a long, smooth drive along the world's longest stretch of flat sand. There is no solitude here, however. In this crowded country, people live in thatched huts all along the beach.

My newfound companions take me to a waterfall, apparently one of the local attractions. It is just a thin trickle coming down the cliff, with a woman in a bright sari gathering water in a large metal pot while naked kids splash around her.

After more bargaining, I get these roguish land pirates to drive me further along the hard sand. The beach goes on seemingly forever, and if we continued for a few hours we would eventually reach Burma. Apparently my time has run out, as we turn into some soft sand dunes, drive around some basic thatched houses, where yards of colorful, filmy sari fabric dry in the sun, then head back.

As we return in the late afternoon, a silver sheen shines over everything, blending the sky, water and wet sand beach without a visible break. Back at the main beach, I await the sunset, a major nightly event here, anticipating the noble elephant of the tourist brochure.

It seems as though at least 2 million of Bangladesh's zillion people are here, along this stretch of sand. While waiting, I chat with a few young locals who insist on getting their photo taken with me. And I watch the beach action, the women in brilliant saris, veiled or with kohl-blackened eyes, and the family groups. Small boys sell peanuts, bead necklaces and chains of sweet-scented jasmine; men stand thigh-deep in the calm sea fishing with long poles or nets; kids play soccer on the sand; a motorcyclist races by.

I am sitting on the hard, sandy beach, finally alone, watching the sun drop like melted butter into the shimmering sea, when from the side ambles a forlorn, cud-chewing black shape.

I wanted an elephant. I get a cow.

INDONESIA

TORAJA

Dead to Rites

March 1987

SOMEWHERE east of Java lie lands of timeless mystery, demons and magic, of ancient rituals, of sultan's palaces, and noisome white tribes roaming village streets. Centuries-old Dutch forts and the debris of World War II lie buried deep in the jungle or in the clear warm seas. Sacred eels dine on fresh chicken eggs, sad-faced orangutans peer balefully from trees, Komodo dragons gorge on carrion - including their fellow dragons.

Indonesia, the world's largest archipelago, stretches 3,200 miles like a great Muslim crescent from west Malaysia to north Australia. Although not much visited, these 13,000 islands with their vast diversity of peoples and cultures, are easily accessible by Garuda, the Indonesian national carrier named for a mythical bird, which flies to most of them.

Sulawesi

From Makassar, now, more dully, Ujung Padang, it is a jarring eight-hour jeep ride north on the trans-Sulawesi highway to the heart of orchid-shaped Sulawesi island. My driver, Captain Hornblower, leans on the Toyota's klaxon as he races past bicycles and buffaloes and tiny ponies pulling cart loads of farm families in traditional dress. Hornblower, in Che Guevara beret and mirror sunglasses, rocks with childlike glee as he forces a bicycle rickshaw and passengers over into a ditch.

A pair of lateen-rigged Bugis pinis ships, part the world's last large sailing fleet, glide along just offshore. Small tin-domed mosques, like over-turned teakettles, dot the crowded road. Women in umbrella-sized cone hats work the rice paddies, and giant, gentle, mud-slathered water buffaloes with horns like Honda handlebars wallow in the ponds. A frantic hour from the airport, we reach the central mountains. Broad rivers brown as a water buffalo's' eyes slice through emerald green, terraced rice paddies reaching like steps up to the peaks.

My destination, Toraja Land, is a full-day journey on this hairy, though scenic, road. The Tana Toraja people, like Southeast Asia's Golden Triangle hill tribes in their mountain fastness, cling to their unique religion, costumes and customs. The Torajans, who it is said "Live to Die," are known for their elaborate funeral rituals. Dead noblemen are mummified and buried or stored in a back room until the family has sufficient wealth in water buffalo and palm wine for a proper wake. It leads to interesting aromas in the houses, a guidebook notes, although the introduction of formaldehyde greatly reduced the odors.

The bodies are finally stashed in caves or buried in Hanging Graves, holes dug in the cliffs, like filing cabinets for corpses. Goggle-eyed wooden effigies, mute guardians in colorful garb, line the railings of balconies built alongside the Hanging Graves. Outside burial caves, youthful entrepreneurs scramble to escort me with kerosene lanterns ("You need two sir, one in front and one behind. Only one thousand rupiahs each") to show us the caves full of skulls and skeletons of ancient relatives. Sulawesi sightseeing involves considerable crunching over ancient bones.

This is a lucky day for us. A nearby village is celebrating a Festival of the Dead, with singing, dancing, religious ceremonies and an animal sacrifice. Along country roads, men carrying

Toraja six-packs -- frothy, tuak palm wine in half a dozen three-foot bamboo tubes slung over their shoulders like crosscut saws -- make for the wake.

In Tallun Lipu village, traditional Toraja houses on stilts with upswept roofs face a muddy common crowded with 14 farmers caressing and murmuring to their water buffaloes. Relatives and friends of the deceased squat in numbered sections under the houses, like privileged baseball fans in box seats. At a command from an electronic megaphone, 14 knives flash at 14 throats and, within minutes, dead buffalo lie in black heaps on the rich red ground. Youngsters rush out with bamboo tubes to collect blood for the stew pot. A young mourner shoots souvenir photographs of his children proudly posing on top of the family beast. A half-dozen ashen-faced Europeans, hands clutching their throats, goggle at this unexpected extra to their package tour.

Moluccas

After the damp, cool Toraja mountain air, Ambon, capital of the former Spice Islands, is South Seas tropical. Near Papua New Guinea, the island is more Polynesian than Asian, with rows of graceful coconut palms arcing over empty beaches, spiky sago trees, clove and nutmeg trees, outrigger canoes and thatched sago leaf huts. A South Seas influence shows in the number of tall church steeples interspersed with domed mosques. Visiting them all would take a month of Sundays.

Only two other whites -- missionaries or businessmen, it is hard to tell with their clipped haircuts, short-sleeved shirts and briefcases -- arrive at Pattamura airport today.

George, a man who could be king, meets us on behalf of Indonesian Tourism. George's father is the hereditary ruler of Tanmbar, one of Moluccas 999 islands. His older brother, the rightful heir, has lived in Amsterdam for decades, and will not return to claim the throne. But George, seduced by the bright Ambonese lights, will likely leave the title to his younger brother upon his father's death.

We ride into the capital in a gaudily decked out van, with gewgaws hanging from the ceiling and "Santa Claus is Coming to Town" playing whenever the driver brakes.

Along the road, shirt-sleeved King George stops to pick cloves from a blossoming tree in the luxuriant jungle, crushing them in his hand to release the rich, sweet perfume of the Spice Islands. These, along with nutmeg, mace and pepper, were the "Green Gold," that made the islands the world's richest for a time, attracting rapacious European adventurers. The Spice Islands have a longer history of European colonization than North America. "In 1674, the British traded Banda, one of these tiny islands, to the Dutch for Manhattan," George adds as a historical footnote.

The Portuguese, British, Dutch and Japanese all had their day here. More Dutch and Portuguese forts with ancient rusting cannons and thick, moss-covered walls molder in their jungle graves here than in the rest of this vast country.

Bailey Bridges across deep gullies and abandoned airstrips recall the bloody Pacific Theater battles during World War II. U.S. bombers flattened all of Ambon city during the war, except for the banana-green mosque. The Japanese scuttled some of their ships in the harbor when they fled, and locals still hear explosions of bombs going off underwater. The well-maintained Australian War Memorial cemetery, including two Royal Canadian Air Force graves, is a somber reminder of past troubles in this paradise. George explains that many of the graves are unmarked, because after the Japanese beheaded captured soldiers, they could not be identified by their dog tags.

As we stop to buy flowers outside the Chinese cemetery, dozens of children shouting "Balanda, Balanda" (Hollander, any white foreigner) besiege us, begging for autographs. In crowded, curious Indonesia, a foreigner with a camera attracts onlookers like a crumb of sugar on the ground attracts ants. At the sacred Waai pool, with water as clear as a mountain stream, a man feeds raw eggs to a long, spotted black eel, a sacred, serpentine pet, too heavy for him to lift from the water. The eel's appearance signifies good tidings and a happy future for us visitors.

On our last evening, George and his friends take us to the town's leading hotel for dinner. Trishaw wheels whisper along the pavement, and sweet Polynesian-like hymns drift from the Gereja (church) Marantha in the otherwise silent evening. The hotel dining room is decorated in standard Southeast Asian Chinese style: acrylic pictures of playful kittens and northern sunsets decorate the wall, while a plastic banana tree, a rude imitation of those lining the road outside, sits in the corner. One of our hostesses goes to the Yamaha organ in the corner to serenade us, we hope with a traditional Moluccan song.

"This is the moment, of sweet Aloha."

LOMBOK

Beyond Bali

August, 1995

THE mysterious stone head, big as a beach bungalow, glowers in the tropical sun like one of the ancient faces of Cambodia's Angkor Wat. Hollow eyes stare out from under a fringe of vines growing over its forehead like bangs. A small, jagged palm sprouts from the top in a spiky punk rock haircut, and mist steams from the mouth and eyes.

It is like a brooding scene out of Apocalypse Now -- until a bikinied figure shoots out of the mouth and lands with a whopping splash in the turquoise, sun-dappled water. Laughter and happy shouts resound across the swimming pool.

This is not a strange, pagan god spitting out human sacrifices, but an imaginative poolside fixture, with its tongue a water slide. The artistic head in the Sheraton Senggigi Beach Resort swimming pool is patterned after the traditional style of mask of the local Sasak people in Lombok, Indonesia. The unique sculpture cleverly adapts local art to modern play in one of Southeast Asia's newest destinations.

Lombok, a 20-minute flight or four-hour boat ride from Bali, was just a stop on the backpackers' long trail from Europe to Australia until recently. Now it is on the verge of major tourist development.

"Lombok is a new place, close to nature," says a Lombok local over poolside Bintang beers. "People save it for the last stop on a tour of Indonesia. It is a place to relax before going home."

Visitors from big-city Jakarta, appreciate the easy island pace. "This is still a fresh area, with no traffic jams and friendly people," a guest explains while wandering the resort's lush grounds.

"Lombok was once an adventure travel destination," he points out. But in the past few years, resorts have made a beach-head in this once remote island, mainly on the wide, sandy cres-cent of Senggigi Beach on the west coast. Now, people are begin-ning to see that it is different, and more couples and families are coming.

Lombok has the same rugged mountain-and-seaside scenery as better-known Bali, but without the crowds. It is easy to ex-plore this 80 by 80-kilometer island by car, although the lack of road signs makes navigating on the back roads stimulating, and sometimes adventurous.

The rental vehicle of choice, a four-wheel drive Suzuki Jimmy jeep, seems unnecessary for the paved roads, but my friends and I soon learn otherwise. Driving is easy, except when weaving around pony carts, motorbikes and trucks in the town. In the countryside, traffic disappears. In an hour along the west coast one morning, we only see a truck hauling coconuts, and a few little pony carts, the popular rural taxis, their steeds not much bigger than Great Danes, clop-clopping down the road.

Lombok's back roads lead to sleepy, rural Indonesia of brown rivers cutting through lush jungles and orderly rice paddies like burnished emeralds turning a silvery sheen as the sun dips low over the hills. In the Pusuk monkey forest, hundreds of curious simians, young and old, line the road, hirsute pilgrims in pursuit of bananas or other offerings from passing cars.

Rustics loiter outside village houses with red-tiled roofs; young boys scramble up tall coconut palms; and women in batik sarongs walk to the fields carrying primitive farming instruments or bundles of firewood delicately balanced on their heads. Small, whitewashed mosques the size of cottages, with pink trimmed wooden windows and domes like silver onions, lie half-hidden in the jungle. On these narrow dirt roads with pot holes big as bath tubs, we appreciate the jeep with its rugged suspension and high clearance.

The winding, dipping coast road north from Senggigi is as stunning as the California Coast, or Kauai, Hawaii, with its high cliffs. The road climbs high up a cliff to give a sweeping view of Bali's volcanoes across Lombok Strait, then drops to run along perfect beaches with outriggers pulled up on the sand, but not a tourist in sight.

Our destination this day is the small port of Bangsal, to catch an outrigger to one of the three small islands known for their tranquillity, and coral. At the end of the short road, village urchins, all budding entrepreneurs, try to get us to park in the shade near their homes for 2,000 rupiahs (US$1). When we park under a palm tree instead, they warn us, "Boss, a coconut will fall on your car."

Looking at the battered Jimmy, I ignore the self-appointed parking attendant's warning.

Shuttle boats leave for the three small islands when they have 15 passengers, for only 1,500 rupiahs (75 cents) each. But it is past noon, and there are only three people waiting. Gili Air, the closest island with a small village, gets the most visitors. Gili Trawangan, the largest, has a party every day with tour boats from Senggigi, they tell us, as though that were a major attraction. So we book a private boat for 35,000 rupiahs (US$17) return to Gili Meno, the quietest island about a 50-minute ride away, and climb aboard the Kontiki, an outrigger with a hull the color of a ripe mango.

As we bounce along the choppy water, we look back to Lombok's majestic Gunung (Mount) Rinjani on the north side of the island. The perfect cone of the 3,726-meter active volcano could have been the model for the hat one of our boatmen wears. The scenic Sidenggile Waterfall on the slopes of the volcano is an hour's hike from the end of the road. Energetic and athletic types climb to the peak to see Segara Anak, a crater lake deep in the caldera. But that three-day excursion, with camping in tents, is best left for another time.

Our destination, Gili Meno, is not totally undiscovered. Basic

rental bungalows on stilts line the beach and a group of temporary islanders, weekend beachcombers, sits at a little open air
cafe sipping fruit juices or Bintang beer and inspecting new ar-
rivals.

Well-used face masks, snorkels and fins hang from a bamboo frame like forgotten objects in a lost-and-found department.
The proprietor asks 7,000 rupiahs rental, immediately dropping
to 6,000, but it seems pricey. Instead, we walk past the bungalows to a fine sand beach near the end of the island. There, a
cheerful old fellow rents masks for only 2,000 rupiahs. Alone,
we snorkel the warm green waters, like swimming in a massive
private aquarium of exotic, radiant tropical fish darting through
the feathery coral.

While Lombok equals the larger Bali in these physical attractions, it lacks that Hindu island's abundance of man-made sights,
the timeless temples, palaces and ubiquitous artwork. However,
those attractions we happen upon have an understated charm.
Narmada, the water palace 12 kilometers west of the main town,
Mataram, is a pleasant spot with the added allure of being de-
void of other visitors when we arrive. The King of Lombok built
this summer palace in 1727 as place of worship -- and a pleasure
garden with a series of swimming pools. The old rogue reputedly had a hidden spot from where he would select village maidens
for his recreation.

On this hot day, it is a serene, riverside setting with a flock of
truant school boys swimming in the Hindu-style temple pools.
Below, the large, modern swimming pool stands empty, while in
an ancient pool nearby, modern plastic peddle boats shaped like
swans stand alongside age-old, moss-covered stone statues.

South of here, in traditional Sasak villages with stilt houses,
locals make pottery, carvings, baskets and weavings. This part of
the island is arid and barren compared with the lush north. At
the end of the road south, through the dry, dusty hills, down the
steep road to the coast, a sign advertises the Matahari Inn. "Kuta
Beach, 1 km, Matahari Inn Hotel and Restaurant, The Place Where

All Nations Are Together. Reasonable Price and Nice People."

Seaweed and coconut fronds cover the large, curved Kuta Beach facing an open bay, fishermen stand ready to launch outrigger canoes and water buffalo graze on the sand vines, but no one swims in the clear water.

The Matahari, the only commercial enterprise in sight, is a pleasant, thatched, open-air backpackers' hotel, with reggae on the music box, but no cold beer. Besides the standard Indonesian staples of nasi and mee goreng and gado gado, the menu offers roesti a la Switzerland and spaghetti Napoli, Bolognaise or marinara.

It is a secluded tropical hideaway. But a Japanese company is building a hotel next door, a new international airport is planned nearby, and the area is going to be the center of new tourist development. Then, this tranquil Lombok Kuta Beach may become like its bustling Balinese namesake.

BANDUNG

A Dutch Treat

January 1998

IT is really better that the train from Jakarta to Bandung takes longer now than it did when the Dutch completed the line in 1886. Then, the train shipped tea from the colonials' mountain plantations to the port. Today, the leisurely pace gives passengers more time to relax and enjoy the scenery on the way to the city where Dutch colonials once went to escape the Indonesian capital's heat and humidity.

In a few pleasant hours, the comfortable, punctual Argogedes train climbs from the steamy coast of Jakarta to the cool mountain retreat 180 kilometers southeast.

So, at 9am on a typical tropical morning, an attractive hostess in airline-style blue uniform greets me on the platform of Gambir Station in central Jakarta. As I settle into my coach seat, the train moves through leafy suburbs, of red tile roofs and green jungle foliage, minarets and domes, and satellite dishes.

The agricultural scene beyond the city, with broad brown rivers, chickens in farmyards, planters in woven cone hats working the rice paddies and children riding large, lethargic water buffalo, is remarkably like that depicted in popular Balinese paintings.

Bandung, the provincial capital of West Java and Indonesia's third largest city, is set on a plateau in the Parahayangan Mountains The City of Flowers' pleasant climate and lush surroundings have provided an escape from the lowlands heat since the mid-19th century, when it was the center of a prosperous plantation area.

About an hour out, the train starts its climb into the scenic green hills of Java, crossing bridges over deep canyons, far above women washing clothes in the rivers. By good fortune, I've been assigned a right-hand window seat going up, with the best views of the valley. I'll remember to pick a left-hand one going down. Higher in the mountains, we pass spectacular rice terraces, like a Hanging Gardens of Bandung.

Bandung may not have the faraway-places-with-strange-sounding-names romantic allure of, say, Malacca or Makassar, Bali or Mandalay, but I first heard of it decades ago, and the name stuck in my impressionable mind. Growing up on the Canadian Prairies in the early ages of black-and-white television, I watched the news about the Bandung Conference of April 18-25, 1955, and the place seemed wonderfully exotic and important.

For a few day that year, the city was the center of world media attention as leaders of 29 African and Asian countries gathered to help determine the future of their newly independent nations and form a new, supposedly nonaligned bloc. Indonesian president Sukarno welcomed such prominent personalities as Indian prime minister Jawaharlal Nehru, Kwame Nkrumah, prime minister of the Gold Coast (later Ghana), president of Egypt Gamal Abdel Nasser, Chou En Lai, premier of China and Ho Chi Minh, prime minister of Vietnam. It was a gathering of the world-shapers of the day, plus lesser-known lights from Algeria, Morocco, Tunisia, Lebanon, Syria, Japan, the Philippines and others.

But this quiet city on a plateau 768 meters above sea level has been a tourist destination for a century, since the time when Indonesia was known as the Dutch East Indies. Dutch colonials rode these very tracks, where this morning rock videos are showing on a TV screen at the end of the car -- fortunately with the volume turned down low. In the colonial days, Bandung was Indonesia's version of the British Indian hill stations such as Ootacamund and Simla. Planters came down from the highlands and administrators and merchants up from the coast to frolic in this lively resort town, with its cafe society and luxury shopping.

Now, as the train rattles up the mountain, the stewardess hands out snacks and cups of water and sells Indonesian style rice and noodle meals. Today, Bandung's attractions are the Sundanese culture (puppet plays, dance performances and angklung music played with bamboo instruments), the surrounding mountains and volcanoes, and its fine heritage buildings.

When I reach Bandung station, I feel I have stepped back half a century, with a vague sense of looking at an old black-and-white movie. The town is a repository of well-preserved colonial buildings, with many fine old residences along tree-lined streets. But when the taxi turns onto the central Asia Afrika street I'm bemused to behold a building resembling a great ocean liner complete with smokestack, railings, decks and porthole windows beached on the plateau; the Savoy Homann hotel.

After checking into my sizable room with a huge balcony, like an outside promenade deck suite on an ocean liner, I look up the hotel's public relations director. The tall, enthusiastic American woman is also executive secretary of the Bandung Society for Heritage Conservation and the local expert on Art Deco architecture.

Over a lime juice in the bright, outdoor Garden Cafe, I get a quick lesson in the style that prevailed between the two world wars, and the merits of Bandung. "Bandung has been a tourist destination for 100 years, long before Bali which is a creation of air travel," she explains. "This was a resort town, a playground of the rich living someplace else. It was a party town, with lots of cafes and cafe society."

And the wealthy Dutch colonials (who at one time planned to move the capital to Bandung), built it in a kind of tropical Art Deco style, with its geometrical shapes and stylized, curvilinear lines. So many of the buildings have been preserved that Bandung shares the curious distinction of being one of the world's three leading sites of tropical Art Deco architecture, along with Miami Beach, Florida, and Napier, New Zealand.

The finest example of the genre is this classic curiosity, with its curved lines, portholes, railings along the balconies like on a ship's deck, even an elevator shaft shaped like a ship's funnel. A mural in the Savoy's lobby depicts a steam train racing across Java -- machinery being a popular Art Deco motif -- with local images including a maiden holding staves of rice, and a reclining water buffalo -- certainly not symbols seen in a Miami Beach hotel. Cast chrome clouds float across the walls of the Sidewalk Cafe, like a ship's dining room with leaded glass, neon lamps, white lacquer chairs and chrome bar stools.

The first hotel on this spot, a bamboo house on stilts, dated back to 1871. Even before the Batavia-Bandung Railway started, the first brick building was built in 1880.in the Greek Revival style and opened as the Hotel Homann. Guests in the early part of the century included Thai King Chulalongkorn in 1901 and Charlie Chaplin and Mary Pickford in 1927.

In 1936, Dutch architect A. F. Aalbers designed this architectural oddity in the super-modern streamline deco style popular in those optimistic days, emulating the grand steamships that brought the Dutch to Indonesia. The hotel opened in 1939 under the new name Savoy. During the Pacific War, from 1942 to 1945, it was the Japanese officers' quarters, then it was the Red Cross headquarters briefly before once more becoming a hotel in 1946.

The current owner, a member of the Bandung Heritage Society, has restored it over the past few years. "We undecorated the place," says the enthusiastic local expert. "We removed the low ceilings and took down the dark wainscotting and painted it white." Renovators also removed the old, frayed carpets to reveal marble floors, and pulled out teak ceilings and wainscotting to reveal Art Deco plaster work.

Lecture completed, my mentor hands me a book on walking tours of Bandung and sends me off to explore this living museum of Art Deco. An afternoon walk along Asia Afrika and Braga streets is a stroll down a Memory Lane of architecture. Just a block from the Savoy, Gedung Merdeka (literally Freedom Building), the venue of the Bandung Conference, was originally the

Concordia, a Dutch social club. It now houses the Museum Asia Afrika, commemorating the historic event. On another note, the nearby Rumah Mata Hari restaurant recalls the legendary WWI Indonesian spy.

The walk takes me along Jalan Braga, once the center for European cafe society and luxury goods shops. The East Indies' first Mercedes-Benz outlet operated on this street and, in the 1930s, when Bandung was "The Parijs van Java" (Paris of Java), Braga was known as "The Fifth Avenue of Indonesia," in a mixed geographical metaphor. Now, Bandung is more famous for its jeans street. Most noteworthy buildings, many with the original stained-glass windows, include the aptly named Majestic movie house, Center Point and the Landmark building, all designed by prolific Dutch architect C.P.W. Schoemaker, who studied under American Architect Frank Lloyd Wright.

But Bandung is not just a city of broad, tree-lined streets and fine period architecture. Like the Dutch before them, Southeast Asians now come here for the fresh mountain air and the cool climate. Up on the volcanoes as night descends, it is long-sleeved shirt and jacket weather, dropping to as low as 5 degrees Centigrade, which feels positively frosty after the tropical heat of the plains below.

So, in search of cool, I hire a car and driver and set out on the most popular excursion from Bandung - to Tangkuban Parahu - which claims to be the world's only drive-in volcano. The road north winds through scenic tea estates and forests up to the volcano, 1,830 meters above sea level. There is a northern woods feel as we climb higher, with the sun slanting through trunks of towering pines like through a half-opened, vertical venetian blind. The forest is empty, except for a few hammock sellers swinging lazily in their merchandise stretched between trees by the roadside, only stirring when a car stops.

I smell the volcano before I see it, when the acrid aroma of a damp match trying to splutter into flames suddenly cuts through the sweet scent of pines. The parking lot is already crowded with tour buses and private cars, and pretty purveyors of bric-a-brac aggressively hounding newly arrived visitors with displays of tourist trash -- furry bags and Davy Crockett-style coonskin hats with the animal tail hanging down the back, bamboo musical instruments, polished stone eggs and black hematite jewelry.

Batting away the junk dealers like pesky flies, I head to the crater pit. From here, I can see ant-like hikers following a path around the rim of the still-active Ratu Crater, with smoke billowing up from the pit below. This is a great walking area, with paths crisscrossing through the forests and leading all the way back down to Bandung. With limited time, I can only hike to the bottom of partly active Kawah Domas (Domas Crater). There is a nominal charge to go down to the crater, plus another for a guide, which is optional. The rate is low, it contributes to the local economy and it provides some company on the way down, so I pay at the office and head down the trail.

Ole has been a guide for 20 years and, despite his advanced age, he scampers down the path to the pit far more agilely than I. The experience reminds me of climbing Mount Kinabalu in Borneo, Southeast Asia's highest peak, many years ago with a local guide who didn't speak a word of English. Although several decades my senior, he scurried up the mountain much faster than I could -- and stopped for smoke breaks whenever I fell too far behind.

The well-marked path, with steps carved into the dirt much of the way, goes down, down, down, 1.5 kilometers to the belly of the beast. Along the way, vendors in bamboo shelters sell refreshments, walking sticks and bundles of short twigs used to make tea to cure rheumatism, although it seems unlikely that rheumatics would be climbing down here. Packets of green powdered sulfur from the volcano are good for the skin, Ole informs me. "Mix it with hot oil and spread it on." I decline the suggestion, fearing ending up smelling like a rotten egg after the treatment.

According to Ole, it is best to come at about 7am before the animals are frightened away, and while black monkeys scamper in the forest. In decades of guiding here, he has seen small black and yellow tigers about 10 times, most recently about six months ago. The wild cats are smaller than Sumatran tigers and not dangerous, he says.

The bottom of the spluttering volcano is like a medieval churchman's vision of hell, as sulfurous pools of evil liquid rumble and hiss, burble and eruct, belching out great clouds of reeking steam. One large pool burbles like a Jacuzzi on overdrive, another spits a spout of sizzling water high into the sky. Ole says it reaches up to three meters high during the rainy season.

At a small refreshment stand, while we wait to buy some soft drinks, Rohana, the stall-keeper, sells 38 chicken eggs to a six-pack of Koreans. It makes his day.

"Asians buy my eggs, especially people from Korea, Singapore and Hong Kong," the egg man says. "Westerners usually don't."

Taking the eggs over to the fumarole, the Koreans put them in brightly colored baskets on a stick and lower them into the bubbling 120-degree pool. After 10 to 12 minutes, they remove the eggs, now hard boiled.

"Delicious, no sulfur taste," the Koreans claim, as they munch through the entire three dozen plus two. Although the crater resembles a mythological inferno, visitors are laughing, romping around, posing before the geysers for group photos and munching on their naturally boiled eggs.

It is a short walk from here back to the main road, and the ride back to the Bandung railway station. Just hours from that Happy Hades, I am on the train once more, winding down the mountain in the soft tropical twilight, snaking around the lush hills, over rushing rivers and deep gorges, heading back to hectic Jakarta.

NEPAL

KATHMANDU to POKHARA

A Soldier's Nepal

June, 1984

"Eight years with the sixth Gurkha Rifles, I never saw a kukrit like this," grumbles ex-Captain Sandy Horner, Sandhurst graduate. He examines the polished, etched, curved knife -- weapon and symbol of Nepal's mountain mercenaries.

"Army-issue kukrits are made in Dharan, Eastern Nepal," says Horner. "Black scabbards, none of this fancy work. Sixteen inches of solid, functional steel. The lads could lop heads off with them."

He scornfully tosses the offensive weapon down among the peacock feathers, Tibetan paintings, prayer wheels, masks and carvings piled before the sidewalk hawker squatting on a stupa in Kathmandu's Durbar Square, a complex of intricately decorated temples, pagodas and palaces.

Nepal, the world's only Hindu kingdom, was closed to the outside world until 1952, when 250 visitors came. Now tourists bring in as much foreign currency as the mercenaries. Culture-seekers clutching the All-Asia Guide admire the holy places and ancient cities, trekker/adventurers in khaki shorts and heavy hiking boots bicycle the rough streets and drug-trippers in billowy, cotton Indian pants smoke the treasured Nepalese hash and savor apple pies and brownies in Freak Street coffee shops.

But even the capital, Kathmandu, with more shrines, pagodas and temples than dwelling places, a wide-eyed, Living Virgin Goddess who is trotted out for tourists, and bovine sacrifices in the main square, seems little affected by the influx.

In the ancient square, this sharp, clear Himalayan day, Nepalese men sport topis (hats), baggy-bottomed jodhpurs and thigh-long, high-collared, slim-cut jackets; bare-legged farmers haul produce in wicker baskets on their backs; and women dangle great gold and jade earrings from pierced ears and noses.

Herds of goats, sheep and cattle graze in the downtown parade square. Dogs with marigold wreaths and red tikka marks on their foreheads for Dog's Day festival sniff at piles of food in the square. Hippies lounging on tall, multitiered stupas gaze dreamily down on the royal drum-and-bagpipe band, dashing in scarlet coats and leopard-skin topis, playing the Colonel Bogie March for Japanese diplomats going into Nasal Chowk, the royal courtyard, for a state function.

"Some 50 to 60 battalions of Gurkhas serve in the Indian army, as well as in the Nepalese army," the retired captain explains, pausing to inspect the band. "Better conditions and more prestige in the British Army. We recruit them straight out of the hills, teach them how to put on boots and socks, turn on a light switch and use a Western toilet, then send them to Hong Kong for military training. Post them to Hong Kong, Malaysia, Brunei, Singapore. It's a proud old tradition, Gurkha soldiers serving under British officers," he states in tones as clipped as his sandy mustache.

"We'll go to the western mountains, where the Gurungs, the major martial caste, are recruited," says Horner. "I want to see the burra-sahib, the old man who served as my senior officer 14 years ago. They show great love and respect for their commanding officers, you understand."

The dawn's early light slowly tinges the Himalayas reddish-orange, the color oozing down from the tips like strawberry sauce poured on a blob of vanilla ice cream. We drive away from the Soaltee Oberoi Hotel past cow's garlanded with marigolds and colored with saffron or vermilion this Cows' Day Festival.

"The five day Tihar Festival takes place during the last three days of the dark half of the lunar month in November, and the following two days," Horner says as our driver negotiates around cows, three-wheel scooters and buses topped with swaying passengers.

"The festival of lights honoring Laxmi, Goddess of Wealth and Good Fortune starts with Crow's Day, then Dog's Day, then Cow's Day. It's Self-Worship day tomorrow and, finally, Brother's Day. Celebrate with ritual bathing. Burning wicks are soaked in mustard oil, put on small leaf plates and floated on the waters, so the whole countryside is bright with colored candles and butter lamps," he explains, as we pass half-naked men washing in icy mountain streams and village wells out in the countryside.

"Nepal is Hindu, with animistic and shamanistic traditions," the old soldier explains. "They all believe in spirits and ghosts. Each Gurkha regiment has its own priest and temple or shrine, and they celebrate all the Hindu festivals. We'll stop at the Dakshinkali Temple of the bloodthirsty Goddess Kali 'The Terrifying,' for the animal sacrifices."

It is festive down by the temple in a gorge 28 kilometers from the capital, with beer and tea vendors, and children selling garnets and pleading for pencils. Peasants lovingly prepare their goats or chickens for the sacrifice before taking them into the temple, where grinning teenage boys casually cut their throats with long knives.

Warm red blood slicks the ground and dyes the boys' bare arms and legs like scarlet gloves and boots. The farmers plop the sacrificed animals into pots of boiling water, scrape off the fur or feathers and wash the carcasses in the river. Tonight, they will feast.

Outside Kathmandu Valley, in a thick, cold fog, we report to several police posts before breaking out into open country. Peasants along the road pack huge rice bags, firewood and cattle fodder. No beasts of burden share the work, not even wheelbarrows.

As the sun burns off the fog, we drive past farmers in native costume harvesting and threshing rice with foot-powered machines in an Asian Jean Francois Millet scene. Red mud houses, pale green rice and yellow mustard fields, vibrant orange marigold, purple and white chrysanthemums, red khannas, yellow asters and a backdrop of sawtooth mountain peaks piercing puffy clouds complete the setting. Terraced rice fields follow the contours of the steep hills in great thumb-whorl patterns.

Dogs, ducks, chickens and children scurry across the road before us. We stop at a sleazy town where every two-story, open-fronted building calls itself a hotel, for a Nepalese lunch of rice, dahl, spinach and cabbage cooked in charred pots over a wood fire on the ground in the back. Over clay, sake-cup sized containers of raksi, the local rum the ex-captain grows pensive.

"Ate this three times a day in the Gurkhas," says Horner. "Took raksi out on patrol with us in jerrycans." Nostalgia builds a thirst. "Innkeeper, another chotta-peg (small shot) of raksi," he bellows.

A mad, horn-honking drive finally brings us to Pokhara, 200 kilometers from Kathmandu and a center for trekking in the 8,000-meter Annapurna range. The 20,000 trekkers a year who come to Nepal from around the world hire guides and porters (often women) or buy maps, and hike for days or weeks among the Himalayas, sleeping in villages and buying food on the way.

At the New Crystal Hotel, trekkers home from the hills kiss their Sherpas good-bye with hearty farewells: "If yer ever in Houston, y'all come see us, y'hear." Climbers with huge backpacks, crampons and pitons, and clunky mountain boots stomp around the lobby. At the nearby airstrip, lama priests and Tibetan refugees with high cheekbones and mysterious, far-off eyes squat on the ground amid mountainous bundles.

Mule trains and women beasts of burden crowd Pokhara's mud streets. We stop for directions and a Star beer in a shabby shop run by an ex-Gurkha transport driver. His older son is in the army. The younger one sits at a rickety table learning English so that he, too, can follow the family tradition.

Outside, ducks honk like brass carriage horns. The brittle rattle of the Nepalese army machine gun training echoes from a nearby field.

As we approach the Gurkha camp, the rubble road turns to smooth pavement. After the town's subcontinent shambles, the camp's spit-and-polish order seems almost unnatural.

A young English lieutenant with a Basil Fawlty accent, wearing the black, orange and green web belt of the 6 Gurkha Rifles, receives us in the officer's mess. Here, it is all soldier talk peppered with the initial's beloved by military types; 2IC, ADO, RSM, ARO and OC Sahib. (A card on the table reads "From RSM, PMC8 all members WOs/sgts, men, BGC to RSM, PMC8 all members WOs/sgts, men TDBG.")

"England is the favorite posting for the Gurkhas," the lieutenant explains. "This is because of the sights, and the friendly people in the pubs, who treat them well."

"They are also posted to Belize, Brunei and Hong Kong. None in Northern Ireland, though, because of language difficulties." What?

A Gurkha major arrives in a dump truck ("the staff car," he jokes) to take us to the retirement home of the captain's old soldier friend, Lal Bahudur. His small farmhouse some miles in the country in the shadow of pyramid-like Macchupure (Fish Tail Mountain) is surrounded by fields of marigolds glowing orange in the pale dusk.

The old man's wife, Hem Kumari, greets us warmly at the door, serves tea and biscuits and goes in search of her husband. Cheap Hong Kong souvenirs and black velvet paintings of busty maidens line the walls of the neat little cottage. Kukrit, the Gurkha regimental magazine, sits on the coffee table alongside a framed photo of a uniformed Gurkha officer in Buckingham Palace, waiting to be decorated.

A sound at the back door grabs our attention.

"Remember, they treat their former officers with great honor and respect, so don't be embarrassed," ex-Captain Horner whispers as we rise to meet his old companion.

The arriving Gurkha's face breaks into a creased smile as he recognizes his former commanding officer, laughing and sinking a thin brown finger knuckle-deep in Horner's paunch.

"Ah, sahib, so wonderful to see you. But you are so fat."

KATHMANDU

Wildest Dreams

May, 1998

It is a kaleidoscope of impressions, a dizzying sensory overload of smells, sights and sounds. The balcony of Kathmandu's K.C.'s Restaurant and Bambooze Bar overlooks a scene exploding with action and exoticism, of sadhus (holy men) and trekkers, hawkers, hustlers and hippies, rickshaw drivers and snake charmers with baskets of cobras. The streets form a swarming maze of jostling, variegated humanity, like a crowd scene from an early adventure movie, except the extras are real people.

There is still a lot of weirdness in Kathmandu, and Kipling's oft-quoted saying is as apt today as it was in 1895 when he wrote the poem In The Neolithic Age.

"Still the world is wondrous large--
seven seas from marge to marge
And it holds a vast of various kinds of man;
And the wildest dreams of Kew
are the facts of Khatmandu (sic) ..."

This hermit kingdom was not even open to the outside world when Kipling composed the poem. Even up to the middle of the 20th century, there was no road to Kathmandu, so barefoot porters hauled everything -- crystal chandeliers, solid Victorian furniture, even luxury limousines, up the mountain path from India.

Half a century after it opened to the world, Nepal marches to the beat of a different maadal (drum). Its national flag of two jux-

taposed triangles is the only one in the world which is non-rect-
angular. Its time zone is out of synch with the rest of the world,
15 minutes behind India and five hours and 45 minutes behind
Greenwich Mean Time. And it even has odd-numbered currency
denominations, with 25-rupee bills.

The Nepalese capital is still rustic, with the air of a farm village in the shadow of the Himalayas. Cow dung on the roads
is as great a pedestrian hazard as the relentless hawkers selling
everything from Buddhas to Tiger Balm. Livestock wander the
streets past cyber cafes offering full Internet services; goats graze
on garbage outside temples; and clucking chickens peck at the
ground in small courtyards. Daniel Wright, a surgeon based with
the British residency in the 1870s, described the city unkindly as
"... a dunghill in the middle of latrines."

As I ponder these harsh words, a Gurkha soldier slides his
kukrit (large curved knife) out of its sheath and says, "Twenty
dollars," startling me from my reverie. These Nepalese mountain mercenaries can reputedly decapitate an enemy with a swift
blow of their lethal trademark blades. But when he asks "How
much?" I realize the soldier is selling his weapon.

The incident is frightening because of the setting. It is in the
15th century, in medieval Nepal, and fresh blood glistens on the
cobblestones from animal sacrifices. Or it could be the 15th century, until a Japanese man comes into the cobbled courtyard, and
shoots the soldier -- with his Sony Handycam.

While still messy and rubble-strewn, Kathmandu charms the
most jaded of travelers. I first visited in 1969, when Nepal had
been open to outsiders for just over two decades, and the city
is still identified with that time. Nepal's attraction for the early
hippies, the later freaks, and contemporary backpackers is readily apparent: the capital city is cheap and exotic, with a tolerant
attitude to foreigners' foibles.

In the late 1980s, 20 years after the hippie invasion, writer
Pico Iyer stayed in Freak Street, anticipating the last stronghold
of the turbulent hippie era. "I had great expectations for Kath-

mandu -- subject of Cat Stevens songs, longtime Mecca of the hippies, sometime colony of the professional idealists of the Peace Corps," he writes in Video Night in Kathmandu. He was disappointed in his quest. After exploring Kathmandu's bizarre streets and alleys, Iyer grumbled, "I could have easily found all this in Washington Square."

Despite Iyer's comments, Kathmandu still seems to be a throwback to 30 years ago -- although it is now much more than just a hippie haven. "The old Freak Street was for hippies, for hash heads, hash cakes and hash potatoes," says a local hotel operator. Then the Kathmandu Guesthouse opened in nearby Thamel, and the district took over as the travelers' center, with restaurants, hotels and tour operators who offered trekking trips, whitewater rafting and jungle sorties.

"Thamel is the Left Bank, the Greenwich Village, the Soho of Kathmandu," exclaims author and local character Dubby Bhagat, with his writer's vivid imagination and the outsider's love of his adopted home.

My wife, Marnie, and I have joined old friends Jug and Bunny Suraiya and their school friend Dubby for lunch in the Patan Museum garden cafe. Jug is a senior editor at the Times of India in New Delhi, and the couple visit Nepal frequently. We hadn't seen them, our only friends in the entire Indian subcontinent, in many years. Then, week earlier, we ran into them in the Shangri-La Hotel coffee shop in the town of Pokhara in western Nepal, and shared many beers and memories there and back in this city. Another wild dream is made a fact in Kathmandu.

The Suraiyas had also visited Kathmandu in those heady, hippie days. For travelers then, Kathmandu was a destination for buffalo burgers and apple pie. "We used to go to the Vishnu Chai and Pie Palace and the Eden Hash House," Bunny recalls from her early visits.

"These aren't hippies, they're trippies," she adds, referring to Kathmandu's current crop of travelers. And they are trekkies as well. The biggest difference on the streets now is the bright blues,

reds, yellows, greens and purples of the trekkers' outdoor clothing, set off against the vivid orange and magenta of the ascetics'
robes as they mingle on the crowded streets of Thamel. As Iyer
noted more than a decade ago, "And as surely as the eighties had
eclipsed the sixties, so trekking seemed mostly to have usurped
questing. These days, more people come to Nepal to improve
their muscles than to expand their minds."

And they are wealthier. "Backpackers today all have a wallet
full of credit cards," says an adventure tour operator living part-
time in Nepal.

At the museum cafe, Marnie orders the Nepali set lunch and I
get a biryani, while our Indian friends eat sandwiches and ham-
burgers. Over lunch, I get Dubby to sign his book, Peak Hour,
which we found in a bookstore earlier. Bunny had edited the
book about flightseeing tours along the Himalayas, and Jug and
Bunny had named it.

"Dubby's book, Peak Hour, gives a vicarious grandstand
view of the spectacular panorama that unfolds for passengers
who take the 60-minute flight from Kathmandu winging past the
grandest sight on earth: 21 peaks, of which six are over 8,000 me-
tres ..." Jug wrote in the review on the back.

Teeming Thamel's restaurants cater to all tastes; Old Vienna
Inn Austrian Restaurant, Alice's Restaurant, San Francisco Pizza, Euro Pub, La Dolce Vita Ristorante Bar Italiano, and Spam's
Space for "hygienic food and varieties of drink," as though hy-
giene was an exception. Aging hippies and young trekkies loiter
in the Fire and Ice pizzeria and ice cream parlor or the Pumper-
nickel Bakery. Earnest backpackers gather at the Maya Cocktail
Bar, Jesse James Bar, Memory Lane or the Hollywood Restaurant
which shows current movies for free.

The ice ax-and-crampon set favor the Rum Doodle Restaurant
and its 4,000 1/2 Foot Bar, named for W. E. Bowman's amusing
satire on mountaineering, The Ascent of Rum Doodle. The spacious, two-floor restaurant with its a garden and terrace is one
of Kathmandu's most renowned establishments. National flags,

photographs of craggy mountain men and dozens of oversized cutout footprints with names of trekkers and climbing groups decorate the quaint second-floor bar.

Out on the street, young travelers cluster around phone and fax service offices such as Global Net Communications, many no doubt calling home for more money. The Cyber World Cafe sits next to an office for the Holistic yoga ashram and another outlet, advertising ear and nose piercing.

Although Iyer was disappointed in not finding the last haven of the 60s, there is still ample psychedelia (which originated in Asia, at any rate) around Kathmandu. The scent of incense and charcoal smoke fills the air, and the sounds of flutes and cymbals, and wavery, warbly, druggy sitar music seeps from shops selling Asian artwork. The posters of blue-faced gods and elaborate Buddhist thankas (scroll paintings) that once hung in "crash pads" are evidence of just how much the 60s borrowed from the East.

Gaudily attired new wave hippies haunt the streets and coffee shops, the men with matted, dreadlocked hair. Women with shaved heads wearing Mama Cass Earth Mother dresses and rainbow-colored hats plod by, carrying crocheted hippie bags, like home economics knitting projects gone wrong. The Flower Trouser Shop sells retro-60s fashions -- batik bellbottoms and crazy hats, remnants of the Summer of Love.

On Durbar Square, enough trappings to furnish a colony of crash pads are spread out for sale: Tibetan rainbow bags, chimes, masks, psychedelically-patterned bedspreads, brass statues, wood carvings, prayer wheels and puppets. Flute hawkers carry the plain bamboo instruments around on a kind of flute tree, dozens of the instruments sticking out like denuded branches.

One afternoon, just a few blocks from the tourists' ice cream-and-apple pie area, a river of red gushes down the gutter from a freshly sacrificed goat. Small boys splash and play in the blood. Late evening, the restaurants and shops close and Kathmandu goes to bed early. The streets fall deathly quiet, except for the whir of our bicycle trishaw wheels on the cobblestones, and the dark, shadowy alleys turn ominous, spooky. With the unusual architecture, the ancient temples, tiered pagodas, stupas and shrines pressing in all around, the eerie scene seems medieval.

Later, over grog (a local drink) in the K2 Bar in Baber Mahal Revisited, a renovated palace, Dubby educates us about his adopted city. Although Nepal remained isolated from the outside world for hundreds of years, the local people, the Newaris, were amazing craftsmen, wood carvers and architects. The Kathmandu Valley, with its three ancient cities of Kathmandu, Patan and Bakhtapur, is a UNESCO World Heritage Site, with seven monuments on the World Heritage List.

"Chinese pilgrim and writer Fa Hien visited Kathmandu about 400 A.D.," Dubby says. "He marveled at the architecture. He'd never seen anything like it in China." Much later, Nepalese architect Arnikot introduced the pagoda roof to China, and from there it spread all over Asia, according to the author.

"There's a one-eyed yellow idol/to the north of Khatmandu,"
wrote J. Milton Hayes in his 1911 poem The Green Eye of the Yellow God. The writer seems a kind of subcontinent Robert W. Service, and this work, once frequently recited at pubs, is more barrack room ballad than poetry. Still, this was the first thing many people learned about Kathmandu.

In Hinduism, everything in nature is a god, so the religion has a multitude of idols. Some claim that Nepal, a Hindu-Buddhist nation with a strong dose of animism and shamanism, has 33 million gods and goddesses, far more than its 20 million people.

Kathmandu, Hindus have been worshipping at Pashupatinath Temple, one of their most sacred shrines, since 400 AD. Devotees take ritual dips in the fetid, but holy, Bagmati River, a tributary of the Ganges. Sadhus beg for alms and ill-tempered monkeys scamper around demanding banana baksheesh (tips).

A temple hanger-on follows us around, telling us about Pashupatinath in vain hopes for a tip. "There is a sadhu here who has had nothing but milk for many years," he tells us. "Would you like to see the milk man?" The late afternoon of our visit, a family prepares a body for cremation, wrapping it in marigold-hued winding sheets, and stacking firewood on the ghat (steps leading to the river), while hundreds of locals line the riverbank looking down on the activity, like spectators at a sports match. The fact of Kathmandu is, a cremation here is more commonplace entertainment than CNN or MTV.

And you won't see that in Washington Square.

CHITWAN to ANNAPURNA

From Elephantback to River Rafts

Spring 1998

Jasmine Blossom and the massive, squinty-eyed, one-horned Indian rhinoceros face off for several tense minutes. Then the rhino backs down and trots off through the dense bush. No wonder. Jasmine Blossom (Champa Kali) is a five-ton elephant carrying 700 pounds of humanity -- a mahout (driver) and four passengers -- on her back, while the tank-like rhino weighs in at a mere two tons.

This drama is played out in the Royal Chitwan National Park in the Terai, a 360-square-mile subtropical forest in southern Nepal. This Hindu kingdom of yak and yeti (a mythical hairy humanoid), of craggy mountaineers climbing craggy mountains such as Everest, and of maharajahs and memsahibs on elephant safaris pursuing Bengal tiger through the jungle, is an adventure travelers' dream. With the world's highest mountain range, the Himalayas, to the north, and forested hills, rivers and tracts of jungle to the south, Nepal, wedged between China and India is a prime playground for trekkers, climbers, naturalists and nature lovers.

Thamel district in Kathmandu, the capital, is a bustling bazaar for adventure travelers, with hole-in-the-wall outfitters selling trekking trips, whitewater rafting and jungle tours. Tents, sleeping bags, camping equipment and brilliantly colored modern outdoor wear spill out from stores squeezed between incense-scented temples and souvenir shops overflowing with Buddha carvings, prayer wheels and Tibetan paintings. For brilliant color displays, ash-covered sadhus (holy men) in saffron and vermilion robes compete with trekkers in crayon-bright, neon-hued Gore-Tex jackets along Thamel streets.

Budget travelers and backpackers can arrange their Nepal adventures in Kathmandu, while others book trips through international tour operators.

The adventure begins with an eye-popping 225-mile flight from Kathmandu west to Pokhara, the twin-engined Twin Otter flying parallel to the awesome Himalayas. On board Lumbini Airways' 18-seat aircraft, the stewardess hands out wads cotton batten to stuff in our ears (for the noise), candy and cartons of juice. The mountains to our right are a fearsome, jagged wall of white. Below, terraced fields form patterns on the high, dry hills like the whorls of a fingerprint.

In Pokhara's small airport, we get our first experience of the advantage of traveling with an organized company. As other passengers struggle with their luggage and bargain with cab drivers, a crew of Ker & Downey staff in red T-shirts and green sweatpants gathers our bags and ushers the group onto a bus. "That is our army," jokes Umesh, our guide from Kathmandu. The operation is seamless throughout the week.

At the company's office nearby, a dozen eager Western travelers are assigned porters, briefed on the upcoming trek into the Himalayan foothills, and handed ponchos, hats, walking sticks and day packs. After lunch in the Hungry Eye restaurant, we pile back on the bus for the ride up the long and winding road, climbing higher and higher into the Himalayan foothills.

The bus disgorges its passengers at a tiny hamlet with a few shops, where we leave the mechanized world behind for several days of hoofing it. With porters and guides we set off along a path following the contour of the mountain with a stunning view down to the road and river far below. The path is made of wide slate slabs, so walking is easy here. In this rural area of fields and farmhouses, we meet locals carrying huge bundles of fodder, firewood and produce. When it starts to drizzle, the porter hands me an umbrella, and I feel quite silly carrying a brolly in the Himalayan foothills. It works, however, and soon the rain stops.

Despite the heavy trekker traffic, the locals are friendly, greeting everyone with "Namaste," which sounds like "Have a nice day." All along, brazen, bright-eyed children ask for sweets, money, but mostly for "Pen, pen? Sakool (school) pen?" Having been forewarned to discourage begging, the trekkers instead give extra pens to the guide, who will pass them on directly to the local school.

We soon leave humanity behind, following steep stone steps down into the forest where the path gives way to rocky ground and tricky walking. The path crosses a basic bridge of four logs thrown across a stream, traverses an old rock slide, passes a few rough stone farmhouses and finally reaches a swaying suspension bridge crossing the Modi River.

After two hours of brisk walking, we reach Sanctuary Lodge, where staff meet us with welcoming glasses of chilled lemon juice. The pleasant, peaceful lodge, with its clipped lawn set above the rushing jungle river is among the most comfortable in the whole Annapurna range.

While most trekkers stay in old, and not always clean, teahouses, Ker & Downey's three lodges were built especially for foreigners. For Sanctuary Lodge, 800,000 stones cut from the river and surrounding hills were carried to the site to form the walls. Porters hauled logs to make the rafters from jungle three days away, as well as carrying in all of the kitchen equipment and a dozen or more solar panels to heat water. When we flop onto our beds at the end of a day's hard trekking, we appreciate the amenities: Western toilets that flush, clean sheets and hot showers.

The next few trekking days follow a pattern. The morning begins pleasantly, if a bit early, with "bed tea," tea or coffee brought to the room. The custom was introduced, no doubt, by the British Army, which recruited local men as mercenary troops, the legendary Gurkhas. Breakfast at 7:30 am includes muesli with boiled milk, fried or boiled eggs, hard toast with local jam or Indian peanut butter, fried potatoes with thin slices of onion and slices of orange, banana or other fruit.

Then it is onto the well-marked stone trails or mud paths, through the forests of conifers, rhododendrons and bamboo, and up mountainsides on the edge of the Annapurna Massif. In Swahili, they say "pacey, pacey," (slowly, slowly), while hiking. In Nepali they say "bistaari, bistaari." There seem to be no directions in the Nepalese hills, just up and down, and no distances, just estimated walking time. Plenty of time is left for the treks, and anyone reasonably fit can do the hikes. The age span of this group ranges from 30s to 70s, and Umesh recalls leading an 81-year-old-American woman up these trails.

In the forest, we hear cuckoos and barking deer. Scarlet rhododendrons just starting to bloom add brilliant patches of red to the somber green. Along the lower slopes, we pass clusters of basic stone farmhouses, fields of corn and potatoes and grazing milk cows. The air is brisk and fresh here, smelling of jasmine, the forest and fresh cow dung, while the scent of freshly popped popcorn comes from darkened houses in the tiny villages. Bees buzz around hives like small beer kegs hanging from the rafters of every home. Across the valleys, the terraced mountainsides look as though a giant comb had been run through them, gouging out parallel grooves to make fields.

"Happy Hour" in the lodges has the happiest prices of all - drinks are free. Tired, but elated trekkers sit around a blazing fireplace (or kerosene heater) recounting the day over Tuborg beer, Challenger whiskey or vodka and orange juice. Fireside snacks include crispy pappadums topped with onion and chopped tomato, delicious Nepalese-style deep-fried mashed potato balls or local popcorn.

Guests are well-traveled, their conversations sprinkled with tales of Marrakesh's open market, giant turtles in the Galapagos, sunrise on Mount Kilimanjaro, polar bears in Churchill, Manitoba, and temples in Thailand.

"They dropped a snake around my wife's neck to take a picture and wanted me to pay for it," one man chortles. "She almost had a heart attack."

And there is lively chatter about the day's events. "This was the hardest thing I ever did in my life," says a lady from Dallas, Texas. "The trekking was really tough, but I've wanted to do it all my life, and I feel so good about myself. "When I was out there, I forgot about the kids' lunches, the car pool, everything."

"The last time I came last in anything was in a Nice Guy Contest," groans a graying Californian with the bulky shape of a former athlete who straggles in after the rest.

Meals are hearty and plain, using local produce. Tonight it is tasty mashed potatoes, cheese omelet and some curry vegetables. While a few guests linger over coffee, most, weary from the exercise and bracing mountain air, slip away, and the lodge falls silent.

On the last full day of trekking, along a rare flat stretch, we approach what seems like a mountaintop mirage, the tiny village of Pothana framed by the immense, snow-covered Annapurna Range. About a dozen small stone buildings straddle the trail: the See You Lodge and Restaurant, Hotel Fishtail, the Shangri La and the Heaven's Gate guest houses, many advertising "solar hot shower." They are typical of the inns where those on "Teahouse Treks" stay.

Souvenir sellers have set up shop here, spreading their wares on the road. One inn has a roadside al fresco snack shop with white plastic garden tables and chairs and large sun umbrellas. An elderly woman with a row of a dozen golden rings adorning her pierced outer ear, like a Nepali peasant punk rocker, sits in the sun serving tea, coffee and cold drinks to passing trekkers in their designer hiking gear.

On the last stretch of the day, a mule train passes, the pack animals bustling up from Pokhara like they own the road. Recalling the advice from the briefing on donkey etiquette, I take the high side or risk getting knocked down the cliff.

Our last night on the mountain is in Basanta Lodge, a 200-year-old house that is more basic than Sanctuary, but in a breathtaking setting. A 6:30 a.m. knock on the door next morning brings us outside to a view of the sun rising over the magnificent Himalayas, stark, white, awesome and somehow intimidating. Over "bed tea" we sit outside watching the sun slowly wash over the jagged peaks of Annapurna South, Hiunchuli and 22,890-foot-high Macchupucchare, Fishtail Mountain, which has never been climbed because it is sacred to the local people.

From here, it is an easy walk along straight flat, smooth, stone or dirt paths, through an area of meadows, cultivated fields and stone farmhouses. After an hour-and-a-half, the path suddenly drops down, down, down, zigzagging thousands of feet to the valley. And there, waiting by the roadside, is our bus, and the 20th century.

The aptly named Shangri-La, Pokhara's only luxury hotel, provides a welcome break between the rigors of the mountains and the river, a chance to do laundry, rest and catch the news on satellite TV. The small town was once a stopover on the ancient trade route running from India over the high Himalayan passes to Tibet. Today, the long stretch of outdoor equipment stores and trekking outfits lining Pokhara's Lake Plewa is like Thamel, without the temples.

In restaurants such as the Hungry Eye, the Amsterdam or the Enlightened Yak, with its rooftop terrace, trekkers gather for bargain-priced meals of pasta, pizza, grilled chicken or buffalo steak.

Back at the Shangri La, a Japanese tourist passing the swimming pool sees the perfect pyramid of Fishtail Mountain reflected in the swimming pool. "Paramount Pictures, Paramount Pictures," he exclaims excitedly, rushing off for his camera. Indeed, it does resemble Paramount's perfect peak symbol. "All it needs is a circle of stars," agrees an Indian lady sipping tea under an umbrella.

The two-hour bus trip south to the rafting site, offers roadside cameos of traditional Nepali life. The highway is chaotic with three-wheel tractors, swaying buses top heavy with passengers squatting on the roof, and farmers packing huge rice bags, firewood and cattle fodder, like walking haystacks with only their bare legs showing below. Village men are more formally attired in baggy-bottomed, pipe-stem jodhpurs, thigh-long, high-collared, slim cut jacket and flat-topped topi hat, like a soft fez. Women in butterfly bright saris flutter around village wells, and dogs, ducks, chickens and children scurry across the road before us.

Wheat, corn and yellow mustard fields follow the contours of the steep terraced hills in parallel patterns. Lowland Nepal is a blaze of floral color this spring morning. Further down the valley, buffalo with wooden yokes work shimmering, emerald green rice paddies where snowy-white egrets settle like flecks of white ash. Vibrant orange marigolds, purple and white chrysanthemums, red khannas and yellow asters form a brilliant foreground to sawtooth mountain peaks piercing puffy clouds behind us.

Down on the rocky riverbank for our next adventure, we don helmets, grab paddles stow our cameras in a waterproof drum and board an inflatable blue raft. The raftsman sitting on the back with oars gives us a cursory lesson in raftsmanship: "Forward paddle please, back paddle please," then we push off, drifting lazily downstream to the milky Seti River.

Aside from monsoon time (June to September), the river is placid, so this is mainly a float trip. It is peaceful away from town, with just a few farmers walking along a path running above the river or brazen boys playing on the banks.

Brilliantly colored birds with long pointed red beaks, turquoise backs and yellow breasts flit through the jungle, kingfishers, swallows and suncatchers swoop and dip along the banks. Keen birders identify the obscure species - brown-headed, storkbilled kingfishers, large pied wagtails, river chats.

"Someone should publish bird books with rubber pages for whitewater rafting," mutters a frustrated watcher, unable to identify a particularly colorful species.

A few fields give way to a jungle of palms, poinsettias, bottle brush trees, papayas and bougainvillea. Along the stony banks, country folk wash clothes, cook meals in sooty pots over open wood fires and fish with nets on wood frames. The only riverine traffic we see all day is the wreck of a dugout canoe stuck in the mud on the bank, and another ferrying women with huge bundles of fresh, green fodder across the river.

When the rapids come, they hit with a shock. Squeals of mock terror erupt as waves of water wash over us, and we bounce down river like a rubber duck in a Jacuzzi. But the water is not cold this time of the year, and the churning rapids are just rough enough to get our hearts beating and keep us alert. At noon we stop at the pebbly riverside for lunch, prepared by the Hungry Eye in Pokhara. Boiled egg deep-fried chicken cutlet, cheese sandwiches, juice drink, oranges and banana.

On slow stretches, we paddle occasionally, without overly exerting ourselves, but on the rapids we work frantically to the polite raftsman's commands of: "Forward please, backward please, stop please," as the inflatable thuds over the foaming water like a pickup truck over a rutted dirt road. Soon, we are so wet, we feel like extras in the movie Titanic.

Sunny Seti River tent camp, set back from a rocky beach, is a haven of peace with a thatched roof dining hall, clean communal bathrooms and showers, and lots of hot water. Changing out of our wet clothes, we sit outside our tents sipping coffee, munching chocolate biscuits and trying to identify the day's sightings from a "Birds of Nepal" book.

Next morning, after another few hours of drifting interspersed with a few moments of action, the Seti runs into the Tirusali, and soon after we pull over to another beach where transportation to the Royal Chitwan National Park jungle awaits.

After a comfortable two hours drive, we pole across the

broad, placid Rapti River on a narrow boat to reach Temple Tiger Lodge. One of several jungle resorts in the Terai, it is Nepal's version of a basic African game park resort. Meals are served in an open-air dining area with a huge, tent-shaped thatched roof, and small cabins on stilts are spread out through the forest. Accommodating is summer-camp basic, but comfortable, with kerosene lamps (bring a flashlight or electric lantern) and, once again, hot showers and flush toilets.

With no TV, telephones or discos, evenings are quiet at the lodge, so guests sit around a campfire recounting jungle stories. The Royal Chitwan National Park is a rare conservation success story, a resort guide explains while logs flicker in the fire pit. Until 1951, the area was a hunting reserve where maharajahs mounted on elephants bagged up to 120 tigers in a single expedition. In 1970, the area was declared a wildlife reserve, mainly to protect the one-horned Indian rhinoceros. By then, only 80 of these large, low-slung pachyderms survived. Today, more than 500 rhino, more than 25 percent of the world's population, graze in the park's forests and elephant grasslands, and Chitwan exports them to other reserves.

The park's 46 species of mammals include four kinds of deer, sloth bear, wild boar, leopard, king cobra and the elusive royal Bengal tiger -- but no more maharajahs.

During the day, resort guides take guests on dugout trips down the Rapti River, where the main attraction is observing the avian antics of hundreds of brilliant birds. Binocular-clutching bird watchers whisper in hushed delight as they pick out iridescent blue kingfishers, black ibis and others of the 400 types in this park. Birdsong fills the morning air, and the guide identifies the "brain fever" and the "one more bottle" birds from their calls (which sound like they are singing out these words). In the rising heat, I can identify with the latter's plea.

On long walks through the forest, we spot jungle fowl fluttering on the ground like bright fighting cocks, little brown-horned barking deer trembling like Bambi, long slithery mongooses and a flash of black as a wild boar crashes through the jungle under-brush. In the morning mist, monkeys cavort in the trees, making fantastic, Tarzan-like leaps from branch to branch, while a croco-dile, an ominous dark green flattened shape, basks in the sun on the opposite bank of the river.

But elephant rides through the jungle are the resort's prime attraction, and at the cruel hour of 4 a.m., the call comes for the dawn ride (along with coffee and tea delivered to the door). There is nothing like waking up in the jungle, with its hooting and clicking, crying, rustling, chirping, whistling, wailing and trilling, to make you realize how noisy Nature can be.

Before first light, we step from a high mounting platform onto our ambulatory conveyance. This is not a caparisoned and gaud-ily painted circus elephant, but a working beast with plain wood howdah, unadorned cushions and simple harness. Four passen-gers ride each elephant, with the mahout, wielding a thick stick and a vicious-looking long metal hook, squatting on the great beast's neck. The mahout talks to his charge constantly, nudg-ing it behind its mottled ears with his bare foot, urging it on in Hindi (the language of all Nepalese elephants), and occasion-ally whacking it with the steel hook. The jumbo's jockey orders "aggat" (go ahead), and we head into the dense, dew-wet forest towards a riverbank and down the steep bank, the elephant step-ping as delicately as a ballerina.

For several hours we wander through the bush, forest and grasslands where grass higher than an elephant's eye towers over us. The only sounds are the creaking of the wooden how-dah, birds singing in the bush and noisy, squawking pheasants flapping from the tall trees. Along muddy paths, we experience the incredible sense of power as the elephant, an animate bull-dozer, brushes aside giant trees like bothersome twigs. Across the dry riverbed, other guests perched on their howdahs seem to float on the high grass.

Suddenly, the mahout whispers, "Rhino." The huge creature is grazing in the dense undergrowth below us, so close it seems we can reach out and touch its deadly horn. The old male looks as though it was stitched together by a Kathmandu hippie, with great plates of leather stuck on its sides.

Elephant and rhinoceros stand motionless, while we excitedly grab for cameras. When the rhino moves away into the bush a few yards, the mahout guides his steed around in front of it. The rhino moves again, and again we check his path. It is like a giant chess game played with live pieces, with us astride one of the pieces -- the castle.

Finally, the rhino, checkmated, bolts, dashing through the jungle in a noisy retreat. It is the end of the game, and will make another great fireside story.

LUKLA

To Shangri-La and Back

Spring 1998

Squeezed into the little Dehavilland Twin Otter droning towards the high, craggy Himalayas, I am reminded of Lost Horizon. James Hilton's 1930s novel starts with a group of people kidnapped in India and flown to Shangri-La.

"All afternoon the plane had soared through the thin mists of the upper atmosphere, far too high to give clear sight of what lay beneath," Hilton wrote. "Sometimes, at longish intervals, the veil was torn for a moment, to display the jagged outline of a peak, or the glint of some unknown stream. Far away, at the very limit of distance, lay range upon range of snow-peaks, festooned with glaciers, and floating, in appearance, upon vast levels of cloud."

Today's flight from Kathmandu to Lukla, staging point for Everest climbing expeditions, has that same, somehow dated sense of adventure, of approaching a remote and near unattainable place. Viewing the craggy white rampart of the world's highest mountains from the small, basic aircraft, I am as awestruck as the book's kidnapped passengers. "The plane, on that stupendous stage, was droning over an abyss in the face of a sheer white wall that seemed part of the sky itself until the sun caught it..."

After a bumpy, but stunningly scenic, 40-minute flight, it appears we are heading straight into the mountainside, with no air strip visible from the passengers' windows, and no chance of turning back. Suddenly, the STOL (short take-off and land) plane touches down on a dirt airstrip the size of a football field that tips sharply upward, rising almost 200 feet. This is white-knuckle flying.

When the doors swing open, we step into a truly awesome setting, a little niche or terrace in the mountainside surrounded by stunning, rugged peaks. Here at 2,804 meters, the air is clear, fresh and cool. A Russian Sikorsky helicopter that looks like a veteran of the Afghan war is parked on the gravel apron, and dozens of hard-core mountaineers are gathered around the airfield. It reminds me of when I lived in Vanimo, Papua New Guinea, working as a malaria control officer, and the entire town gathered to meet the weekly plane.

There is a great sense of purpose here, of action and energy as climbers prepare for their high-altitude, high-adrenaline expeditions, unloading their packs, boots, ice axes and camping equipment from the plane while others board.

Lukla, a scattering of stone buildings topped by fluttering prayer flags, has a wild, remote end-of-the-world feel. Sir Edmund Hillary, the first man to climb Mount Everest with his Sherpa guide Tenzing Norgay, had this strip built, but on his historic climb, he walked all the way from Kathmandu. A mountain guide says it is several days' walk to the nearest road, and I don't want to be stranded here, so I check in the ramshackle Lumbini Airways office to make sure I can get back today.

The Sagarmantha (Nepali for Everest) Resort, where I stop for tea, is a rough, but pleasant lodge with furniture made of sula, a local wood similar to pine, and bare wood floors. About 30 such lodges operate in Lukla, a surprising number for a village of only about 1,200 people - Sherpa, Tamang and Rais, as well as some Tibetans.

Crossing the field and squeezing through the barbed wire fence built to keep the yaks out, I walk down the only street. In this one-industry town, men are packing yaks, porters are hefting huge woven baskets and numerous intense and earnest climbers are setting off on treks up to the mountains. The guest book at the park information office shows that most visitors stay for a few weeks up to several months. I meekly fill in "three hours" under "length of stay."

In a few minutes I walk to the end of the busy town, stopping where a stupa topped with prayer flags snapping in the brisk mountain breeze marks the start of the trail. From afar comes the rhythmic ringing of yak bells, the whistles of the herder.

Back at the field, I settle in to wait for the flight. An hour after the scheduled arrival, the blue sky is still empty, and I recall the anxiety of sitting on my patrol box in remote Papua New Guinea airstrips waiting for my chartered plane. Finally, the siren sounds to announce the aircraft is approaching, and I see a tiny white speck against the dark green of the mountain. The turboprop aircraft, built to land on remote spots in northern Canada, comes down at a steep angle, kicks up dust as it hits the runway, roars up the steep slope and taxis to a stop.

Taking off is a real rush, as the plane revs up and bumps down the short dirt strip, lifting off just as it appears we will drop off the edge of the mountain. This is adrenaline enough a sport for me.

Back in Kathmandu, it seems positively tropical.

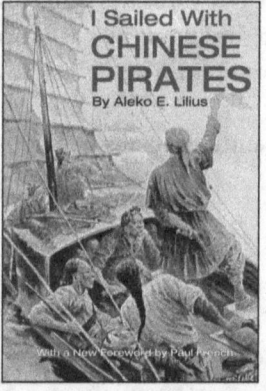
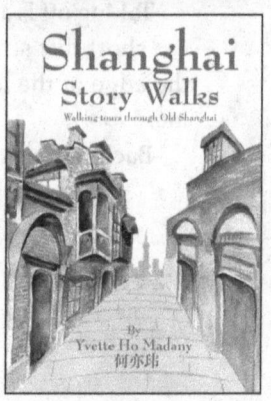

www.ingramcontent.com/pod-product-compliance
Lightning Source LLC
Chambersburg PA
CBHW011234120626
46549CB00009B/3268